Tradition

Concepts in the Study of Religion
Critical Primers

Series Editor:
K. Merinda Simmons, University of Alabama

Books in the series Concepts in the Study of Religion: Critical Primers offer brief introductions to an array of concepts – modes of analysis, tools, as well as analytic terms themselves – within the discourse of religious studies. Useful for almost any course, the volumes in the series do not attempt to assert normative understandings but rather they introduce and survey the various modes and contexts for scholarly engagement with the concept at hand. How, for example, has the term "myth" been used, and what can various definitions allow us to do as scholars? Who in the field is working on the category of race and how? What might be the future of scholarship on gender in religious studies? What are the possibilities and limitations of description or comparison as methodological approaches? Thus, these critical primers provide – but are not limited to – concise overviews of the history of an approach or term. They also present the authors' own critical analyses of the dynamics and stakes present in discourses surrounding these concepts. Including lists of further readings to guide additional consideration of their topic, the books in this series are valuable resources for students and advanced scholars alike.

The series is published in association with the North American Society for the Study of Religion (NAASR).

Published

Comparison
Aaron W. Hughes

Enchantment
Ian Alexander Cuthbertson

Evil
Kenneth G. MacKendrick

Interpretation
Nathan Eric Dickman

Tradition

A Critical Primer

Steven Engler

SHEFFIELD UK   BRISTOL CT

Published by Equinox Publishing Ltd.

UK: Office 415, The Workstation, 15 Paternoster Row, Sheffield, South Yorkshire S1 2BX

USA: ISD, 70 Enterprise Drive, Bristol, CT 06010

www.equinoxpub.com

First published 2024

© Steven Engler 2024

All rights reserved. No part of this publication may be reproduced or transmitted in any form or by any means, electronic or mechanical, including photocopying, recording or any information storage or retrieval system, without prior permission in writing from the publishers.

ISBN-13 978 1 78179 907 9 (hardback)
    978 1 78179 908 6 (paperback)
    978 1 78179 909 3 (ePDF)
    978 1 80050 610 7 (ePub)

British Library Cataloguing-in-Publication Data
A catalogue record for this book is available from the British Library.

Library of Congress Cataloging-in-Publication Data
Names: Engler, Steven, author.
Title: Tradition : a critical primer / Steven Engler.
Description: Sheffield, South Yorkshire ; Bristol, CT : Equinox Publishing Ltd, 2024. | Series: Concepts in the study of religion | Includes bibliographical references and index. | Summary: "This book looks at the concept of tradition in the study of religion. It examines the history of the concept, uses in the discipline, theoretical perspectives (including Indigenous and post/decolonial studies, cognitive science and hermeneutics), and critical perspectives on key thinkers (Halbwachs, Gadamer, Ricoeur, J & A Assmann, Boyer, Morin) and recommendations for clearing the air of a key theoretical tension surrounding the concept of the invention of tradition"—Provided by publisher.
Identifiers: LCCN 2024018306 (print) | LCCN 2024018307 (ebook) | ISBN 9781781799079 (hardback) | ISBN 9781781799086 (paperback) | ISBN 9781781799093 (epdf) | ISBN 9781800506107 (epub)
Subjects: LCSH: Religion—Methodology. | Religion—Study and teaching. | Tradition (Theology) | Religious invention.
Classification: LCC BL41 .E53 2024 (print) | LCC BL41 (ebook) | DDC 200.7—dc23/eng/20240515
LC record available at https://lccn.loc.gov/2024018306
LC ebook record available at https://lccn.loc.gov/2024018307

Typeset by JS Typesetting Ltd, Porthcawl, Mid Glamorgan

Contents

	List of figures and text boxes	vi
	Notes on usage	vii
	Acknowledgments	viii
	Introduction	1
1.	Talking tradition	10
2.	Pure tradition vs. history	35
	Case Study 1: Traditionalism and the denial of historical truth	54
3.	Invention and authority	57
	Case Study 2: Normative tradition in Candomblé	72
4.	Tradition and modernity	77
	Case Study 3: Great and little traditions	91
5.	Agency and reason	94
	Case Study 4: Indigenous tradition and Canadian law	119
6.	Key thinkers of *tradition*	123
	Conclusion	154
	Further reading	161
	Bibliography	165
	Index	186

List of figures and text boxes

Figures

1	Pure vs. historical tradition	37
2	Perennial vs. mystical tradition	50

Text boxes

1	Senses of tradition in two *World Religions* textbooks	16
2	Tradition as MacGuffin	21
3	What is ideology?	24
4	Negative and positive orientalism	27
5	Conceptual binaries of *tradition*	30
6	Tradition as forgery (the Hermetic Order of the Golden Dawn)	43
7	Carlos Castaneda's invented tradition	64
8	Dynamic relations between past and present (Masada)	128

Notes on usage

Italics are used for three things:

1. To indicate when I am talking about a word, not just using it: e.g., *tradition* is a word that refers to tradition.
2. To emphasize words, underlining their importance by *writing them louder*.
3. For non-English words.

When quoting other authors and leaving out part of a sentence, this is indicated by the usual ellipsis (three dots). At points, I flatten text in quotations by invisibly changing lowercase to uppercase letters (and occasionally the reverse).

I use lowercase letters for *east*, *west*, *orient*, *orientalism* and other often-capitalized terms, to underline their constructed nature. I capitalize Indigenous and Indigeneity as a gesture of respect, to acknowledge my own settler status, and to underline critical questions raised in Chapter 5.6.

Acknowledgments

Many people deserve heartfelt thanks:

- Greg Grieve and Richard Weiss for organizing a session on the invention of tradition at the *American Academy of Religion* conference in Atlanta in 2003, and for inviting me to be a respondent; the other participants at that session (Jason A. Carbine, Frederick S. Colby, Susanna Morrill and Greg Johnson); and everyone who engaged in the great discussion session. You all started me thinking about *tradition*.

- Michael Stausberg, Gustavo Benavides, Wouter Hanegraaff, Kevin Schilbrack, Janet Joyce, Ada Jaarsma and 김재영 (Kim Chae Young) for comments on drafts or related earlier pieces.

- Joanne Vermunt and Wendy Witczak, interlibrary loans specialists at Mount Royal University, for chasing down so many publications.

- Merinda Simmons for shepherding the book through the editorial process.

- Mark Gardiner for a decade and a half of conversation and co-authoring on relations between philosophical semantics and the study of religion/s.

- Heloisa, Rachel, Joseph, Anna Maria and the rest of our Brazilian family for their patience with writing time as a family tradition.

- And the many others who have discussed these issues with me.

Elements of the following publications appear here by permission, as per copyright agreements:

Engler, S. (2005). 'Tradition's Legacy.' In *Historicizing 'Tradition' in the Study of Religion*, edited by S. Engler and G. P. Grieve, 357–378. Berlin: De Gruyter.

Engler, S. (2005). 'Tradition.' In *The Brill Dictionary of Religion*, edited by K. von Stuckrad, C. Auffarth, J. Bernard and H. Mohr, 1907–1911. Leiden: Brill.

Engler, S. (2009). 'Review of James R. Lewis and Olav Hammer, eds. *The Invention of Sacred Tradition*.' *Religion* 39(4): 395–396.

Engler, S. (2009). 'Translation, Tradition and the Eternal Present of the Sacred Text.' In *A Bíblia e suas traduções*, edited by C. Gohn and L. Nascimento, 225–241. São Paulo: Humanitas/USP.

Some of the ideas were presented as an invited lecture:

Engler, S. (2017). 'O jogo ideológico da tradição' [The ideological play of tradition]. Programa de Estudos Pós-Graduados em Ciências da Religião, Pontifícia Universidade Católica de São Paulo, Brazil.

Introduction

The concept of *tradition* is central to this book's disciplinary home, the study of religion/s (SoR).[1] Understanding *tradition* helps us understand *religion*. After all, the two words are often used as synonyms. The book asks what this overlap means.

As a first approximation, we can say that the word *tradition* refers to aspects of cultures (and religions) that are passed down from previous generations, and that are accepted as modelling right ways of thinking and acting. Things get complicated right away. Ancient traditions can lose their force, and newly invented traditions can have the same power as old traditions if people *believe* that they are old. Traditions seem to work best when they are seen as scripts to be followed without question; but the selection, interpretation and application of traditions involve active creativity by followers. Some people defend tradition (e.g., as the basis of group identity), and some critique it (e.g., as a tool of colonialism).

As Olivier Morin notes, 'social scientists have increasingly shifted their focus away, from traditions in themselves, to the beliefs that surround them—for instance, beliefs in their immutability' (2016, 38). This leads us to ask what roles these beliefs play in religions. As we will see, the idea of *tradition* can make certain things seem unchanging, divine or eternal. *Tradition* often legitimizes, normalizes, naturalizes, reifies and sacralizes rituals, discourses, values, institutions, social roles and many other things.

---

1. The slash indicates that scholars of religion/s study both individual religious groups (religions) and the overarching category that somehow justifies lumping these all under one generic label (religion).

0.1 Why study tradition?

We already see two important answers to the question 'why should scholars and students of religion/s study traditions and *tradition*?' That word is a synonym for religion, and it points to a key mode in which religions do ideological work.

But why has tradition been seen as something valuable *in itself* by individuals and cultures throughout history? Any answer must start with a basic fact: the things that matter to more than isolated individuals—beliefs, values, practices, institutions, art and artefacts etc.—have effects that last far beyond the short lifespans of human beings. When we are born, we are *born into* a shared something (whatever we call it) that was there before us and that will continue after we are gone. Some of the most complex ideas in the human sciences—*culture, custom, history, religion, memory, tradition*—grapple with this continuity, this linkage of past, present and future. Some sort of intergenerational thread seems to provide a framework of meaning, identity and guidance without which human existence would be atomized, unanchored and disoriented. Or so say those who value *tradition* ...

Religions are often referred to as traditions, but the word *traditional* often labels the opposite of whatever is modern, rational, open-minded, innovative and dynamic. This is not a promising start. How can the study of religion/s (SoR) be relevant today if its subject matter is seen as not even modern?

The relation between memory and tradition is central to religion: tradition is a form of cultural memory. This was the case in societies where religious institutions were important authorities. In ancient Israel, religious memory was invoked to ensure correct behaviour: the *Tanakh* (Jewish Bible and Christian Old Testament) commanded its readers and hearers with the word '*Zakhor*' (remember), ensuring that memory, and by extension tradition, were 'felt as a religious imperative to an entire people' (Yerushalmi 1982, 9). Jan Assmann calls this 'the canonization of the cultural memory', where *canonization* 'means that everything regarded as alien or irrelevant is excluded, whereas everything significant (in the sense of formative and normative) is sacralized, that is, given the status of binding obligation and unchangeability' (2011, 140).

Is this link between tradition and memory still important in the modern world? Or are traditions and religions holdovers and survivals from a distant past? Conservative political philosopher Michael Oakeshott (1901–1990)—a critic of the rationalist, post-Enlightenment dismissal of tradition—emphasized the pragmatic value of tradition and religion as grounds of social cohesion, authority and shared meanings. He pointed to the sharp divide that post-Enlightenment rationalism creates between modern and traditional views, and the dangers that this view presents in the political sphere:

> the Rationalist ... stands ... for independence of mind on all occasions, for thought free from obligation to any authority save the authority of 'reason'. ... [This view is] the enemy of authority, of prejudice, of the merely traditional, customary or habitual. ... If we except religion, the greatest apparent victories of Rationalism have been in politics. (Oakeshott 1962, 1, 3)

On this view, which Oakeshott critiques, both tradition and religion are dead or dying.

But this can't be the whole story. After all, if we are looking for a dead relic of the past, something with at most marginal relevance today, extreme versions of secularization theory are a great example—the much-criticized idea that religion is dying out in the so-called modern world. Traditions are alive and well in the twenty-first century, and the same is true of religions. That is, models of action and thought that are believed to come from past generations continue to be seen as authoritative in many contexts, and this often gives them force to impact the world.

There is work ahead, to sort out what *tradition* means and how it relates to religions. The challenge is to free *tradition* from its prominent but dusty display case in the museum of retro thinking. We can do this by taking a more critical approach to epistemological and ideological issues, and by exploring *tradition*'s relations to social boundaries. Above all, we need to call into question two distorting ideas: first, that tradition is always passive reception (we will look at the importance of active innovation); and, second, that tradition's normative authority is a side-effect of a sort of unthinking habituation (we will look at active ideological uses of *the idea of tradition*).

It makes sense to think that the reason that traditions exist in the first place is *because they work* in certain contexts. Perhaps tradition is rooted in basic challenges of survival:

> [In peasant societies] the margin of subsistence tended to be very narrow. In such societies people simply cannot risk changing practices whose results are predictable and whose outcomes they understand. Peasant societies are inherently resistant to change and prize the ways of doing things which have existed from time immemorial—which meant, generally, at least beyond living memory. There was, then, no great incentive to plant new crops, adopt new technologies, or change the social context of their agrarian societies. One root of traditional attitudes thus lay close to the realities of everyday life. (Emerson 2002)

Traditions have normative force—an implicit idea that it is wrong not to follow them—whatever their origin. If traditions are the tried and true way to avoid starvation, then breaking with tradition seems wrong, because it can be disastrous. The same logic applies to those who see traditional ways as the best path to other goods, like healing and salvation.

Traditions of what we will call the *pure* type emphasize passive reception of truth and models that must be followed. This view of tradition is often found in ancient cultures and current small-scale societies. But this view of *tradition* is not as common as we might think. As Max Weber noted, 'groups approximating the purely traditional type have certainly existed. But they have never been stable indefinitely' (Weber 1978, 263). Even in the ancient world, and much more so in modern colonial and post-colonial contexts, traditions are more dynamic than this. Ideological work is done by the *belief* that tradition is *really* about continuity and passive reception. This (normative) view of *pure tradition* is something that groups fight over. This book tries to describe what is at stake here, without replicating the belief that pure tradition is true tradition. In sum, *tradition* is dynamic and ideological, especially when it is *presented as* ancient, static and unchanging. Scholars in anthropology, folklore studies, history of mentalities, memory studies, heritage studies, Indigeneity, postcolonial and decolonial theory and other areas have been doing this sort of work for decades.

Religions and traditions change as times change, and unpacking *tradition* helps make sense of this. However we define the word, related phenomena are more common in some cultures and groups than others, and they were more important at some points in history than today. But we should be wary of reifying these differences by imposing sharp distinctions between, for example, traditional and modern societies.

Tradition is not a thing but an idea, and its meaning comes not from finding what it refers to but by seeing what other ideas it connects to. Think about the link between religion and politics in the block quote about *rationalism* above. For Oakeshott, the rationalist view of tradition is ideological, and 'the superiority of an ideology over a tradition of thought lies in its appearance of being self-contained' (1962, 12, see 4, 22, 35, 71, 116). This has implications for how we study: investigating *tradition* involves looking at how it unfolds into sets of relations (ideological and anything but self-contained) between beliefs, practices, institutions etc., always in specific contexts. *Tradition* connects. We study it by tracing these links, and by questioning the assumption that they are *simply* rooted in the past.

Here is a view of tradition and religion that refuses to root them in a static past. It gives an example in which both members of a religion and those who study it use the *tradition* label in struggles for authority and status:

> [The Afro-Brazilian religion] candomblé is a clear example of the new roles that have been designed for 'tradition' in the post-modern world. ... Candomblé has become an idiom of 'autochthony' or 'belonging' in a globalising world. As such, it provides Bahian gays, ecologists, black activists and others with a vocabulary that enables them to make the local global, and the global local. (van der Port 2005, 22; see Case Study 2)

Strategic appeals to *tradition* for pragmatic purposes are not a new thing among Afro-diasporic communities. Centuries ago, maroon societies in the Americas—formed by escaped enslaved people—found that appeals to shared African identity helped to solidify their communities. Central among 'the principles that served to integrate them [were] ... a recently forged Afro-American culture and ... a widely shared ideological commitment to things African' (Price 1973).

So, which is it? Is tradition, like religion, always conservative, culturally and politically, or even pre-modern? Or is it a powerful post-modern tool for progressive activism and theorizing? We will see that it is both of these things and many others in between. We will ask which particular threads of *tradition*'s conceptual tangle allow it to do its varied work.

Given tradition's complexity, this book does not tell a neat, unified story. What else would we expect when *tradition* intersects with three of the thorniest concepts in the human and social sciences? It is often used as the opposite of *modern* and a synonym for *religion* and *culture*. It is also related to other complex concepts: e.g., agency, authority, belief, canonization, cognition, collective memory, communication, community, continuity, cosmopolitanism, custom, discourse, dis/re-enchantment, habitus, heritage, identity, ideology, individualism, innovation, history, legitimization, memory, mimesis, norms, origins, patrimony, postmodernity, power, practice, rationalization, ritual, secularization, temporality, translation, transmission etc. (see Nyíri 1992). Tradition shapes and is shaped by—it reflects and is reflected in—all these and many other ideas. With this in mind, this book explores a selection of related questions and themes, offering critical analyses and drawing out implications for SoR.

0.2 The weight of tradition

In the Broadway musical *Fiddler on the Roof*, the lead character, Tevye, introduces the song 'Tradition' by explaining,

> Because of our traditions, we've kept our balance for many, many years. Here in [the village of] Anatevka we have traditions for everything: how to eat, how to sleep, even how to wear clothes. For instance, we always keep our heads covered and always wear a little prayer shawl. This shows our constant devotion to God. You may ask, how did this tradition start? I'll tell you—I don't know. But it's a tradition. Because of our traditions, everyone knows who he is and what God expects him to do.

Fiddler on the Roof is about the erosion of traditional life in a *shtetl*, a small Eastern European Jewish community in pre-revolutionary

Russia, at the beginning of the twentieth century.[2] As director Jerome Robbins put it,

> 'We have to establish the traditions at the beginning and then the audience will see how they're breaking down. That's the show.' ... The forces breaking down the traditions would press from both the inside and the outside. In the first instance—modern children challenging their parents' staid ways—the generational conflict would make the story universal. At the same time the violent antisemitism of czarist Russia would exert pressure externally. (Solomon 2013, ch. 3)

A key message of *Fiddler on the Roof* is that tradition shapes identity: e.g., 'Actors perpetuate, and allow themselves to be shaped by, traditions because they perceive them to be at least partially true. Tradition is not only something constructed by prior subjects, but also contributes to the construction of subjects, insofar as it is prior to them' (Grieve and Weiss 2005, 7).

Many things are passed down in human cultures, but only some of these have the weight of authority that is associated with *tradition*. Tradition is not just a *descriptive* recognition that people and cultures happen to repeat themselves. It has *normative* force.[3] This is a key reason why it is so complex:

> It is easy to see how a general word for matters handed down from father to son could become specialized, within one form of thought, to the idea of necessary respect and duty. ... [W]hen we realize that there are traditions ... and that only some of them or parts of them

---

2. First produced for the stage in 1964: direction and choreography by Jerome Robbins; lyrics by Sheldon Harnick; music by Jerry Bock; and book by Joseph Stein. A film version was directed by Norman Jewison for MGM in 1971.

3. *Descriptive* claims are about facts, about the ways things (supposedly) are. *Normative* claims are about values, about the way things (supposedly) should be. Descriptive claims about a tradition note what it says and how people use it and act in response to it. Normative claims believe that a given tradition is *the right* (or wrong) way to act. Scholars tend to make descriptive claims and insiders normative claims about traditions. This book often makes *descriptive* claims about people's *normative* views: it *describes value judgments* that groups make about their traditions. We will also ask whether scholars sometimes end up making a mistake, by believing normative claims as if they were descriptive facts (see Case Study 2).

have been selected for our respect and duty, we can see how difficult Tradition really is. (Williams 1983, 319)

Issues of ideology, authority, power and politics lie close to *tradition*'s surface.

As soon as we start to investigate tradition, many questions arise. Is it a sort of thing, passed on within a social group, language or culture? Is the continuity of tradition an automatic effect of social and institutional (or superhuman) structures or forces, is it a strategic construct, or does it sit somewhere in between? What does it mean that people's own traditions, but often not others', seem natural and legitimate? How is tradition similar to other types of transmission, communication or translation? What is the source of its moral force? Can traditions change, or does that mean that they stop being traditions? Why do so many groups deny that their traditions change, even when they obviously do? At the most basic level, who or what makes tradition happen and how? And what does all this have to do with religion/s?

0.3 Overview of the book

Six chapters take different lines of sight on the complex concept of *tradition*. The result is a series of cross-sections, not a sequential laddering of ideas. This helps partly unravel the knot of *tradition* because it does not accept (or reject) the idea that tradition is some definite *thing* out there in the world. Instead, it explores bridges between *the idea of tradition* and other concepts. The link between tradition and religion is in the background of all these discussions.

Chapter 1 reviews some initial ways of thinking about tradition and *tradition*. It looks at ways that *tradition* has been used in SoR and also at concepts used to analyse *tradition*, by scholars of sociology, anthropology, folklore studies and cultural memory studies etc. Chapter 2 looks at pure religious tradition, the belief that supernatural forces protect tradition from the forces of history, maintaining it unchanged. Chapter 3 looks at issues surrounded the idea of *invented tradition*. Chapter 4 highlights conceptual relations between *tradition* and *modernity*, above all their ideological work. Does it matter whether views of the origin, age and continuity of a given tradition are actually true? Or is all that matters whether people *believe* that those stories are true? Chapter 5 looks at the questions of agency and reason. It asks whether *tradition-as-agent*—like religion-as-agent and ritual-as-agent—is more than just a metaphor. Does *tradition* take religion out of our hands by telling a story of why it has never been in our hands? If *tradition*, like a stage magician, makes something disappear from human hands over here, in whose hands does it reappear over there? Chapter 5 also highlights the place of dynamic views of traditions among Indigenous and subaltern (marginalized) groups. Chapter 6 looks at selected academic views of *tradition*, noting the strengths of each, and noting how each presents a view of *tradition* that is limited by the authors' assumptions, conceptual work and theoretical agendas. The book ends with brief thoughts on how SoR can better work with the issues raised by discussions of *tradition*.

In sum, *tradition* is religious, ideological, historical, social, cultural and political. It gets work done because people believe certain things about it. This book shines light on some of those beliefs and some of that work.

Chapter 1

Talking tradition

Tradition means many things. It is a 'shaggy amalgam' of overlapping ideas (Noyes 2009, 248). It seems too vague to be of any use for the study of religion/s (SoR). The word *tradition* tells us that something in the past somehow shapes something in the present, in different ways, in some groups more than others, with varying effects. If *tradition* just refers to cultural transmission over time, then what aspect of social life is *not* traditional (Radin 1937, 62)? This chapter starts the work of clarifying tradition by looking at some conceptual distinctions and typologies: ways of trying to sort out and keep straight different issues.

1.1 *Tradition* in translation

Many languages do not have a word for *tradition*. As a result, the most obvious association of this English word—the normative force of things that are passed down unchanged from past generations—is not always central when *tradition* is used to translate ideas from other cultures. For example, note the emphasis on *groups of words*, not a thing called *tradition*, for the Cree First Nation(s):

> In the Cree language, there is no one word that stands for *tradition*. Rather there are groups of words that convey something of how the Cree people express the English term. For example, the Cree dictionary, with participation of over 100 Cree elders, decided that *kayasohkisitwawin* meant something that had inner strength. There are also words such as *kiseyinew mamitoneyiht tanowin* that convey the meaning of a great mystery that is solid and carries on. Some derivatives of these words convey the meaning of a strong current in a river. *Isinisiwin* also carries the meaning of intelligence, wisdom and

brilliance. All of these encompass what *tradition* conveys, and they might be used depending on context. The online Cree app also lists *aniskototamowin* which conveys the meaning of motivation/reason for doing something. As you can see, a variety of terms may reflect what we call *tradition*. (Earle Waugh, personal communication; see Waugh, Cardinal and Leclaire 1998)

Many cultures speak of *their own ways*, without insisting on the idea of identity with the past. For the Niitsítapii (Blackfoot), a common translation of *tradition* is *niitsítapia'pii*, which refers to Blackfoot (or Indigenous) culture.[1] If tradition is *the way we do things*, how does this imply connection to the past? If all *our* authentic choices are by definition traditional, that would seem to include radical innovation under the category of tradition. Seeing this as problematic in any sense would be a mistake: it would impose assumptions that come packaged with the English word *tradition*.

I had the privilege of participating in a workshop with Siksika Elder Kent Ayoungman. The group was talking about the Nation's historical record of images painted on a sacred bison-hide robe. Ayoungman mentioned that he and another Elder had added a new symbol to this generations-old sacred object, in order to represent the government-imposed residential school system and its destructive impact on their community. I asked him if this new symbol that the two of them had invented was traditional. 'Of course', he said.

This takes us past a simple contrast between tradition and innovation. There is a difference between actions performed as an Elder and the normal range of actions of members of the community. When an Indigenous or tribal Elder, *acting as an Elder*, does something *new*, this is not a break with the past, because that Elder's learning, teaching, values and way of life all exemplify and instantiate *the way we do things*. Where is tradition if not in the model of the Elders, in the way that they walk the community's path? The best word for the new symbol on the sacred bison-hide robe of the Niitsítapii is not *tradition* but *niitsítapia'pii*.

A different sideways slip-in-translation occurs in Japan, where 'several Japanese words can be translated as "tradition"' (Asoya

---

1. Blackfoot dictionary: https://dictionary.blackfoot.atlas-ling.ca

2006, 57). One of the most important of these partial translations overlaps with a particular conception of culture. The word *bunka* emerged in the early twentieth century, and it often points to tensions between tradition and modernity in Japan:

> This idea was employed in part as a means of juxtaposing true culture qua superior, traditional lifestyle to emerging patterns of urban society ... *Bunka*, however, was not simply the intellectual domain of those interested in preserving a real or imagined traditional society. ... In rural areas, in particular, *bunka* is a concept often employed in slogans devised to imaginatively represent a town's character to outsiders, and to remind residents that their town is at once technologically progressive and democratic, while retaining traditional values associated with the rural countryside. (Traphagan and Thompson 2006, 3)

The emphasis is not on the influence of the past in the present, but on a *spiritual realm* that marks differences within Japanese society:

> Culture [*bunka*] springs from the inner spirit of every person and is 'indistinguishable from personality or the qualities of being over doing, feeling over accomplishment, and madness over reason.' Restated, one's 'cultural life' springs not so much from one's character as from one's natural and often irrational personality. (Tamanoi 1998, 144–145; citing Minami Hiroshi)

This emphasis on individual feeling seems opposed to the shared constraints on action that are associated with tradition. Once again we see that ideas built into the English word *tradition* do not transfer well to all linguistic and cultural contexts. The lesson is to pay more attention to our own presuppositions.

Part of what *tradition* conveys often gets lost in translation. *Tradition*'s relation to the past is complex, and it becomes more so from a cross-cultural perspective. Continuity with the past is refracted through community values for the Blackfoot Nation, and through individual inner life and local communities in Japan. We should be suspicious of any alleged one true meaning of *tradition*.

1.2 *Tradition* in English

In Latin, the words *trāditiō* (delivery) and *trādere* (to hand over, deliver) both derive from *dō, dare* (to give), alongside other derivates, such as *datiō* (the act of giving), *datum* (present, debit), *prōditor* (traitor), *reddere* (to give back) and *vendere* (to sell) (de Vaan 2008, 174). Where Latin has both a verb and a noun, English has no verb: people receive tradition, but no one *tradites* it.

The word's origin and early history in English frame it as the act of handing over (from Latin via French). The *Oxford English Dictionary* (OED) shows that a majority of early meanings in English, many now archaic, emerge from Christian, and later Jewish and Muslim, views of authority: concerning beliefs passed down from generation to generation. The importance of preserving that which is passed down is silhouetted by a third cluster of meanings: tradition is also betrayal, the delivery of oneself or others over to Satan, the surrender of Christian scriptures to persecuting authorities.

Here is a partial list of meanings of 'tradition' in the *OED*, in chronological order with dates (CE) of first recorded usage given in parentheses:

- that which is passed down, above all orally, from generation to generation (1380);
- Oral Torah (1380);
- an ordinance delivered orally (1382);
- teaching (1384);
- religious doctrine not found in scripture, but with comparable authority (1425);
- betraying a person to another (1483);
- instruction, delivery of information, usually oral (1500);
- transferring the possession of objects (1540);
- Christian teachings passed down orally from the time of the early Church (1551);

- the action of handing down or passing on beliefs, rules customs 'by tradition' (1591);

- customs or procedures having almost the force of law, based on immemorial usage (1593);

- custom or normative usage more generally, later losing the sense of transmission over time (1597);

- tradition quasi-personified, generally in the role of a speaker (1658);

- the Sunnah of the Prophet Muhammad (1718);

- in Church history, the surrender of early Christian scriptures to persecuting authorities (1840);

- teaching the Creed to [Christian] catechumens (1888);

- a literary, artistic or musical style followed by other people (1900).

The sense of the word in Latin is handing over, donating, giving; all are acts that take place in the present. This synchronic sense survives in English in the word 'extradition' (surrendering an alleged criminal from one jurisdiction to another for trial). By the time *tradition* first appeared in English, its sense had shifted to an inter-generational handing down or passing on, an act that takes place over a long period of time. This diachronic sense is basic today, and the heart of the term's relation to religion. There are, of course, comparable terms in other languages, e.g., French *tradition*, Portuguese *tradição*, Greek *paradosis* and, reflecting older uses, Russian *predanie* and German *Überlieferung* (Boudon and Bourricaud 1989 [1982]; Noyes 2009, 235). The third cluster of meanings, relating to betrayal, has fallen by the wayside.

1.3 *Tradition* in the study of religion/s

Because *tradition* and *religion* are often synonymous, you might think that the study of religion/s (SoR) would be a leader in using the term carefully, and in clarifying its different meanings. You would be wrong. Uses of *tradition* in SoR are all over the map.

Meanings of *tradition* in SoR are both narrower and broader than those in the dictionary. They are *narrower* because certain meanings have been left behind: e.g., transferring possessions in a transaction; the act of oral instruction in religious doctrine; surrendering scriptures to persecutors; and betrayal. They are *broader* in two ways. (1) They are more religiously inclusive, leaving behind narrow references to the Abrahamic religions. (2) They split into a wide spectrum of meanings related to the general idea of passing down information from generation to generation. The discipline echoes theoretical discussions in sociology and other disciplines, pushing the raw dough of *passing down* through a conceptual pasta machine, squeezing out many strands of *tradition*. At the same time, these strands have a tendency to stick together as they are boiled in our disciplinary pot.

The basic problem in SoR is vagueness. Here are the uses of *tradition* in a single chapter on Buddhism: it is a 'tradition diversified in time' that bears a certain historical relation to 'Vedic traditions' and to 'a number of religious traditions of ... [East Asia] such as Confucianism and Daoism in China, Shamanism in Korea and Shinto in Japan'; it includes 'various ascetic traditions', a 'monastic tradition', 'lay traditions', 'scholastic traditions', 'meditation traditions' and 'ritual traditions'; as a whole, it consists of 'Chinese Buddhist traditions', 'Tibetan traditions' and the 'Southern tradition'; alternatively, it consists of 'Mahāyāna traditions' (with their 'philosophical and commentarial traditions'), 'Buddhist tantric or Vajrayāna tradition' (which is divided into 'four traditions', with their distinct 'traditions of interpretation') and 'Theravāda tradition' (which reflects 'Pali tradition' and includes the 'Thai Theravāda forest tradition' and the 'forest monk tradition in Sri Lanka'); and all of these are related to 'ethnic cultural traditions' (Cantwell and Kawanami 2002, 49, 48, 73, 72, 53, 51, 71, 63, 58, 75, 80, 52, 55, 70, 68, 66). What does this give us, beyond a generic sense that we are dealing with some type of system, group or form of practice that is characterized by some sort of continuity with some perception of the past? If that is tradition, what is not?

When *tradition* becomes so fuzzy, how can we make sense of a reference to 'Buddhist values and traditions above any specific school' or the claim that 'creativity is evident in the ways in which tradition is interpreted' (Cantwell and Kawanami 2002, 69, 68)? Given the word's apparent lack of descriptive purchase, we must consider the possibility that *tradition* is an empty placeholder, a loose frame for conceptual tensions that lie deeper, a cover for ideological work.

Textbooks of the introduction-to-world-religions type illustrate this conceptual spaghetti well, because of their broad, descriptive approach. Text Box 1 provides a list of different senses of *tradition* found in two 'world religions' textbooks chosen randomly from my shelf: Christopher Hugh Partridge's edited *Introduction to World Religions* (CP; 2005); and Warren Matthews's *World Religions* (WM; 2011). (Creating a similar list is a useful exercise.) Citations are limited here to literal uses of *tradition*, leaving aside occurrences of *traditional, traditionally* etc. Feel free to disagree over how the citations are grouped or labelled. The basic point is clear: SoR's tradition on *tradition* is scattered. This list offers an initial sketch, not an exhaustive typology (for example perennialist views do not appear here—see Chapter 2.4).

Text Box 1 Senses of *tradition* in two *World Religions* textbooks

1. *A religion*
   - 'Congregational worship takes place at the gurdwara, one of the central institutions in the Sikh tradition' (CP 228)
   - 'When Buddhism joined these nature religions, each tradition affected the other' (WM 178)
2. *Received wisdom in a broad sense*
   - 'Tradition tells how Indrabhuti Gautma's enlightenment was obstructed by his supreme attachment to Mahvira' (CP 167)
   - 'Tradition has attributed to Confucius the revision of five Chinese classics' (WM 194)

3. *A national, cultural or regional set of beliefs*
   - 'The Three Purities of sectarian Daoism ... were not foreign to Chinese tradition' (WM 185)
   - 'according to [Australian] Aboriginal tradition ...' (CP 462)
   - 'Western tradition has been severe in condemning witches' (WM 390)
4. *A sub-set of beliefs or practices within a religion*
   - 'Some Hindus branches out from the tradition of the Brahmins and the Vedas. They never denied these traditions, but they did go beyond them' (WM 78)
   - 'the Jewish mystical tradition known as the Kabbalah' (CP 278).
   - 'He stressed the need for commitment to [Jewish] tradition, but with adjustment if necessary' (CP 275).
5. *A formal doctrinal statement within a religion*
   - 'One [Christian] tradition teaches that since the time of Adam and Eve, humans have been influenced by sin so pervasive that only God can overcome it. The other tradition is that humans have a capacity for both good and evil' (WM 324)
6. *An informal statement of belief*
   - 'There is a tradition that the Buddha specifically recommended preserving and transmitting his teachings in local languages ...' (CP 196).
7. *An institutionalized form of religious practice*
   - 'examples of female gurus who participate in the classical guru tradition' (WM 85)
   - 'As Buddhism moved eastward from India, the tradition of bhikkunis disappeared' (WM 142)
8. *The cumulative products/positions of institutional authority*
   - 'A few reformers challenged the basic authority of the medieval church, preferring scripture over tradition' (WM 313)
9. *The teachings or practices of a specific religious figure*
   - 'Some witches, in the tradition of founder Gerald B. Gardner ... perform the rituals nude' (WM 389)

10. *Religious custom, law or norm*
    - 'the law or tradition taught by the Buddha' (WM 414)
    - 'broke Buddhist tradition by eating meat' (WM 131)
11. *Pre-modern aspects of a religion*
    - 'All Jews, along with members of all religious denominations today, contend with conflicting influences. One option is to cut off as far as possible from modern influences and seek refuge in tradition' (CP 308)
12. *A body of oral or written doctrine or teachings*
    - 'Sikhism has a pious biographical tradition of its founder' (WM 162)
    - 'These are the only two texts that Digambara Jains accept as belonging to the ancient scriptural tradition' (CP 171)
13. *A body of non-factual wisdom or teachings*
    - 'They would classify much of our information about the biography of Confucius as legend or tradition rather than fact' (WM 188)
14. *An established cultural practice*
    - 'Anthropologists have identified in dozens of diverse tribes a tradition of 'two-spirited' people' (WM 28)
    - 'Because of my cultural tradition I had an arranged marriage ...' (CP 233)
15. *A body of artistic or cultural knowledge and practice*
    - 'The title of the festival was changed to Hola and the tradition of martial arts remains associated with it' (CP 232)
16. *An academic or scholarly area or approach*
    - 'belonging more to a scientific than to a humanist tradition' (CP 22)
    - 'the sociological and symbolist tradition of the Durkheimians' (CP 22)

Sources: CP = Partridge (2005); WM = Matthews (2011)

When a term can convey so many different things, we are left with the lowest common denominator of *tradition*: passing-down-from-generation-to-generation. This fails to draw the sorts of distinctions—e.g., between types of source materials and types of authority—that are supposedly the hallmark of SoR. It also imposes a misleading assumption: that tradition is static not dynamic, imitation not creation.

There are different types of lack of clarity about tradition. Sometimes we find straightforward vagueness. What sense of *tradition* is involved in the claim that 'Bruce Lee brought the meditative tradition of the martial arts into American living rooms' (Eckel 2000, 143)? Sometimes we find ambiguity. For example, in a single sentence, we can find *tradition* referring to both a religion and a general appeal to the authority of the past: 'New Religious movement, whether in the Christian, Buddhist or any other tradition, are not in the strict sense revivals of tradition ...' (B. Wilson 1991, 204). It is often possible to get a general sense of what *tradition* means in a given context. But context is not always enough: e.g., 'Krishna ... is depicted in several forms, which might indicate that he is a coalescence of traditions' (Molloy 2010, 98). Are these different streams within a religion, or theological schools, or popular beliefs, or iconographic styles, or ...? SoR is not immune to the problem of using *tradition* in unclear ways.

Why do scholars *choose* to use over-generalized descriptions like *the Islamic tradition, Hindu tradition, Judeo-Christian tradition*, or *pre-modern tradition*? There are no useful details here, because each is a plurality. If we lump together all sub-types of Islam as one tradition—Sunni, Ibadi, Ithnā 'Ashariyyah, Nizari Isma'ili, Dawoodi Bohra, Alevi, Druze, Ahmadiyya, etc.—we can only do this by ignoring important differences. The most that such vague uses can do is to signal an abstract and de-contextualized contrast between one broad group and another, e.g., *Mahayana tradition* vs. *Vajrayana tradition*. By losing sight of complexity, over-generalized appeals to *tradition* contribute to the misperception that religions are somehow timeless and unchanging (McCutcheon 1997, 35). Vague uses of the idea of *tradition* make local, concrete traditions invisible.

All this might leave sceptics wondering if, as scholars of religion/s, we even know what we mean when we use the word *tradition*. This is a warning to step back and be critical. Critiques of *religion* have become an important sub-genre of work in the study of religion/s (e.g., McCutcheon 1997; Fitzgerald 2007; Nongbri 2013). If we are so critical about *religion*, why are we so naive and uncritical about *tradition*?

1.4 Conceptualizing *tradition*

This section looks at some distinctions and typologies that can be useful in certain contexts. They overlap with each other. None of them tell us *the truth* of tradition: some might be useful for a given case or context.

Here is a first useful tool for making sense of *tradition*. We can distinguish three levels of *tradition*-talk:[2]

- *Particular traditions (zero-order)*. For example, a religion is often called *a tradition*: e.g., 'The Dawoodi Bohras are a Shi'a Muslim tradition'.

- *General ideas about tradition (first-order)*—whatever it is that makes traditions *traditional*. For example, tradition is seen as following how previous generations thought and acted: e.g., 'Tradition is passive reception of past authority'. This is *one* view of what all traditions have in common. We will see many more.

- *Ideas about ideas about* tradition *(second-order)*—critical analysis of the nature, scope, functions and ideological effects of *tradition*-talk. For example, a key theme in the book is that tradition is often *seen as* passive reception of aspects of the past, and that this *belief* has social effects, whether it is true or not.

Zero-order views are untheorized descriptive labels. First-order views are found in religious/insider discourses and some uncritical scholarly/outsider works. Second-order views are found in critical scholarship that asks questions *about* first-order views. This is just a conceptual schema for guiding interpretation in specific contexts. It is not meant to suggest that these levels represent independent *things* in the sphere of tradition. This book works at all three levels to explore various conceptual networks that link to the idea of *tradition*.

---

2. Paul Ricoeur made a very similar distinction between *traditions*, *tradition* and *traditionality* (see Chapter 6.2).

Another important distinction is between the content of tradition and the mechanisms that transmit it, between 'the idea of *what* is passed on and the process *by which* it is transmitted' (Tanner 2006, 230, original emphasis). Edward Shils uses *traditionality* for pointing to tradition as process: 'Traditionality is compatible with almost any substantive content' (1981, 16). (I avoid this term because it is used in different ways, see Chapter 6.2.) Often, what matters is the way that people treat the contents of tradition, not the nature of those contents (see Text Box 2).

Text Box 2 Tradition as MacGuffin

It is useful to distinguish between the *content* of tradition (beliefs, practices, artefacts etc.) and the *motivations* that these provide for people's actions (preservation, interpretation, defence, even violence against those whose traditions are different).

British screenwriter Angus McPhail coined a word for the thing that motivates the action in a film: a 'MacGuffin' (McArthur 2003, 21). Film director Alfred Hitchcock pointed out that it doesn't matter what a MacGuffin is. All that matters is that it motivates the characters:

> a MacGuffin is actually nothing at all ... It's not important. ... The MacGuffin ... [is] the device, the gimmick, if you will, or the papers the spies are after. ... The theft of secret documents was the original MacGuffin. So the 'MacGuffin' is the term we use to cover all that sort of thing: to steal plans or documents, or discover a secret, it doesn't matter what it is. ... The only thing that really matters is that in the picture the plans, documents, or secrets must seem to be of vital importance to the characters. To me, the narrator, they're of no importance whatever. (Cited in Truffaut and Scott 1985, 138)

It often makes sense to see tradition's *content* as a MacGuffin. It motivates people, shapes their identities and drives ritual and social action, but we can analyse its effects independent of what the particular content happens to be. What matters to scholars of religion/s is that tradition's content matters to religious people.

We can distinguish *traditional content* from *traditional lineages*: i.e., 'anything which is transmitted or handed down from the past to the present' as opposed to 'a temporal chain, ... a sequence of variations on received and transmitted themes' (Shils 1981, 12–13). It is also useful to keep in mind that the *carriers* of tradition are a separate issue, referring to distinct social roles in the passing on of traditions, like Elders, priests, scribes etc. (Schönpflug 2009).

The content or materials of tradition vary: practitioners can spend their entire lives learning the complex nuances of a single set of beliefs, practices, symbols, artefacts, roles etc. Processes of tradition are more general: e.g., normalization of ritual; technologies of memory; mechanisms of canonization; publication of norms; modes of habituation, education, apprenticeship and initiation; writing, memorizing and performing; mimesis, reproduction and copying; conservation and preservation; rediscovery, reclamation and reappropriation etc. Though details of religious traditions vary, similar processes of transmission are found. We can also distinguish chronological phases in processes of tradition: e.g., *emergence, consolidation* and *transmission* (Hammer 2016). Processes of tradition can be seen as outside of history, as history at work, or as examples of social construction. The more we emphasize the latter options, the more we see traditions as plural, variable and selective: a tradition is 'the construction of a continuity over and above actual discontinuities, a continuity that is installed, fictitious yet effective' (Gisel 2017, 12).

The content vs. process distinction is not the same as that between form (or scheme) and content. Both the content of tradition and the processes by which it is passed down are already meaningful. Tradition's content is not pure data or uninterpreted raw material, and overemphasizing transmission as a distinct issue can lead to limitations (see Chapter 6.2). Both are discursive and open to ideological critique. The distinction can be helpful for beginning to focus our attention on the *work*, not just the *stuff*, of tradition. But from other perspectives, it makes sense to analyse the two together, for example when exploring relations between ideological concepts of *authentic* and *invented* traditions (see Chapter 3).

Tradition as process is not all-encompassing or automatic; it is piece-meal and constructive. Above all, it is selective: 'the process of tradition is ... a process of selection' (Shils 1981, 26). This underlines the value of studying the forms, properties and mechanisms of tradition's transmission. These offer fertile ground for comparative SoR. Does it come as a surprise that scholars of religion/s often follow religious practitioners in emphasizing tradition as content (Costa 2006, 28-29)? We get hung up on the details. We describe beliefs and rituals, as opposed to comparing more systemic and analytic aspects of religions. We list details more than the many processes that transmit, receive, alter, negotiate and invent these. This book makes a case that SoR should focus more on the latter.

Another important distinction is between the (alleged) *descriptive* fact that traditions are transmitted and their *normative* force (see page 7, footnote 3). Arnold Van Gennep (1873-1957) underlined

> the double sense of the word *tradition*, the first implying only 'that which is transmitted', from one being or generation to another, with no discontinuity, and the second having a coercive nuance, 'that which must be preserved as it is, without modification.' To say that something is 'traditional' often means that it is imposed, that it must be carried out or accepted without any change. (Van Gennep 1975, 62-63)

Ideology is central here (see Text Box 3). Any step beyond the unthinking repetition of tradition involves seeing tradition *as tradition* and contemplating the possibility of its being different: 'Every critique or modification of a tradition involves a consciousness of what is being criticized or rejected and hence, to that extent, self-awareness' (Rahman 1982, 10). Of course, the choice to speak and act as if a given instance of tradition is passed on automatically—even when we know it is constructed and ideological—is one of many strategic possibilities.

Talal Asad underlines that this point applies not only to traditional people but also to scholars and students who study and write about *tradition*:

> To write about a tradition is to be in a certain narrative relation to it, a relation that will vary according to whether one supports or opposes the tradition, or regards it as morally neutral. The coherence that each party finds, or fails to find, in that tradition will depend

> **Text Box 3** What is ideology?
>
> This book talks a lot about the ideological role of tradition, but *ideology* means different things (Stråth 2013). To start with, we are not interested in the idea that an ideology is a particular political viewpoint, like socialist or libertarian.
>
> In this book, *ideology* refers to a belief or system of beliefs with three characteristics:
>
> - *Reification:* it is held by members of one or more social groups to be true in a manner that is obvious, natural, real, legitimate and/or divinely sanctioned, etc.
> - *Contingency:* from the perspective of others, it can be seen as false, inconsistent, confused or otherwise offering a mistaken view of reality.
> - *Hierarchy:* belief in its truth plays a role in establishing and/or maintaining unequal material, social and symbolic relations between groups.
>
> From this perspective, *tradition* is often ideological: it is used in struggles of power; it can put one group up and other groups down.
>
> Ideology is most effective when the powerless believe that their marginalization makes sense. But it can have profound effects whether it is believed by the powerful, the powerless, or both (but not if no one believes it). As an example of the first case, slave owners have sometimes believed that they *just are* superior and so have a right to enslave others; enslaved people disagree. (Ideology can take the place of real and threatened violence, but violence can do its damage without ideology.) As an example of the second case, women in some religious and cultural contexts accept their exclusion from much of economic and political life because they believe the ideological claim that this is their divinely-given nature. As an example of the third case, some members of all four Hindu castes believe in the caste system. Even some Dalits—outcasts considered beneath all four castes—accept their fate, at least in this life because *that is just the*

> *way things are.* Ideological beliefs can be false, true or undecided. What matters is that people *believe* them.
>
> Ideology can be hierarchical in the sense that those who oppress others can also be oppressed by those with more power. For example, in colonial systems, 'the utilitarian rationality of bureaucratic imperialism implied an ideology of bureaucratic self sacrifice and imperial manners. The bureaucrat is both perpetrator and victim, both master and slave. The bureaucrat subjects others to rule by virtue of being a subject himself' (Haldar 2007, 139).
>
> Academic uses of *ideology* tend to take one of two positions: (i) a normative view that critique is an ethical imperative and that scholarship must be activist, trying to change social inequality and oppression as these are reified and legitimated by ideology; or (ii) a more descriptive view, that critique involves revealing the contingent relations between concepts and social locations and groups. This helps explain two polarized approaches to *the critical study of religion*: a Marxist-influenced approach (e.g., Roland Boer), and a historicizing approach (e.g., Russell McCutcheon and Craig Martin) (Engler 2016a).

on their particular historical position. In other words, there clearly is not, nor can there be, such a thing as a universally acceptable account of a living tradition. Any representation of tradition is contestable. ... Declarations of moral neutrality, here as always, are no guarantee of political innocence. (Asad 2009 [1986], 24)

This underlines the value of appealing to the concept of *ideology*.

Polish historian of ideas Jerzy Szacki distinguished between three dimensions of tradition, three 'ways of approaching the problem of links between present and past' (cited in Krygier 1986, 255):

- the *objective dimension* (the things handed down, the objects, texts, discourses, institutions etc. that exist in the present after having been transmitted by or received from the past);

- the *process* of transmission (techniques and structures for passing on elements of culture over time, e.g., from one generation to another); and

- the *subjective dimension* (the valuation of the past and of its legacy or presence in the present, and, associated with this, the defence and critique of tradition).

Authority and ideology are crucial to the third, subjective, dimension. The processes here are not those of passing on tradition but those by which tradition comes to be *seen as* determining what and how people *should* believe and act. This normative, value-laden, dimension invokes issues of authority and power.

Ann Taves extends Shils's distinction—between content and temporal chains of tradition—into a three-fold distinction that complements Szacki's: 'tradition$_T$ (T = things handed down), tradition$_L$ (L = lineage of chain of variants) and tradition$_A$ (A = sources of authority or legitimation)' (Taves 2011, 114). This underlines that religious beliefs about tradition work because people believe them, not because they are true.

The subjective dimension reveals two different views of tradition's relation to time: unchanging (immune to the forces of history) vs. dynamic (constituted in part by those forces). The *tension between* these views—not just the fact that there are two views—is central to processes of tradition: 'Taking a non-essentialist stance relative to tradition$_L$ and tradition$_T$ means understanding tradition$_L$ and tradition$_T$ as historically constructed products of contestation rather than as guarantors of truths revealed at the beginning and handed down over time' (Taves 2011, 117).

This normative force provides the basis for a different angle on the topic. The primary view of tradition is that it is a type of authority in itself: tradition has authority *because it is tradition*. When tradition comes to be consciously maintained and policed, a new idea gets layered over this one: on top of tradition as authority comes the idea of the keepers of tradition as authorities. Traditions can establish and maintaining institutional authority: certain roles or people have authority *because they preserve or interpret tradition*. This makes traditions and views of *tradition* into prizes in struggles for power.

Some scholars point to the solidification of tradition, a process very much like Max Weber's idea of the routinization of charisma:

> Tradition ... is always an ambiguous concept, both because traditions are always defined by later ages and because, once established, a tradition is soon reified into an orthodoxy, losing its original freshness and innovative capacity. ... Dogmas, creeds, confessions, theologies, ethical codes, rites, sacraments, religious institutions, in short, all the elements of tradition, not only define a religion but also enable its survival. (A. Davies 1999, 20)

A related lesson is that tradition is always some particular group's tradition. If *tradition* (as a tool for talking about religions and other traditions) is cut free from a discussion of specific groups, it risks a crippling lack of precision.

Text Box 4 Negative and positive orientalism

At several points in the book, we will see the idea of *tradition* being used to portray *other* people as backwards, non-modern, passive and irrational. This ideological move is related to orientalism: a distorted view of *the non-west*. Orientalism has had a toxic effect on portrayals of religions like Islam, Hinduism and Sikhism (Abdel-Malek 1963; Said 2003; Inden 2000; King 1999; Mandair 2009). (In Germany and France, 'Orientalism' remains a common description for the academic study of Islam and Islamic cultures. Its scholars, for obvious reasons, distance themselves from negative orientalism [Johansen 2004].)

Orientalism—though always a distortion—is not always negative. It has two dimensions, descriptive (supposed facts) and normative (value judgments laid over these). This makes it very similar to the relational model of *tradition* discussed in the following section. In descriptive terms, orientalism sees *the west* as modern, progressive, scientific, dynamic etc. and *the east* as traditional, archaic, religious, spiritual, mystical, static etc. In normative terms, value judgments can be either negative or positive. Critiquing orientalism involves two steps: correcting the distorted description of east and west; and critiquing the ideological work of the overlaid value judgments.

Negative orientalism (the most well-known type) adds a disparaging value judgment to the false dichotomy between east and west, holding that the characteristics associated with the west are good. There is also a *positive orientalism*. It agrees with the descriptive view but inverts the value judgment (Sedgwick 2004, 266; Granholm 2014, 22–24; Baumann 2015, 19–21). Positive orientalism has been prominent in esoteric currents since the founding texts of Rosicrucianism in the early seventeenth-century (Ackerman 2007). The *Fama Fraternitatis,* one of the foundational texts of Rosicrucianism, tells us that Christian Rosenkreuz, the group's founder, travelled east to find the true, trans-historical traditions that he hoped would inspire a 'general reformation' and bring about a new spiritual era:

> in Damascus ... he heard by chance about the wise men of Damcar in Arabia and the great wonders they performed and how nature was an open book to them. ... There he learned the Arabic language better ... [and] took his physics and mathematics ... At Fez he made the acquaintance of the Elementary Inhabitants ... who revealed to him much of what they knew ... and thereby found an even better foundation for his own belief, a foundation which is in exact harmony with the whole world, and whose impress is wonderfully evident in all periods of time. (Anonymous 2016 [1614–1616], 16–18)

In Theosophy, Helena Blavatsky claimed that she was passing on ancient teachings from the East, that she received from Ascended Masters, adepts who had preserved a pure lineage of spiritual knowledge in Tibet. Traditionalism, a type of perennialism, also holds that the Orient is where true spiritual knowledge has been preserved: it sees the West as a corrupt and degenerate civilization (see Chapter 2.4 and Case Study 1).

1.5 A relational model of tradition

It is helpful to look at *tradition* in relational terms, as related to some words and opposed to others in specific contexts. In the same way, the idea of *sacred* often takes on its meaning in contrast to *profane* (Engler and Gardiner 2017). And *culture* is often defined in contrast to *nature*. *Tradition* too becomes clearer in relation to other concepts. When this is the first step, the second is often ideological: attaching value judgments to one side or other of the resulting conceptual binaries. (The logic is similar to that of *orientalism*—see Text Box 4.)

In both religious and non-religious cases, the concept of *tradition* or its opposites function by claiming the normative high ground in relation to other concepts (Engler 2005a, 359–361; 2005b; 2009a). Paul Ricouer made this point about the concept of *modernity*: 'The term "modern" has indeed changed partners several times (ancient, but also old, traditional), while at the same time binding its fate to different synonyms (recent, new). What is more, the paired terms continue to be accompanied by favorable, pejorative, or neutral connotations' (Ricoeur 2004, 306). The contrast between popular and elite religion has the same relational dynamic: '"Lived religion" evokes a contingent series of oppositions: actual vs. idealized, embodied vs. abstract, experiential vs. doctrinal, folk vs. official, heterodox vs. orthodox, hybrid vs. pure, lived vs. mandated, local vs. global, nonexpert vs. expert, rural vs. urban' (Engler 2016b, 795).

Tradition is a useful concept not because it *refers* to what is passed down but because it *connects* to other ideas in particular contexts, through relations of similarity and difference.[3] It takes on its meaning in binary relation and opposition to other concepts. *Tradition* tends to be associated with the ideas in the first column of Text Box 5 and opposed to those in the second column. (What value judgments get added to this set of distinctions is a separate issue: some groups see one column as good, and other groups take the opposite view.) A particular case of tradition will have many, but not all, of the first set of

---

3. On the importance of variability (heterostasis) as well as similarity (homeostasis) in making sense of complex concepts, see Josephson Storm (2021, 89, 110, 116–118, 154, 177, 180).

characteristics and be opposed to many, but not all, of the other. The relation is a polythetic or family-resemblance one, not of necessary and sufficient criteria (see Engler and Gardiner 2024).

Analysing *tradition* involves clarifying the relational tensions between these concepts. For example, invented traditions can claim the characteristics of the first column while, in fact, operating according to the logic of the second. The conceptual networks

---

Text Box 5 Conceptual binaries of tradition

Traditional	Non-traditional
Old	New
Ancient	Modern
Past	Present
Backward-looking	Forward-looking
Archetypal	Novel
Irrational	Rational
Unintentional	Intentional
Habitual	Spontaneous
Continuous	Discontinuous
Accepted	Invented
Received	Newly created
Mimetic	Inspired
Repetitive	Innovative
Echo	Voice
Scripted	Improvisational
Hand-me-down	Brand new
Conserved	Fresh
Preserved	Freshly minted
Conservative	Progressive
Static	Dynamic
Original (from the beginning)	Original (newly created)
Unitary	Plural
Local/Parochial	Global/Cosmopolitan
Constraining/Binding	Liberating/Freeing

among concepts in a given column tend to be dynamic, even though the opposite is claimed to be the case: 'Traditions are continually negotiated, and shifting. They can never be fully grasped, because individuals and groups are always adapting them to fit personal, historical, and cultural circumstances' (Morrill 2005, 142).

These descriptive binaries are enabled, enacted, empowered or energized when they are superposed with normative binaries. *Tradition* gains its purchase where the conceptual pairs come with value-judgments superimposed: where the Text Box 5 binaries (old vs. new, static vs. dynamic, and received vs. innovated etc.) becomes aligned with a different set of binaries (good vs. bad, right vs. wrong, authentic vs. inauthentic, acceptable vs. unacceptable etc.). (Compare this to negative and positive orientalism, discussed in Text Box 4.) It is this superposition of normative and conceptual polarities that makes *tradition* such a broad and effective label, with great powers of legitimization through identification with established authority. This helps explain the ideological functions of *tradition*, i.e., why holding or denying this high ground has great strategic value for both conservative and reactionary forces.

There are three critical questions to ask:

- Which descriptive oppositions are implicit in a given case of *tradition* (ancient vs. modern, received vs. invented, imitative vs. creative, static vs. dynamic, unitary vs. plural, universal vs. particular, continuous vs. discontinuous etc.)?

- How is this first set of oppositions aligned with a second normative set, i.e., normative distinctions (good vs. evil, useful vs. harmful, authentic vs. inauthentic, orthodox vs. heretical etc.—with one side or the other held to be good and its opposite bad)?

- How do the links between these *two sets* of conceptual oppositions or binaries legitimize and reify specific social, institutional and ideological structures (e.g., kingship can sanctioned by sacred tradition if *tradition*, i.e., column 1, is aligned with *good*; or certain traditional modes of social relations can be seen as dysfunctional and out-of-date, if *tradition* is aligned with *bad*).

Here is the recipe: describe tradition in black-and-white terms; add a polarized value judgment; and use the result in ideological and power struggles. The crucial step is the third one, where the doubled sets of binaries (the descriptive portrayal of tradition with an overlaid normative frame) is used to legitimize an individual, a group, or a set of values, or social structures/institutions.

This is how *tradition*—whether invented from whole cloth or authenticated by divine authority—can be both *traditional* and *radical*, depending on what sort of priest, prophet or scholar is claiming or investing its mantle.

1.6 Chapter summary

This chapter lays some general conceptual groundwork.

Not all languages have a word for *tradition*. When that word gets translated into other languages, different ideas get emphasized. Sometimes, the idea is one of beliefs and practices seen as legitimate and representative of a group, for example, as lived and performed by model members, like elders. This is a common view in Indigenous communities and nations. If *this* is the meaning of tradition, then the idea of identity with the past is secondary. Sometimes a possible translation expresses a form of spirituality. If *this* is tradition, it can point to individual expression; and that contradicts the usual view that tradition shapes the beliefs and actions of an entire group. Ideas considered essential to *tradition* often get lost in translation.

The core meaning of *tradition* in English, since the 1300s, is of *something passed down from generation to generation*. This links other words to *tradition*: for example, *authority, custom, habit, morals, practice, ritual* and *value*. Other meanings—like *betrayal*—have become less common. The decline of this sort of active meaning of *tradition as something that people do* leaves only the idea of passive reception: tradition becomes something that just happens, without people having much choice; it is not something they *make* happen.

SoR emphasizes this same core meaning of tradition as something passed down through time. This means that the tendency to call religions *traditions* brings a bias toward the past, as if *true* religions are always ancient and religious people are always living in the past. If we look at how *tradition* is used in SoR texts, we find such a wide range of overlapping meanings that there seems almost no point to using the word. Students and scholars of religion/s should think about the various meanings of tradition, being clear on which they find and which they intend. Best practice tip: either define *tradition* or avoid the word as much as possible.

A first step for making sense of the complex range of meanings of *tradition* is to look at some of its proposed dimensions: e.g.,

- *Content* (things passed down).
- *Lineages* (themes and variations over time).
- *Carriers* (types of people who play roles in transmission).
- *Processes* (transmission, emergence, consolidation, transmission etc.).
- *Normative evaluations* (whether reified or constructed).
- *Social effects* (functions of traditional authority).
- *Social boundaries* (the line between those who follow a tradition and those who do not).

This list raises several points. The contents of tradition are often irrelevant for critical and historical study (though insiders tend to disagree): the processes and social effects of tradition can be compared regardless of what particular things are passed down. On the other hand, we should try to study the processes of tradition within the contexts of specific groups, not as universal phenomena (see the discussion of Ricoeur in Chapter 6.2). We should distinguish between what people believe about tradition (true or false) and the social and ideological effects of traditions. This also applies to those who study tradition/s: all viewpoints are contestable. A final useful distinction is between two views of meaning. The first is a referential view, which sees the meaning of *tradition* in terms of finding what thing out there in the world this word refers to. The second is an interpretational view, which sees the meaning of tradition in terms of exploring what connections the word has with other concepts. The latter view is more useful for a book on such a complex idea.

The concept of *ideology* is central, because *tradition* often plays this sort of role. What this means is that (i) certain ideas about tradition are often held to be true (legitimate, natural, god-given, just the way things are, etc.), even though (ii) other people have good reasons for rejecting those ideas; and (iii) believing in those ideas gives some people more power than others. From this perspective, it often doesn't matter whether ideas about tradition are true. What matters is that *belief* in those ideas can lead to some people being marginalized and excluded and to others having more power and resources.

Key take-home points—*The word* tradition *means so many things that we need to be clear about what meanings we find and what meanings we use. A good start is (i) to spell out connections to other ideas and (ii) to pay attention to the social and ideological effects of beliefs about tradition.*

Chapter 2

Pure tradition vs. history

The goal of this book is to articulate some of the competing agendas and assumptions that are built into the concept of *tradition*. With that in mind, it is useful to start with the prototypical case of traditions that are *believed* to have three related characteristics: they are passed on without change; they are received passively (people cannot change them or neglect parts); and they have great authority as models of thought and action.

Pure, unchanging tradition—most often a religious view—is different from views of tradition used in historical/critical approaches to the study of religion/s (SoR). Some religious insiders see their tradition(s) as static, ahistorical and unalterable, untouched by time's corrupting influence. Scholars of religion/s see traditions as historical and subject to alteration. This point is crucial, because even scholars often see *tradition* as referring to the pure type. Tradition is better understood not as pure tradition itself but as characterized by *rhetorical appeals to the idea of pure tradition as a strategy of authority.*

The belief that tradition is unchanging is often central in the construction of tradition, *even if the belief is false.* Beliefs that tradition is received, not constructed, are part of how tradition is constructed. Hitchcock put his finger on the key point (see Text Box 2): the MacGuffin (the thing that people chase after in an action film) must seem important to the characters, but what matters to the filmmaker is its impact on the actions of and relations between those characters. Scholars of religion/s are like film directors: we investigate how tradition works: insiders believe certain things about it, but whether these beliefs are true or not tends to be a side-issue. The authenticity, legitimacy, authority, purity and truth of tradition are ideological constructs, not transparent facts; they might or might not be relevant, depending on research goals and on the contexts of particular groups.

2.1 Pure tradition and religionism

Edward Shils, in his classic book *Tradition*, distinguished between the 'real past' ('the past of hard facts') and 'the perceived past' ('the past which is recorded in memory and writing' and which is 'capable of being retrospectively reformed by human beings living in the present') (1981, 195–196). This distinction is more complicated than it seems. First, determining what happened in the past is not a straightforward process. In general, the most we can hope for is more or less probable accounts. Second, the study of history provides evidence that traditions do in fact change, even though members of religions often believe the contrary:

> the post-Enlightenment antinomies—tradition and change; tradition and progress; tradition and modernity—rest on a deep misunderstanding of the nature and behaviour of traditions. ... Although authoritative interpreters police the present to see that it does not stray too far interpretation of the past, it is impossible for traditions to survive unchanged. (Krygier 1986, 251–252)

Traditions claim continuity with the past. Sometimes, often with religions, this continuity takes the extreme form that we are calling *pure tradition*, which we will contrast with *historical tradition*. Tradition seems most religious when it is seen as shielded from decay, exempt from change, outside of history, beyond human interference, in a sense, transcendent. For example, the authority of Tibetan 'treasure revelation' reflects its status outside of history (Gayley 2007). This term refers to a certain type of texts from the early phase of Buddhist propagation in Tibet. They are believed to be found and uncovered in the landscape itself, as opposed to being preserved by people and institutions. By being preserved at a distance from human knowledge and activity, treasure revelation is more authoritative than oral or written tradition. Its authority rests on the claim that—because it was preserved outside the corrupting flow of history—its relation to ancient origins is purer. To give another example, the Rosicrucians—with their perennialist view of tradition (see Chapter 2.3, 2.4 and Case Study 1)—were believed to have reclaimed original esoteric knowledge, side-stepping history's eroding force: they 'were thought to have rediscovered Adam's knowledge in Paradise' (Åkerman 2007, 159).

Pure and historical are extremes on a spectrum of views, and extreme views of the former deny history. Figure 1 illustrates this core contrast with historical tradition. To see tradition as historical is to see change as an inevitable result of historical transmission: something is always lost, added or altered in the moves from generation to generation. The view that tradition is pure denies this. To use a pertinent metaphor, signal loss is inevitable in any process of transmission or of communication (if context's role in meaning is recognized). There is always some difference between what is sent and what is received, due to the effects of intervening time and space, physical materials, ambient conditions, cultural and linguistic contexts etc. Extreme views of pure tradition have faith in the possibility of lossless transmission over a timespan of thousands of years. It is as if all the intervening generations between the origin of tradition and its present reception never existed. The present generation is believed to receive tradition in *the same form* in which it originated: the effects of history—its changes and alterations—do not exist.

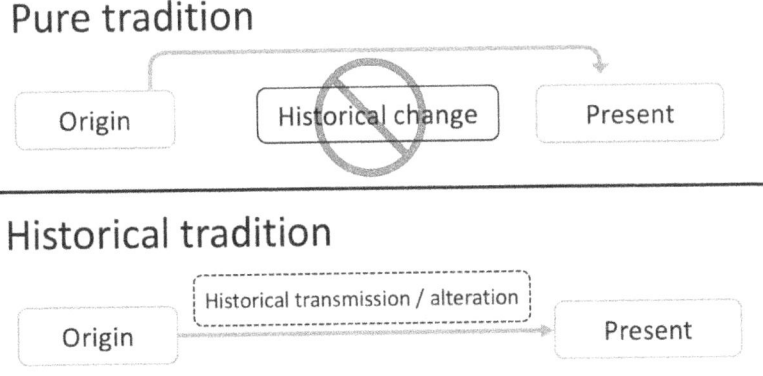

Figure 1 Pure vs. historical tradition

History is side-stepped as the present is plugged back into the pure tradition's origin.

If history is the study of how things were and how they have changed, then, for believers in pure tradition, history is irrelevant. If a tradition is the same today as it has always been, then the only history is the history of Heresy, of how *other* groups diverged from the one true path. For pure tradition, two things matter: the *origin* and the *continuity* of tradition. In SoR, it makes sense to look at what is *believed* to be the case about these two things.

It is useful to think of traditional beliefs as composed of two levels: (i) tradition's content; and (ii) the claim that this content *is* tradition. The founding metamyth of pure tradition is the insistence that it is genuine, authentic, unchanging, transmitted without error etc. This is a *metamyth* because it is a myth about the nature of myths: 'metamyths ... perform an important function in the self-justification of any religious tradition, the essence of which is the perpetuation of the myth that things have not changed when, in fact, they have' (Doniger 1995, 113).

Of course, pure traditions reject others' metamyths as false. Think about the following view of how traditions work themselves out in society:

> Claims of 'tradition' are made in mutual dependency on one another, in constructing *alternatives* in a religiously 'productive' framework of pluralism. That traditions ... are claimed in a situation of competition implies that we have to scrutinize these claims with regard to identity formation. Like identities, traditions are not found but negotiated in a complex process of cultural exchange. (von Stuckrad 2005, 223; original emphasis)

This makes sense if we think of *pure tradition* as something that different groups *claim* for themselves. As scholars of religion/s, we focus on the nature of those claims and their interactions in specific contexts: we do not ask which tradition is the true one.

Claims to pure tradition are found in some aspects of some religions. Modern and liberal religious groups tend to accept the historicity of their traditions. A selected emphasis on pure tradition is more characteristic of orthodox or conservative groups. This not a sharp distinction: these types are the endpoints of a spectrum, abstract models useful for analysis. The pure end of the spectrum tells us something important about religion/s.

Orthodox Christianity is a good example. *Tradition* (*traditio* in Latin; *paradosis* in Greek) plays a foundational role in this type of Christianity. St. Athanasius of Alexandria (296/8–373) offered a clear statement of the normative force of historical transmission, back through the Church Fathers and the Apostles to Christ: 'let us look at the very tradition, teaching, and faith of the Catholic Church from the beginning, which the Lord gave, the Apostles preached, and the Fathers kept. Upon this the Church is founded, and he who should fall away from it would not be a Christian, and should no longer be so called' (Athanasius 1951, 133–134). A twentieth-century Orthodox voice illustrates the ahistorical nature of this tradition on *tradition*:

> Tradition is not a principle striving to restore the past, using the past as a criterion for the present. Such a conception of tradition is rejected by history itself and by the consciousness of the Orthodox Church. ... Tradition is the constant abiding of the Spirit and not only the memory of words. Tradition is a charismatic, not a historical event. (Florovsky 1972, 47)

This is the heart of pure tradition, a metamyth of purity that emphasizes an error-free process of transmission. This metamyth is accompanied by another: the view that the religious tradition in question is true. These claims of inerrant transmission and true correspondence to origins reflect and support each other. Belief in a supernatural origin often serves as the hinge that links them. Supernatural forces can explain the origins and continuity of tradition, protecting it from the erosive processes of history. A lot depends on how we define *supernatural*. For now, it is enough to note that religious pure tradition transcends history *because of* its supernatural origin, often in divine Revelation. Its purity is a sign or warrant of its divine truth, and its origin guarantees error-free transmission, beyond the eroding effects of historical change.

Ancient Mediterranean views of history clarify this relation between pure tradition and religion. In some ancient Greek views, everything this side of the moon (in the sublunary sphere) is subject to change; but beyond the moon (in the aetheric sphere of the planets and stars) everything is eternal and unchanging. Pure tradition brings a spark of unchanging aetheric light down here, below the moon, into the realm of history and change.

The idea of *the secular* is related to this. *Saeculum* was a Roman concept for a unit of time—*era* or *century*—but it shifted in early Christian thought: 'the definitive connotation of the secular as "this worldliness" is bound up with contrasts and complementarities between the heavenly city and earthly existence; between the eternal time (of God) and the time of the "saeculum" or "century"' (McLennan 2015, 130). The contrast between religious and secular—at least in terms of these early origins of the latter term—was that between outside of and inside of time, between beyond and subject to history. This reflects the contrast between pure and historical tradition.

The pure vs. historical distinction is related to a distinction between two approaches to the *scholarship* of tradition/s and religion/s: religionist and historical-critical. As a first approximation, a *religionist* approach accepts certain basic beliefs of religious insiders as true. In this case, religionist scholars accept the core claims of pure tradition. Chapter 2.4 looks at the presence of perennialist views in SoR in order to illustrate this point. It is one example of how religious beliefs (as opposed to beliefs *about* religion) serve as central categories in certain approaches within SoR.

By contrast, historical/critical approaches—including many theoretical and methodological lines from anthropology, critical theory, cultural studies, economics, history, legal studies, literary theory, philology, philosophy, political science, psychology, social theory, sociology, women's and gender studies, etc.—recognize the necessity and value of translating insider discourses into discipline-specific academic discourses. This involves reflecting on the concepts and categories used in analysis, with due attention to epistemological, semantic, ideological and other issues. The historical/critical scholar of religion/s aims to make sense of religious phenomena not from a (quasi-)religious but from a humanistic or social scientific perspective.

This distinction cannot be a stark black-and-white one, as if religious people and religionists, on the one hand, and historical/critical scholars, on the other, have different discourses. That belief would lead to mutual incoherence and methodological solipsism. It would leave scholars with no reason to claim that they are talking about the same thing as the people that they study (Engler and Gardiner 2013).

2.2 Truth, belief and social boundaries

Does tradition's normative force—its power to tell people how they *must* act and to have them act this way *because* of the tradition—depend on its being true? To say *tradition is true* is to attribute truth to the set of beliefs that make up a tradition, including metabeliefs about its origin, nature, transmission, scope and authority. A tradition is *true* for several related reasons: if it originated when and how it is believed by its traditionalists to have originated; if it was transmitted without distorting that origin; if the beliefs that make up its content meet criteria of truth; if its relevance and authority are as believed, etc. Truth is relative to some extent: traditions can be more or less true in all these senses. In addition, different conceptions of *truth* can apply.

If we accept that religions are social and cultural phenomena, key questions involve the roles, impacts and functions of tradition. The issues of how traditions work and whether they are true are related in some cases and not in others: whether they are is a question to be investigated, not an assumption to start with. In this context, the association of *tradition* with a specific social group, as opposed to a historical lineage of normative authority, can be misleading.

The case of Landmarkism, a late-nineteenth-century wing of the US Southern Baptist movement, illustrates the flexible relation between issues of truth and group boundaries. Landmarkism was distinguished by its doctrine of pure tradition. Members believed that the one true Christian church (theirs) was part of a 'visible, definable, continuous, historical succession' of churches, recognizable by their adherence to certain landmark doctrines: 'since the time of Jesus there had always existed an unbroken line of true churches, which was now expressed in the Baptist denomination' (Tull 1975, 7; Hall 2002, 119). Where historians see the origin of the Baptists in the radical wing of the sixteenth-century Protestant Reformation, these Baptists saw themselves as heirs to an unbroken and unchanging tradition stretching back to the origin of Christianity.

Tradition's role in marking and sustaining group boundaries is related to but separate from its doctrinal role. As a distinguishable sub-group of Baptists, Landmarkism had largely disappeared by the mid-twentieth century: in that sense, the tradition was dead. However, its distinguishing view of *tradition* lived on. A 2010–2011 study of students at Southern Baptist colleges found that

> over 39 per cent said that Baptists could be traced as a denomination from John the Baptist to the present day Baptist churches. Sixty-two per cent said that … Baptist churches can be traced through groups of various names back to the first church in Jerusalem. … Over 98 per cent of those surveyed could not identify Landmarkism from a list of multiple choice answers. (Maples 2018, 205)

A doctrine of pure tradition was once the distinguishing characteristic of a sub-group, but now it is a view held by southern Baptists in general. The close relation between social boundaries and a particular theological claim dissolved, but the latter survived.

Beliefs about social boundaries are themselves aspects of tradition and, as such, can be effective even where they are false. For example, Landmarkism held that 'the doctrine of an unbroken succession of Baptist churches was necessary in order to identify the true church. … Baptists were known down through the centuries as: Novatians, Donatists, Phrygians, Galatians, Armenians, Paulicians, Paterines, Vaudois, Albigenses, Lollards, Waldenses, and Anabaptists' (Maples 2015, 133–134). This distorts historical facts. These groups bear only superficial similarities, more so in some cases than others. This is not a critique. It just underlines that the issue of truth is secondary. This tradition's metamyth supports claims of theological authority because followers *believe* it, not because it reflects the views of historical experts. What else would we expect, if we believe that our tradition was founded and maintained by an all-powerful supernatural being?

Sometimes belief in pure tradition is immune to historical critique or other conflicting evidence. In other cases, the introduction of alleged new facts can undermine its authority (see Text Box 6). This tells us something about SoR's relations to its objects of study. If denying the historicity of tradition (by making it pure) increases its

---

Text Box 6 Tradition as forgery
(the Hermetic Order of the Golden Dawn)

When authority is based on invented traditions, it can be undermined if that fact is made public. A dramatic example is the decline of the Hermetic Order of the Golden Dawn, the most important esoteric and magical group of the late nineteenth and early twentieth centuries.

In 1886, prominent British occultist William Wynn Westcott (1848-1925) came into possession of descriptions of a series of rituals. He soon founded the Order, along with Samuel Liddell Mathers (1854-1918). The group's authority was based on a perennialist view of tradition (the historical transmission of timeless or ancient truths): a series of letters from an important German adept guaranteed that the Order's rituals and teachings were rooted in ancient truths.

However, the crucial 'correspondence with the supposed German adept Anna Sprengel was fabricated by Westcott in order to provide the Order with a convincing pedigree'; 'Westcott also created a spurious history for his Order, claiming descent from a hybrid body that conflated a genuine masonic lodge at Frankfurt with a fictitious Rosicrucian Society' (Pasi 2005, 1169; Gilbert 2005, 545). Rising tensions between Westcott and Mathers led to the erosion of the group's authority. Mathers made

> an extraordinary claim about Westcott that undermined the integrity of the Golden Dawn and threatened to destroy the Order. Mathers claimed that he alone had ever been in communication with the Secret Chiefs and that Westcott had forged the original correspondence with Anna Sprengel. What he seems to have failed to recognise is that if the members of the Order believed him then they would realise that the Golden Dawn was an utter sham, based on forgery and deceit. (Gilbert 2005, 549)

authority, then historical/critical scholarship can be a direct threat to that authority. SoR can be *rightly* seen as a threat by many of the people we study. Scholars can be easy to ignore because they are outsiders. On the other hand, scholars are sometimes seen as allies in religious claims of pure tradition (see Case Study 2).

There are *exclusive* and *inclusive* extremes along a spectrum of views of pure tradition. These vary in the extent to which other groups are seen as sharing the same pure base. In exclusive pure tradition, the emphasis on inerrant transmission of genuine tradition results in sharp doctrinal, ritual, institutional and social boundaries: only *our small group* has true tradition. Inclusive views open up the scope of *tradition*, if only to traditions seen as sharing the same source. The official Catholic position on intercommunion (whether other Christians can share in the Eucharist) is relatively exclusive. It excludes Protestants on the basis of their churches' failure to preserve tradition:

> Ecclesial communities derived from the Reformation and separated from the Catholic Church, 'have not preserved the proper reality of the Eucharistic mystery in its fullness, especially because of the absence of the sacrament of Holy Orders'. It is for this reason that, for the Catholic Church, Eucharistic intercommunion with these communities is not possible. (*Catechism* 1993, ¶1400)

The language of an ecumenical Catholic-Lutheran document published by the US Conference of Catholic Bishops is more inclusive: 'Despite all remaining differences in the ways we speak and think of the eucharistic sacrifice and our Lord's presence in his supper, we are no longer able to regard ourselves as divided in the one holy catholic and apostolic faith on these two points' ('Eucharist' 1967).

In sum, claims that religious tradition is passed on pure and unaltered, insulated from historical change, are something to be investigated by SoR for their social and ideological effects. Pure religious traditions assert both the truth of beliefs and the accuracy of transmission. Historical-critical scholarship asks other questions about the conditions and effects of these claims. It investigates the processes that lead to and result from the inception, transmission, reception, reconfiguration and (re-)invention of traditions in specific contexts.

SoR—if it aspires to be at all critical—should investigate *tradition* and traditions in light of the same profane historical processes that are fenced off by pure tradition. I say this not because I insist that it is *the truth*, but because it is more productive given the goals and contexts of SoR.

2.3 Ancient perennialism

Exclusive appeals to the authority of tradition played a role in debates over authority in ancient Europe. As cited below, Wouter J. Hanegraaff writes that early Christian apologists appealed to a certain concept of 'Tradition' (2012, 17). In this context, we can contrast perennialist and emerging Christian views.

A perennialist view of tradition was prominent in some cultures of the ancient Mediterranean. It was and remains central to esoteric currents. This reflected 'the idea that there exists an enduring tradition of superior spiritual wisdom, available to humanity since the earliest periods of history and kept alive through the ages, perhaps by a chain of divinely inspired sages or initiatory groups'; this view has had various names, 'prisca theologia, prisca sapientia, pia philosophia, (philo)sophia perennis, perennial philosophy, perennial wisdom, "the wisdom of the ancients", or simply "Tradition" with a capital T' (Hanegraaff 2005, 1125). This is very different from the idea that tradition accumulates, sediments or builds up over historical time. It is also different from the Christian idea of Revelation.

Early Christianity developed a sense of tradition that contrasted with this perennialist view. Christianity faced an uphill battle in being accepted as a *religion* in Roman culture because it was, at that time, a new development. It was traditionless:

> the assertion of modern origin was equivalent to the assertion of historical insignificance. Nothing could be both new and true. It was a general conviction of the age that the oldest was always best, that the present was an age of decadence, a low point on the universal cycle; that the 'ancients' were nearer to the gods and the beginnings of things and therefore knew much more about them. ... Judaism at least has the advantage of being traditional. Christianity, on the other

> hand, has no tradition and hence no authority for its doctrines. ... In comparison to Judaism ... Christianity is far worse. It has no native tradition upon which to base its doctrines. ... Put simply, Christianity is a deliberate distortion of the ancient theological tradition. (Droge 1989, 4, 78, 80)[1]

The *ancient theological tradition* that Droge refers to—from which Christianity was excluded because it was a recent innovation—was not historical but trans-historical. This perennialist view of tradition was taken up by some early Christian theologians. It reflected

> the basic assumption (peculiarly unhistorical to us, but quite natural to them) that all the great sages represented one and the same, timeless and universal wisdom tradition. ... Apologeticism—the polemical defense of one's own position as superior to others—was central to the ancient wisdom discourse from its very beginning, and 'Tradition' was the symbolic capital over which the various participants were competing. ... The unquestioned assumption they all held in common was that antiquity equaled superiority. ... (Hanegraaff 2012, 16–17)

However, Christian authors began to develop a distinct sense of *tradition*. They inverted these evaluations of religion (good because ancient) and superstition (bad because new):

> Why are we ungrateful? why do we grudge if the truth of divinity has ripened in the age of our time? Let us enjoy our benefits, and let us in rectitude moderate our judgments; let superstition [*superstitio*] be restrained; let impiety be expiated; let true religion [*vera religio*] be preserved. (Minucius Felix 160–250 CE?, 38.7)

The true religion to be preserved was a new Christian tradition that had arrived on the scene not long before, inspired by *Revelation*.

The Christian view of tradition differed from the perennialist view in two main ways. First, Christian Revelation emphasized recent Revelation and transmission via a more recent set of identifiable figures: 'In the early Fathers tradition means the revelation made by God and delivered by Him to His people through the prophets and

---

1. Droge paraphrases/cites *The True Word* (*Alethes Logos*) by Celsus, a second-century critic of Christianity. Passages of that book are preserved only in the work of Origen (184/185–253/254 CE) who cited them to argue against them.

apostles. It denotes something "handed over," not something "handed down"' (Livingstone 2013). Second, it was narrower in doctrinal and social terms, being identified with a small set of Christian texts, in contrast to the perennialist emphasis on the presence of one true tradition that included Egyptian, Assyrian, Persian, Zoroastrian, Orphic, Pythagorean and sometimes Jewish and other currents.

The development of modern perennialist views began during the Italian Renaissance (Sedgwick 2023, 27–31). Marsilio Ficino (1433–1499) and Giovanni Pico della Mirandola (1463–1494) thought of pre-Christian philosophers not as pagans but as ancient theologians (*prisci theologi*). Agostino Steuco (1498–1548) labelled these ancient teachings *perennial philosophy* (*philosophia perennis*). The lineage of transmission included Noah, Zoroaster, Moses, Orpheus, Hermes Trismegistus, Pythagoras, Plato and the Neo-Platonist thinker Iamblichus. English Hebraist, classicist, theologian and philosopher Ralph Cudworth (1618–1688) dealt with the criticism that these ancient thinkers were polytheists by suggesting that their apparently anti-Christian views were just the external or *exoteric* side of their ideas: beneath those lay a secret monotheistic theology. This was a key step in the growing link between perennialist thought and esotericism.

2.4 Perennialism and religionism in SoR

Perennialist views continue alive and well, and they have had a direct impact on academia, including the study of religion/s (Sedgwick 2023, 35–37; see Case Study 1). As noted above, historical/critical and religionist approaches in SoR can be contrasted. The former take a human- or social-scientific view of how academic knowledge claims should be supported; the latter include some theological modes of supporting knowledge claims. Perennialist views are a third sort of approach, seldom acknowledged in SoR. That is, we can contrast two different religionist currents in SoR: *crypto-theology* holds that religion is about faith, and that history studies, at most, traditions that reflect this; and *perennialism* holds that religion is about true tradition, and that history studies, at most, contingent features that reflect this. Note the contrasting place of *tradition*.

Some scholars—sometimes characterized as holding a *crypto-theological* position—hold that religion is a *sui generis* phenomenon, something only accessible through religious experience and not through history. From this perspective, tradition is a side-issue. For Max Müller (1823–1900),

> religion means at least two very different things ... a body of doctrine handed down by tradition ... [and] a faculty of faith in man, independent of all historical religions. If we say that it is religion which distinguishes man from the animal, we do not mean ... any special religion; but we mean a mental faculty, that faculty which ... enables man to apprehend the Infinite under different names, and under varying disguises. (Müller 1873, 16–17)

Wilfred Cantwell Smith proposed that the study of religion/s should rest on a distinction between 'cumulative tradition' ('the entire mass of overt objective data that constitute the historical deposit ... of the past religious life of the community') and 'faith' ('an inner religious experience or involvement of a particular person; the impingement on ... [them] of the transcendent, putative or real') (W. Smith 1964, 141). Müller's distinction between tradition (as found in historical religions) and universal faith and Smith's 'tradition-faith analysis' (1964, 176) both categorize tradition under history and faith under the timeless. This has the effect of downplaying or marginalizing historical/critical approaches, because they do not deal with the primary aspect of religion, the quality of faith that is found in all religions. Historical/critical approaches play at most a supporting role of cataloguing details and variations. The religionist core is transhistorical and transcultural.

If we keep our eye on the ball of *tradition*, perennialism is a different religionist approach, with seldom noted implications for SoR. It takes history seriously, but in an esoteric not critical light. It illustrates how the religionist view converges on insider views of the purity of tradition and of the negation of history. *Perennialism* refers to a set of religious, esoteric and philosophical belief systems that distinguish true traditions from false. True traditions have an authentic relation to a primordial (often pre-historic and eastern) 'original Tradition seen as the mother of all others' (Faivre 1999, 8). By contrast, false traditions and religions have lost the thread of true Tradition. The perennialist views of tradition are not always extreme views of pure, static, unchanging tradition. The idea that one true Tradition is passed on from ancient times tends to emphasize this, but a degree of historical change can be accepted.

The perennialist view of tradition is still contrasted with the Christian view, as found, for example, in Orthodox Christianity. The Orthodox Christian Church's claim that tradition is charismatic and ahistorical itself depends on a nuanced tapestry of institutional and traditional authority. This historical tradition about *tradition* here tempers the radical view that *true* tradition is ahistorical.

Perennial tradition involves an esoteric appeal to a line of tradition that reaches further back and that emphasizes the continuity of that knowledge throughout that history (Hanegraaff 2012, 8–12). Ancient ideas of *prisca theologia* (primal theology) and *philosophia perennis* (perennial philosophy) played prominent roles in Renaissance esoteric thought, eighteenth-century Christian theosophy, nineteenth-century occultism and modern Theosophy (Faivre 1999; Hanegraaff 2005). And it is found within SoR (see Case Study 1).

Scholars who hold that all religions share a common core tend to argue one of two things (see Figure 2). They either hold that all true religions share a common origin, with core beliefs and practices passed down over time, so that religions are like the branches of a single tree; or they hold that a common experience lies behind all religions, e.g., Aldous Huxley's view that mystical or hallucinogenic experiences reveal this common core. The former is continuous, involving ongoing transmission of tradition (receiving the core). The latter is discontinuous, involving repeated re-discovery through mystical experience (perceiving the core). The word *perennialism* is often used for both of these views. However, following usage in the study of esotericism/s—where the concept is central—it is better to limit *perennialism* to the first of these senses: the path of unchanging tradition, not that of inner experience. We can use the term *mysticism* for the second sense (keeping in mind that this is a complex and debated concept).

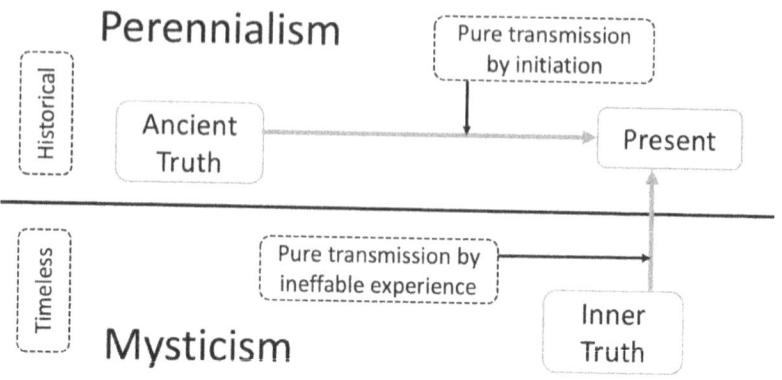

Figure 2 Perennial vs. mystical tradition

Huston Smith—a former President of the American Academy of Religion—is one of the most well-known advocates of this perennial sense of tradition. Smith held a soft, hybrid form of perennialism. His idea of *wisdom traditions* emphasized both the experience and tradition paths: he was influenced by Huxley and by Traditionalist Frithjof Schuon (1907–1998).

Smith's perennialism shaped his views of religions and how they should be studied. Throughout most of history 'primordial tradition' with its mythic dimension was a form of 'human unanimity', until it experienced a 'collapse' in the face of modernity and science (H. Smith 1992, 5; see 54n23, 158). As a result, modern forms of religion are debased, because they have lost touch with tradition: 'In religion modernity demythologizes tradition to accommodate it to its one-story universe' (H. Smith 1992, 6). The study of religion/s should be conducted in a religionist mode, rejecting historical/critical methods: 'science ... can glimpse a land across the river, but its methods do not enable it to enter that land' (H. Smith 1992, 116). For Smith, non-perennialist (i.e., historical/critical and social scientific) approaches to the study of true tradition/s and religion/s are doomed to fail, because 'true reality is never the most obvious': we should recognize 'the mistake of reductionism—spirit reduced to metamorphosed matter (Darwinism), truth reduced to ideology (Marxism), psyche reduced to sex (Freud ...)'; rejecting historical/critical approaches 'sets us against the modern outlook and turns us back toward tradition' (H. Smith 1992, 41). Because truth is timeless, having been passed down without alteration, it can be found here and now—if you know where and how to look. History, as a perspective on human society and culture, is dangerous and misleading: views of historical progress are central to the modern outlook that has resulted in our separation from primordial traditions (H. Smith 1992, 120).

For Smith, SoR should seek capital-t Tradition and reject modernity. This involves rejecting a historical perspective: the only part of the past the scholars of religion/s should value is the pure tradition that stands outside of history. Our personal, academic and civilizational quests are one and the same: 'it concerns truth, truth of the kind that is timeless. … If we have appealed to past ages it is because we see them as having been bathed in such truth to a degree that we are not' (H. Smith 1992, 146). Huston Smith's presidential plenary address to the American Academy of Religion is a striking rejection of a historical/critical study of religion/s in favour of perennialism (1989; see Sedgwick 2004, 166).

Where Müller and W. C. Smith see tradition as historical, opposed to (but leaving room for) faith, Huston Smith places false tradition on the side of history: true tradition is moved over to the timeless, ahistorical side of the ledger. This is pure tradition as a vision of the true object of SoR. From this perspective, the historical/critical study of religion/s is locked out, unable to arrive at a true account of religious phenomena: the majority of scholarship in SoR is marginally useful at best, because it is conducted by those outside pure tradition; only insiders (members of religions and religionist scholars) can have access to that Tradition.

In sum, perennialism undermines historical/critical SoR. The two are irreconcilable and incommensurable because perennialist 'doctrines derive from metaphysical intuitions, and … like mystical theophanies, metaphysical intuitions are ultimately ineffable' (H. Smith 1987, 554). Ineffable, according to the OED, applies to what 'cannot be expressed or described in language; [is] too great for words; transcending expression; unspeakable, unutterable, inexpressible'. What can we add to that?

2.5 Chapter summary

This chapter looks at the idea of *pure tradition* (unchanging, unaltered, immune to the forces of history). This is contrasted with *historical tradition*, which sees tradition as something that changes over time. The idea of pure tradition has great power, even if it is not true: the *belief* that tradition is unchanging has great force. This means that the difficult, sometimes impossible, work of doing historical research into the origin and trajectory of a given tradition can turn out to be useless. If tradition's social effects are based on belief not facts, then whether the belief matches the facts is often irrelevant.

Tradition has normative power: it shapes how people think and act because they see it as the right way of doing things. This raises questions about the relation between tradition and truth. The belief that tradition is truth often takes a powerful form in religious contexts. More orthodox and conservative religious groups often portray themselves as those who have the one and only pure, authentic unchanged tradition. This idea can help form, strengthen and maintain those groups. But the idea of *pure tradition* does more. Some groups have an exclusive view of pure tradition (*only we are truly traditional*) or a more inclusive view (*a few others share this with us*). These dynamics go back to ancient times and are found in many cultures.

Perennialist views of tradition have been influential in Europe for thousands of years. This is the view that there is a stream of ancient tradition kept alive over the ages, and preserved in certain living communities. Early Christianity was excluded by mainstream Roman culture at first, because it had new ideas, not perennial truths. Some Christian authors soon claimed their own perennial truths, in order to tap into the authority that came with having this sort of tradition. But a Christian sense of tradition soon emerged: based in Revelation at a point in history, not in ancient transmission; and more limited to specific (i.e., Christian) groups.

Perennialist views are more characteristic of esoteric streams and groups, and these have played a role within SoR. Critical perspectives that reject theological influences in SoR often fail to note the presence of perennialist views, which are also religionist. The twentieth-century perennialist (esoteric) movement of

Traditionalism has had a significant impact (Sedgwick 2023). Perennialist influences in SoR can be more exclusive or inclusive. Scholars of religion/s influenced by perennialist ideas tend toward the latter extreme, some even seeing most religions as expressions of the same ancient spiritual truth.

Traditionalism illustrates the tension between religionist and historical/critical approaches to studying traditions and religions. If the understanding of religious traditions is only possible for insiders, then there can be no academic SoR: we would have nothing to study. Even if we were members of a tradition, there would be no way for non-members to understand it, even if we tried to explain it to them. This book sides with historical/critical approaches to studying traditions and religion, not because we can prove that these approaches are *true*, but because religionist, hard-insider views of *tradition* and *religion*, like perennialism, are less *useful* for studying the public faces of religious beliefs and practices.

The task of the academic study of religion is to investigate the historical, social and ideological processes (all at times *religious*) that constitute traditions, and to analyse their conceptual presuppositions and implications. This tells us a lot about our own academic traditions about *tradition*, and so about *religion*.

Key take-home points—*The pure view that tradition is most authentic when it repeats the past is often found in more orthodox and conservative religious groups and also in many esoteric groups. Esoteric perennialist ideas and groups (which see religious truth as passed down from ancient times) illustrate the power of that idea. They also show why that view of tradition is something that scholars of religion/s should study, but not a view that they should use to define their object of study.*

Case Study 1: Traditionalism and the denial of historical truth

The movement initiated by twentieth-century French esotericist René Guénon—Traditionalism or the Traditionalist School—is a clear example of the link between essentialist, perennialist views of tradition and the explicit denial of historical/critical methods.

Beginning in 1906, Guénon (1886-1951) became involved with the study of esotericism, occultism and spiritualism, including high-level participation in Masonic groups. From 1912 to 1923, reflecting his study of Hinduism and his indoctrination into a small Sufi order, he criticized and rejected these esoteric groups and their claims to constitute authentic initiatory traditions. His own distinctive views were established in 1927 with his classic book, *La crise du monde moderne* (*The crisis of the modern world*) (1994). Guénon moved to Cairo in 1930 and spent the rest of his life there, learning Arabic, integrating into Egyptian society, practising Sufism and writing Traditionalist books and articles (Quinn 2005).

The heart of Traditionalism is the view that false religions reflect and maintain the modern West's lack of sacred knowledge: 'parasitic vegetation must not be confused with the very Tree of Tradition' (Guénon cited in Sedgwick 2004, 58). These regressive inversions of pure and authentic Tradition are entered into through *counterinitiation*. This view informed Guénon's broad idea of *tradition*: 'the identification of tradition with the entire civilization is fundamentally justifiable', but this only applied to eastern civilizations (including Islamic societies), where true Tradition had been preserved (Guénon 2009, 94). This is possible on the view that primordial Tradition is unified, despite any appearances to the contrary. Italian Traditionalist Julius Evola, for example, saw Tradition as a set of principles that belonged to the unchanging metaphysical world (as opposed to the changeable physical one): 'This whole can be called "tradition" in the singular mode, since values and principles are basically the same throughout, notwithstanding obvious variations in historical form' (cited in Ferraresi 1987, 111). Guénon taught that the 'traditional world has been swept away ... by degenerative and spiritually involutional processes. ... The "modern world" ... is a pure and simple negation of Tradition' (Evola 1994, 12).

The *Traditionalist school* also includes the work of related thinkers, most importantly Ananda K. Coomaraswamy (1877-1947), Frithjof Schuon (1907-1998), Julius Evola (1898-1974), Seyyed Hossein Nasr (1933-) and Alexander Dugin (1962-). The writings of Guénon, Schuon and other traditionalists had an important impact on religious thinkers such as Thomas Merton (1915-1968) and Henry Corbin (1903-1978), as well as on academic scholars of religions, including Huston Smith (1919-) and Jacob Needleman (1934-) (Quinn 1997, 40-41; Sedgwick 2004, 162-167). Mircea Eliade (1907-1986) was influenced by Traditionalism, though scholars differ about how much:

> some central and characteristic concepts of Eliade's thought derive some of their features—in some cases fundamental ones—directly from his reading and his use of the works of the traditionalists. This is true in particular of the concepts of anthropo-cosmic correspondence, of the symbol, of the sacred centre, of the 'cyclical' quality of traditional time, of human construction as a repetition of cosmogony, of sacrifice as reintegration, of androgyny, and of the archetype. (Spineto 2001, 68; see also Quinn 1997, 36, 42, 101, 140, 209, 269; Wasserstrom 1999, 38, 40, 44-47; Urban 2001, 440; Sedgwick 2004, 109-116, 162-167, 189-192; 2023, 55-59; Ingram 2008, 211, 219n268; Hanegraaff 2012, 306; Asprem and Granholm 2013, 42)

There are different emphases within this modern take on perennialism. Mark Sedgwick distinguishes between 'hard' (*overt*) and 'soft' (*non-overt*) Traditionalists (Sedgwick 2004, 111, 269). There are also more and less exclusive formations. Guénon, Coomaraswamy and Schuon are exclusivist, relegating almost all religions to the category of non-authentic, regressive instances of counterinitiation. By contrast, Huston Smith's emphasis on *wisdom traditions* exemplified a more inclusive vision of religious pluralism: 'Don't search for a single essence that pervades the world religions. Recognize them as multiple expressions of the Absolute which is indescribable' (H. Smith 1994, 277; see Sedgwick 2004, 165-167; 2023, 61-63).

Soft Traditionalism has left its mark on SoR. A comparison of two contemporaneous articles on Islamic views of evolutionary theory illustrates its unacknowledged influence (Alam 1992; Danner 1991).

Both authors were university professors: Shah Manzoor Alam in India and Victor Danner in Bloomington, Indiana. Alam wrote an article that is rooted in quranic interpretation. Danner, on the other hand, was secretly a leading member of the most important group of Maryami (Muslim Schuonian) Traditionalists in the USA (Sedgwick 2004, 161–162). His article brands the West as corrupted by 'evolutionism'—i.e., a regressive belief in progress—an accusation that is more Traditionalist than Muslim. Note the irony: the American Religious Studies professor—not the Muslim scholar—presents the more radical religionist view, with his presuppositions obscured. Another example is *The Sacred Pipe*, an influential text on Sioux beliefs and practices, written by Traditionalist Joseph Epes Brown, another follower of Schuon (Brown 1989; see Sedgwick 2004, 123).

How can perennialist claims regarding these *contacts with metaphysical reality* be assessed? Guénon was explicit that ideas passed down by the sorts of written sources that historians use as evidence can tell us nothing about Tradition: 'No tradition has "come to our knowledge" by "writers" ... Their works have only provided us with a convenient occasion to present it, which is quite different' (cited in Borella 1992, 336). Writing as a follower, Jean Borella clarifies how Guénon's ideas were supported:

> Guénon calls on only the intrinsic evidence of the truth. ... [He] means that, by definition, metaphysical doctrine possesses its truth within itself, that it does not depend at all on a reference to any authority but only on the assent of the intelligence that becomes aware of it. Moreover, a direct teaching given by an authentic representative to a qualified mind communicates a deeper comprehension of the religion or tradition than any scientific study. (Borella 1992, 336–337, original emphasis)

For Guénon, 'it was an absolute and indispensable requisite to believe a profound religious or metaphysical doctrine or principle in order to understand it' (Quinn 1997, 25; see Faivre 1999, 33). The result is a strong version of insiderism, one committed to a relation of untranslatability or uninterpretability between insider and outsider languages (see Gardiner and Engler 2012, 245). The contrast with historical/critical SoR could not be sharper.

Chapter 3

Invention and authority

Keeping in mind the book's goal of drawing out different assumptions and agendas that come bundled with *tradition*, this chapter takes a look behind the curtain of that concept's work. Where the previous chapter looked at the idea of pure tradition, this one looks at invented traditions. The key point is that traditions can claim authority whether they are ancient or invented last week, as long as people *believe* that they are passed on from the past.

Some traditions are ancient. Others are invented and presented as old. Drawing a sharp line between the two is difficult. The past does not exist anymore, only memories, stories, texts and artefacts etc. *Some* of these things that are left behind—many falling under the heading of *tradition*—become sites of divergent interpretations and valuations. This is prominent in the modern world, because memory and tradition have become less a taken-for-granted shared backdrop and more a series of self-conscious projects: 'there are *lieux de memoire*, sites of memory, because there are no longer *milieux de memoire*, real environments of memory' (Nora 1989, 7). Granted that the study of religion/s (SoR) achieves more useful academic results (not *true* by all definitions of that word) by taking historical/critical approaches, there remain important questions about how best to do this. The idea that some traditions are true and some false is a valuable test case.

Some scholars suggest that it is important to distinguish authentic from invented traditions. Others argue that all traditions, including academic discourses, are invented. This chapter explores both these views, underlining the relative nature of judgments regarding *genuine* tradition and the play of ideology across the entire spectrum of relations between traditions and their putative sources. When we start to focus on *how tradition-talk is used*, not on the historical status of traditions themselves, our attention shifts to perceptions. As Hungarian folklorist Tamás Hofer writes, 'it is generally understood that traditions are continuously created and recreated in the life of any modern society and that it is difficult to draw a dividing line between the "invention" of a new tradition and the creation of a new "tradition awareness" for an old one' (1984, 135–136).

3.1 The invention of tradition

Imagine that you have invented a brand-new religious idea or practice. How would you get people to believe in it, to see it as legitimate or authoritative? One important strategy in the history of religions has been to claim that the innovation is not yours and not new: it is a tradition. As historian of Christianity Ronald Knox put it, 'Your prophet who passes for an innovator in the eyes of his contemporaries does not admit the charge; he claims, rather, to be restoring the godly discipline which flourished in apostolic times, now overgrown with neglect' (1950, 9). But who gets to decide, and how, whether a tradition is old or faux-old?

Historical work can be useful for uncovering the origin of certain traditions and the conditions of their transmission. Olav Hammer looks at the Swedish traditions of Lucia Day, a 13 December celebration of the coming shift to longer days after the darkest point in winter: 'much of the modern Lucia tradition ... was created within the space of a few years around the turn of the twentieth century, and received a major boost when it was publicized by a Stockholm newspaper in 1927' (Hammer 2016, 719). But the rituals continue. How could this tradition still be a tradition, when an important scholar of religion/s has *outed* their invented status? Perhaps what people believe and do matters more than how scholars label things.

A simple distinction between authentic and invented traditions tends to miss what matters most: *beliefs* about the authenticity and authority of *tradition*. Seeing tradition as *the given* ignores the strategic value of claiming the high ground of tradition in struggles for power. Polish anthropologist Bronisław Malinowski (1884–1942) emphasized that myth is 'a hard-working active force' (1961, 101).

Recent scholarship extends this insight in seeing *tradition* as a strategic device that must be analysed in specific contexts: 'tradition is actively constructed and ... its importance for any given group is situational: each social and cultural context generates different uses for tradition as a legitimation strategy'; it is 'a category that cannot be removed from the historical and hermeneutic contexts in which it is being employed'; the meaning of *tradition* 'is not determined by the static purity of its "ancientness," but rather by how its "ancientness" is imagined and used' (Hjelm 2005, 121; Hawley 2005, 317; Grieve 2005, 280).

The *invention of tradition* became an important idea starting with a 1983 book of that title (Hobsbawm and Ranger 2012).[1] The various authors emphasize political uses of visions of the past and new secular rituals in the United Kingdom and its colonies from the late 1700s to the early 1900s. Eric Hobsbawm and Terence Ranger argued that the usual reason for inventing tradition is to legitimize authority, by associating some belief, practice or institution with a positively valued conception of the past. As Max Weber noted, 'In the pure type of traditional authority it is impossible for law or administrative rule to be deliberately created by legislation. Rules which in fact are innovations can be legitimized only by the claim that they have been "valid of yore"' (1978, 227).

The invention of tradition involves creating an alternative version of the past that legitimates something new. Invented traditions 'are responses to novel situations which take the form of reference to old situations, or which establish their own past by quasi-obligatory repetition ...' (Hobsbawm and Ranger 2012, 1; see Sarot 2001, 30). For example, the medieval Muslim scholar Ibn al-Hajj (c.1258–1336) attempted to legitimate a new ritual development, the Night of the Ascension festival, by linking it to practices from the first generations of Muslims: 'Ibn al-Hajj presents a discourse in which a notion

---

1. For anthropologists, the spark for these discussions came a year earlier, in a special issue of *The Australian Journal of Anthropology* (then *Mankind*), titled *Reinventing Traditional Culture: The Politics of Kastom in Island Melanesia* (Keesing and Tonkinson 1982).

of tradition is constructed in the service of a reformist agenda' (Colby 2005, 48).

Hobsbawm and Ranger suggest that the invention of tradition—and the '(re)-invention' of 'extinct' traditions—became more frequent in modernity, as 'the old ways' of genuine traditions became threatened by rapid social transformation (1983, 4-8). Re-making tradition is another useful strategy for adapting to changing social circumstances (see Case Study 2). For example, in an act of 'cultural recalibration' by incarcerated Native Hawaiians, a traditional ritual, Makahiki, became 'temporally compressed and symbolically condensed to meet the conditions of its new contexts' (G. Johnson 2005, 207-208).

Both those with and those without power use the *tradition* label in struggles for legitimacy and authority. The invention of traditions by the British in colonial India helped prop up the power and authority of an Imperial centre: a 'ritual idiom [was] created to express, make manifest and compelling the British construction of their authority over India'; but the same idiom could be appropriated by the colonized: 'Indians ... came to develop a public political ideal of their own ... that in effect ... used the same idiom that their British rulers employed' (Cohn 1983, 208-209).

A look at the role of sacred texts in the (re)invention of tradition helps illustrate the complexity of these processes. James R. Lewis and Olav Hammer draw several useful distinctions (2007, 1-17). Some innovations are seen by insiders as recent—as in the writings of L. Ron Hubbard (Rothstein 2007) and Carlos Castaneda (Hardman 2007; see Text Box 7)—and, for others, 'the crucial legitimating events are projected centuries if not millennia in the past', as with the Latter Day Saints (Lewis and Hammer 2007, 5; see D. Davies 2007). Some invented traditions bestow legitimacy on their own community's beliefs and others seek to delegitimize the beliefs of others. On the one hand, an existing tradition can be attacked as inauthentic, for example in attempts by anti-cult groups to delegitimize the Family Federation for World Peace and Unification (FFWPU, formerly the Unification Church) by claiming that Sun Myung Moon's book, *Divine Principle*, was plagiarized (Chryssides 2007). On the other hand, a counter-tradition can be invented to undermine an existing one, for example, the *Protocols of the Learned Elders of Zion* was a false story of Jewish tradition that attacked Jewish tradition (Partridge and Geaves 2007).

The misattribution of authorship is an important mode of the invention of religious traditions. It takes three forms: texts written pseudepigraphically (said to have been written by a well-known historical figure, like an important earlier religious leader); texts later attributed to such figures; and texts attributed to people who never existed. All are effective strategies for framing innovation as tradition, in planning or in hindsight. Scholars, as well as members of religions, have been responsible for this invention of authorial tradition. Michael Stausberg looks at 'Zoroaster as a figure of authorization and a screen of ascription', and he finds that 'the study of Zoroastrianism is an example of modern scholarship actually producing a pseudepigraph' (2007, 178).

Lewis and Hammer also distinguish between traditions that claim legitimacy by attributing the authorship of texts to figures within one's perceived community—as is the case with the Hebrew Bible (P. Davies 2007) and the New Testament (Thomassen 2007)—and those that do so by 'projecting one's beliefs onto … exotic others'—a modern European and North American strategy of appealing to Asian or Indigenous beliefs and practices (Lewis and Hammer 2007, 8). The latter strategy is often found in positive orientalism (see Text Box 4).

In sum, there are many ways of inventing traditions of different types, but the motivation for doing so is the same: to claim the normative authority that comes with tradition's perceived connection to a valued vision of the past.

3.2 True and false traditions

Inventing tradition is a tactic for claiming normative authority. This is often done in two steps: re-imagining the past in terms of present norms; then claiming that the authority of this view of the past legitimizes that set of norms over its competitors. Present concerns are projected onto the past, and the past legitimates the present: these two linked moves produce perceived continuity. From this perspective, tradition is 'a modern construct, something that allows a particular group to inscribe themselves and their values on an earlier time or space. This temporal or spatial period is upheld as the standard by which to live in the present' (Hughes 2005, 54). To broaden this point (replacing *modern* with any contemporary moment in history), the same dynamic of claiming the authority of tradition has been going on for thousands of years.

Some scholars argue that *all* traditions are invented. Jocelyn Linnekin and Richard Handler argue that tradition, being 'symbolically constituted', is tied to a specific context of social and ideological relations: 'Tradition is invented because it is necessarily reconstructed in the present, notwithstanding some participants' understanding of such activities as being preservation rather than invention' (Linnekin and Handler 1984, 275, 279). Linnekin asks, 'how do we defend the "real past" and "genuine" traditions if we accept that all cultural representations, even scholarly ones, are contingent and embedded in a particular social and political context?' (Linnekin 1992, 250). As James W. Turner puts it, 'From an anthropological perspective, all tradition—indeed culture itself—is invented, in the sense that it is a product of deliberate experimentation with, and recombination of, symbolic elements present in the repertoire of actors' (1997, 348).

This view has its value, but it has two complications. First, it positions scholars, professional outsiders, as the adjudicators of authenticity (i.e., defining it as an ideological stance): 'Like the people who are characterized as "inventors of tradition," these scholars claim discursive authority by virtue of the way that they construct their own distanced position with respect to tradition' (Briggs 1996, 460). That is, this view imposes an assessment of what is *really* the case about *genuine* tradition, based on a certain line of thought within the late-twentieth- and early twenty-first-century Euro-American social sciences. Second, by making a universal judgment, this view makes no useful distinctions. The philosophical point is interesting, but it doesn't help us study traditions. Calling *all* tradition *invented* ignores the fact that it is the *perception* of strong links between current and past phenomena that gives *tradition* its normative force. It is not helpful to label all traditions *cultural representations*. It makes more sense to explore the *processes of representation* that lead to the range of views of *tradition* that we find in religious (and, for that matter, academic) discourses.

Hobsbawm and Ranger's collection provides the classic statement of the opposite view, that we can distinguish genuine and invented traditions: 'insofar as there is ... reference to a historic past, the peculiarity of "invented" traditions is that the continuity with it is largely factitious' (Hobsbawm 2012, 2). This implies that it is fairly easy to distinguish between non-invented and invented traditions.

There are five problems with this view. First, we often lack firm historical evidence to assess how well traditions correspond to their origins, or how accurately they were transmitted over time.

Second, this distinction is often irrelevant: claims to authority are premised on the belief that traditions are accurate and true, not on the actual status of those claims. If people believe that an invented tradition is authentic, this gives it authority. Examples abound in three edited collections that have looked at the invention of tradition in religions (van Henten and Houtepen 2001; Engler and Grieve 2005; Lewis and Hammer 2007). The reverse is also true: labelling a true tradition as false can undermine its authority.

A third problem with drawing a sharp distinction between authentic and invented traditions is that the viewpoints from which we can make judgments about tradition are themselves historical, cultural and ideological (as Linnekin emphasizes; see Case Study 2). This calls into question the ways that scholars categorize things as being within *this* tradition and not others. Scholars can criticize each other's views by labelling them as part of this or that academic tradition. The line between authentic vs. invented distinction gets very complex (see Text Box 7).

A fourth problem with the authentic vs. invented distinction is that religious communities are often quite clear that their traditions are dynamic and changing: the necessity of continuity with previous tradition is often balanced with a pragmatic emphasis on altering traditions to make them more useful in specific contexts (see Case Study 4). Questionable assumptions about stability and continuity as essential to *tradition* are built into the authentic vs. invented distinction.

Text Box 7 Carlos Castaneda's invented tradition

Carlos Castaneda's work illustrates how discursive contexts call into question the *authentic vs. invented* distinction. In the 1960s, Castaneda invented an indigenous Yaqui *man of knowledge*, Don Juan, and his shamanistic tradition (1972). He presented his fiction as ethnography and received a PhD degree from UCLA on that basis. He invented an Indigenous tradition in a work of fake scholarship.

In a sense, Castaneda's work is part of a tradition of fictional scholarship, including, for example, Thomas Carlyle's *Sartor Resartus* (1831), Jorge Luis Borges's 'Pierre Menard, autor del Quijote' (1939) and Vladimir Nabokov's *Pale Fire* (1962). Does it matter that these works, unlike Castaneda's, were *presented* as fiction? Things are not so simple. The *fictional* frame is imposed by readers as much as by authors: Castaneda's books are fictional scholarship, but they were accepted as real scholarship by his discipline's academic gatekeepers. It is too simple to insist that the intention to deceive is what distinguishes true from false tradition. Castaneda had already published two books on the teachings of don Juan before he submitted the third as his dissertation (Lochle 2014, 81). He published the same fictional text as both a mass-market book and PhD dissertation.

It is a mistake to reify categories like literary and academic genres, fiction and non-fiction; or authentic and invented traditions. These distinctions are *often* helpful guidelines, but they can get in the way. After all, Castaneda's invented traditions are still believed to be true by many readers of his books.

Things get even more complicated if we ask about the *effects* of Castaneda's dissertation. It is seen as a gateway text in the tradition of reflexive ethnography (a self-aware form of presenting research that is associated with the 'writing culture' debates in the 1980s; Clifford and Marcus 1986). Castaneda's academic trajectory 'forced anthropology to confront the myth-making element in ethnography and to accept that there is no "true" ethnography' (Hardman 2007, 52). Stefan Lochle argues that Castaneda was both innovator and trickster:

> Castaneda managed to obtain the title of PhD for a fictional account about alleged anthropological fieldwork ... [which was in fact conducted] in the UCLA library. ... He also transformed and taught in that he helped to lead towards a new paradigm in anthropology which ... bestows on him traits of the culture hero as the facilitator of (new) cultural techniques. Even if Castaneda has been dismissed as a hoaxer and an anthropological imposter his work did manage to change and transform culture. (Lochle 2014, 94)

Inventing tradition normalizes, legitimizes and naturalizes religious innovations, and this works even in cases where the innovations are recognized as new. Sangyé Gyatso (1653–1705), a regent of the fifth Dalai Lama, defended the pre-eminence of his Gandenpa/Gelukpa tradition within Tibetan/Vajrayana Buddhism by walking this fine line:

> Sangyé Gyatso explicitly combin[ed] ... established traditions claiming venerable authority with new rites and ceremonies. ... [He] considered himself to be initiating new customs ... Yet he also took great pains to link these new examples of religious activity with classically dictated ritual forms. ... The Dalai Lama died just like the Buddha, Sangyé Gyatso tells us, and yet everything from the way in which the Dalai Lama's remains were preserved to the rituals of commemoration were clearly and self-consciously contemporary innovations that needed to be persuasively argued for. ... In the very act of drawing these connections between tradition and innovation he reveals how necessary it was to actively maintain ... calendrical and memorial rites and through persuasive writings ... [to contextualize] the establishment of new ceremonies. The effect of such histories—be they of festivals, the New Year, or the death of the Buddha—was precisely to authorize his own innovations ... (Schaeffer 2006, 194–195)

This tug-of-war between tradition and innovation also underlines the issue of truth. The truth or authenticity of tradition is more than a matter of accurate correspondence with the past. It also involves functionality within a specific religious context: doctrinal harmony, appeal to central concepts, rhetorical persuasiveness, perceived ritual efficacy etc. The (re)invention of tradition must fit with existing traditions, but, at the same time, it alters the religious landscape. Correspondence to religious reality and construction of that reality go hand-in-hand. Innovative tradition must honour established tradition even as it alters, rewrites, subverts, appropriates or replaces it. This harmonizes continuity and innovation.

A fifth problem with imposing a sharp distinction between authentic and invented traditions is the normative evaluation that goes along with it: not all cultures and religions think that false, invented or innovative traditions are worse than ancient ones.

The issue of historical authenticity in the Jewish Tanakh (which Christians call the Old Testament) and in the Christian New Testament illustrates this point. Einar Thomassen notes that the concept of literary forgery was current during the period of the formation of the New Testament and played a role in the formation of the canon (2007). This underlines pseudepigraphy (attributing the authorship of texts to famous figures) as a theological problem. Thomassen notes five potential strategies for dealing with this problem: *denial*; *minimization* (insisting that pseudepigraphy was common); *rationalization* (shifting emphasis from authenticity to usefulness for the church); *selectivity* (distinguishing more and less authentic parts of the canon); and *revision* (excluding pseudepigraphy from the canon). This illustrates a range of insider perspectives regarding the invention of tradition, and it implies that the role of the scholar of religion is to investigate, not resolve, these differences.

But was this theological problem seen as acute? Philip Davies tells us that 'the Old Testament, when measured against a yardstick of "authenticity," fails as often as it passes. It is full of spurious attributions and spurious events. On balance, its history is more invented than recorded' (P. Davies 2007, 275). However, the *yardstick of authenticity*—with its sharp distinction between true and false—had little relevance, because these were texts 'whose cultural world was deeply immersed in invention and fantasy and whose authors saw no reason to disappoint their readers with the literal truth, ... a culture in which historical reliability simply does not count or matter' (P. Davies 2007, 275; see Corrigan and Harrington 2007, 241–243). The distinction between authentic and invented tradition was of little importance in this historical and cultural context. Modern scholarship tends to place an emphasis on true as opposed to false accounts, but it is a mistake to impose this normative judgment on other communities without checking first. The relevance of the authentic vs. invented distinction and its relation to normative stances is an empirical issue to be investigated.

3.3 Folklore and fakelore

National folklore illustrates how complicated the true vs. false or authentic vs. inauthentic distinction gets. Richard M. Dorson distinguishes 'folklore' and 'fakelore', where the former is an authentic folk tradition and the latter an ideological construct (1950; 1976). Dorson expresses surprising confidence that it is easy to tell the difference between the two:

> A couple of minutes of handling a book of collected folklore can suffice to inform probing folklorists as to the general character of the goods they hold. Does the collection contain items of folklore as they were actually told, word for word, or are the tales or materials paraphrased? Are the tellers, singers, and carriers of the folklore—the informants—identified, and not just by names but with some personal details? (Dorson 1986, 463)

The history of folklore suggests that Dorson is overly optimistic here. For example, starting in 1760, James Macpherson (1736–1796) began to publish a series of supposed translations from the Gaelic compositions of Ossian, a famous bard and warrior from the third century. The final military victory of England's domination of Scotland had occurred in 1746, and the Gaelic language and Scottish Highland culture were being marginalized. Macpherson's works were celebrated by many (especially Scots) as authentic affirmations of the vitality of ancient Scottish culture; they were criticized by others (mainly English and Irish) as invented traditions and fakes. The truth lies somewhere in the middle:

> The notion of a tangled web barely begins to describe the Ossianic mess. ... Laborious scholarly analysis eventually demonstrated that none of these manuscripts represented an 'original' in the strict

sense of the word and, to make matters even more complicated, most scholars now doubt that Macpherson could even have read the Gaelic manuscripts in his possession. Does this mean he was an impostor and a fake? What many Ossian specialists argue today is that this is the wrong question to ask. Macpherson did not have recourse to an ancient Gaelic original, but he did base his works on traditional written and oral Gaelic material ... Macpherson's Ossianic corpus cannot be termed 'authentic' by some narrow definition, but as folklorists in recent decades have increasingly suggested, authenticity is a highly elusive and problematic category. (Ziolkowski 2013, ch. 1; see Trevor-Roper 2012).

More was going on this same period than the straightforward issue of truth and falsehood. There are many comparable examples of how the presence of folkloric tradition was seen as support for the legitimacy of claims of national cultural identity: for example, Wilhelm and Jacob Grimm and their famous collection of 'Children's and Household Tales' (1812–1856); Vuk Karadžić (1787–1864) and his collections of South Slavic (Serbian) folk poetry; and Elias Lönnrot (1802–1884) and the *Kalevala*, the Finnish national epic that he first published in 1835 (Ziolkowski 2013, ch. 1; Dundes 1989).

The Grimms drew most on the knowledge and memories of middle and upper-class acquaintances—including French-speaking descendants of Huguenot refugees—as opposed to *authentic* peasant informants, and their methods did not aim at preserving their sources:

> The Grimms did not believe in the existence of an original and fixed oral text of a tale that later renditions only imperfectly reproduced, but instead in an essential narrative core that was expressed in multiple variants. Their notion of this core verged on the mystical; it could be apprehended, communicated, and appreciated by persons imbued with the proper spirit, a special sensitivity to fairy-tale truth. While a certain fairy-tale style was acknowledged to exist, consistent verbatim recording was not necessary to document this style. (Ziolkowski 2013, ch. 1; see Kamenetsky 1992, 110)

Karadžić included examples from family members, his own memory and submissions from amateur contributors. In addition, he cut material that did not reflect the aesthetic that he was aiming for, and he left out dialect forms and popular vocabulary in order to reflect and construct a standard Serbian vernacular language (D. Wilson 1970, 317–320).

Lönnrot edited and reorganized his raw material extensively: 'the editing principles and the artistic goals adopted by Lönnrot inevitably meant that the poetic material gradually became homeless in his hands, it ceased being the product of a particular local culture and merged to form a mixture into which Lönnrot dipped as required' (Honko 1990, 211).

Various critical issues arise. Political and cultural ideologies were central to the reception of these new traditions, which underlines 'the impossibility of drawing a clear and distinct line between folklore and propaganda' (Ziolkowski 2013, Conclusion). The supposed originals used to inform these traditions were manuscripts reflecting oral or written sources from many centuries before, which raises questions about the accuracy of transmission: 'In the midst of all this uncertainty and partisanship, the notion of authenticity recedes, a tantalizing will-o'-the-wisp whose illusory reality fades on closer examination' (Ziolkowski 2013, ch. 1).

To return to Dorson's breezy insistence that it is easy to tell the difference between folklore and fakelore, he emphasizes superficial aspects of textual criticism. He ignores scholarly and editorial impacts on these national folklores. Nor does he address ideological and other distorting assumptions and normative frames.

Ironically, Dorson himself exemplifies these distorting frames. He criticizes Paul Bunyan—the giant woodsman with his enormous axe and blue ox—and later figures in the same mould, like Pacos Bill, John Henry, Tony Beaver and Febold Feboldson. He criticizes them for their ideological implications:

> These comic demigods are not products of a native mythology, but rather of a chauvinist and fascist conception of folklore. They must be 100 per cent native American supermen, all-conquering, all-powerful, braggart and whimsically destructive. By such distorted folk symbols the Nazis supported their thesis of a Nordic super-race, and touted Hitler as their greatest folklorist. (Dorson 1950, 336)

Dorson's uses 'native' here to refer to white, European immigrant cultures in the USA. He mentions 'the Indians' and gives an example of fake Chippewa mythology, but he treats the many Indigenous cultures of North America—'one illustration will do'—as just another 'ethnic group', alongside Finnish, Flemish, German, Irish, Italian and other immigrant communities (1950, 340–342). Dorson's defence of 'genuine American folklore' takes 'America' and its settler ideology for granted (1950, 337). This underlines that folk vs. fake, true vs. false, authentic vs. inauthentic distinctions are not the most important part of the story. Ideology lies deeper. To understand it, we need to interrogate the function of beliefs about tradition, not the historical realities of authenticity.

3.4 Chapter summary

Is it possible to find clear evidence that a tradition started the way people believe it started, and that it continued down over time unchanged from then until now? Opinions differ.

At one extreme, some scholars distinguish authentic and invented traditions. *Invented traditions* are new ideas and practices that are presented as if they were old, innovations masquerading as traditions. Why would anyone bother to invent something, and then pretend that they didn't? Why portray innovation as ancient? Because tradition often comes with normative authority built in: old ways are best. The topic of invented traditions is very relevant for SoR.

There are also problems with the idea that some traditions are invented and others authentic. (i) Historical evidence can be hard to come by. (ii) Invented and authentic tradition work the same, as long as people believe that they are authentic. (iii) The, often academic, viewpoints from which we can make judgments about tradition are also historical, cultural and ideological. (iv) Many traditions are quite open about the fact that they change over time. They walk a strategic line between tradition and innovation. This undermines the whole idea that a tradition must be a simple case of static repetition to be authentic. (v) Who gets to decide what is authentic and what invented: are scholars of religion/s the absolute judges of people's religious traditions?

At the other extreme, some scholars say that all traditions are invented: those we study, and our own academic traditions. This view doesn't help us study traditions: we still need to explain why people *believe* that some traditions are true and what effects this has.

National folklore traditions illustrate how elusive and problematic the category of authenticity is. These traditions are both authentic and inauthentic, and they have ideological leverage because of that blurred status. They tell us that interested uses of *tradition* as an idea are more important than the alleged historical realities of authenticity.

Key take-home points—*The idea of invented traditions tends to get distracted by questions of truth (how do we know?) and relativism (aren't all traditions invented?) Belief in tradition does more work than historical facts do. Analysing tradition as a relational term helps understand this: (i) tradition is associated with some ideas (ancient, unchanging etc.) and opposed to others (modern, dynamic etc.); and (ii) this contrast is associated with value-judgments (one of these sets of ideas is good and the other bad). The following case study shows how scholars can end up taking sides in these disputes.*

Case Study 2: Normative tradition in Candomblé

Candomblé is the most well-known of the many Afro-Brazilian religions.[2] It consists of Brazilianized elements of West and Central African traditions brought by enslaved people from various cultural and linguistic groups in those regions (Verger 1993; P. Johnson 2002; Parés 2007; Silva and Brumana 2016). European esoteric influences are also found in some Candomblé terreiros (Walker 1990). At the heart of the religion are the *orixás* (pronounced "oh-ree-SHAS"), powerful and positive entities/deities who incorporate in initiated members. Initiation is a crucial moment, when members become full practitioners of the religion, entering into a life-long ritual relationship with one *orixá* in particular and with a nested series of doctrinal and ritual secrets (Prandi 2005). Faced with persecution by Christians, enslaved Africans in Brazil made Catholic saints central to their discourse and rituals. They identified each *orixá* with a saint, mapping authentic African symbolism onto the imposed Christian frame. This allowed them to continue to honour their *orixás* in an indirect, safer way.

Candomblé highlights ideological issues of debates over *tradition*:

> Although Orisha religions [like Candomblé] offer textbook examples of 'invented traditions', tied to globalization and the emergence of new collective identities, one should not be content to simply identify them as such. What is required is the careful delineation of the specific historical processes by which these traditions were both maintained and reconfigured over time by actors making choices in novel situations. (Cohen 2002, 32)

Starting in the mid twentieth century, both insiders and scholars began to re-position Candomblé by de-emphasizing its acknowledged

---

2. Other Afro-Brazilian religions include Batuque, Cabula, Mesa de Santa Barbara, Jarê, Omolocô, Quimbanda, Tambor de Mina, Tambor de Nagô, Xambá and Xangô. Others have a greater proportion of Indigenous elements: e.g., Babaçuê, Batuque Paranaense, Candomblé de Caboclo, Catimbó, Jurema, Pajelança, Terecô and Toré de Xangô. There is a spectrum between Afro-Brazilian *religions* and ritual forms of dance and procession: examples toward the latter end of this spectrum include Candombe, Canjerê, Caxambu (Cucumbi), Carimbó, Congado (Reinado), Jongo (Bendenguê) and Suça (see van der Poel 2013; Engler and Brito 2016).

Afro-*Brazilian* nature and its syncretism. *Tradition* became an ideological battleground.

The strategic privileging of *authentic* Africanness led to a certain type of Candomblé being seen as the most pure and authentic. The *Nagô* family in Candomblé has Yoruba roots: i.e., reflecting characteristics of this religious and cultural grouping, not limited to a single linguistic group, mainly in what is now Nigeria. *Nagocracy*—ideological emphasis on the greater authenticity of Yoruba elements—is prominent in Candomblé and among scholars (Sousa Júnior 2005, 9; see Ferretti 2001; Lima 2003). This ideological stance itself seems to have African roots: J. Lorand Matory attributes it to 'Lagosian Renaissance-inspired discourses of Yoruba superiority', where previous scholars had considered it either an authentic tradition or one invented by scholars (Matory 2005, 97, see 25, 43–45, 63, 89).

The legacy of Eugênia Ana dos Santos (1869–1938) was central. *Mãe* Aninha, founder and head of the Axé Opô Afonjá *terreiro* was one of the most famous *mães de santo* (saint mothers) in Salvador, Bahia. She said, 'My sect is pure Nagô [Yoruba]. ... I have revived a great part of the African tradition ...' (Parés 2004, 186; see Matory 2005, 126). *Mãe* Aninha and her associate, 'Professor' Martiniano do Bonfim (1859–1943), introduced an institutional innovation, the twelve *obás* (ministers) of Xangô, and they claimed that this was inspired by the political organization of the Oyo kingdom. There is no counterpart for this among Yoruba groups in Africa: it was an invented tradition (Parés 2004, 186).

Starting in the 1930s, intellectual elites in the Northeast saw Candomblé, including the *Nagô terreiros* led by *mães de santo*, as sparkling examples of the new national ideological emphasis of *mestiçagem* (hybridity) and 'the myth of three races' (African, Indigenous and European), as the key to Brazilian character, a view that was critiqued in the 1960s for being racism-blind (Matory 2001, 172; DaMatta 1987, 58–85; see Engler 2009b, 557, 568; Fernandes 2007, 38–48, 59–63; Magnoli 2009, 143–162). Police persecution of Afro-Brazilian religions in Salvador was selective: 'most of the terreiros suffering from this repression were non-*Nagô* and headed by men, while there are no reports at all of assaults on the main *Nagô-Ketu* traditional houses' (Parés 2004, 195; see Engler 2023).

Roger Bastide (1898–1974), René Ribeiro (1914–1990), Edison Carneiro (1912–1972) and other early scholars of Candomblé noted that members of the religion were using academic studies of Candomblé in the construction of their social and religious identities (Bastide 1973, 168n111; see Silva 1999, 150). These scholars produced 'literary and social-scientific discourses that were remarkably like the political and religious discourses of Professor Martiniano and Mãe Aninha' (Matory 2001, 180; see Motta 1996; Despland 2008). To this day, Candomblé's *tradition* is inseparable from the beliefs and practices of 'the close-knit congregations of anthropologists and priests in Salvador' (van der Port 2005, 10n15).

Continuing a long history of transatlantic influences (Matory 2005), many less important Candomblé leaders sought to claim more authority in the face of the dominance of the major *nagô* groups by travelling to West Africa to investigate the 'tradition of the orixás', and this led to tensions between their *terreiros* and the recognized *traditional* Bahian *terreiros*, both groups claiming to be more traditional (Epega 2006; see Verger 1993). Religious debates in Brazil over de-syncretization and re-africanization became politicized in light of anti-racist activism (Agier 1995, 254–258; Selka 2007a; 2007b, 22–26).

The case of *caboclo* spirits tells us more. *Caboclos*—Indigenous spirits—are common to many Afro-Brazilian religions:

> the caboclo spirits are the 'owners of the land'; they represent the Indians who lived here before the arrival of the whites and the blacks. When they descend [incorporate] in the *terreiros*, they wear feather headdresses, dance with bow and arrow, smoke cigars and drink wine. ... When they tell of their origin, they present themselves as inhabitants of a 'mythical village' ... not locatable in time and space. (Silva 2005, 87–88; see Engler and Brito 2016, 143–145)

If the *orixás* index the *Afro-* part of *Afro-Brazilian*, then *caboclos* index the *Brazilian* part. They play a larger role than is recognized—or admitted—in traditional *terreiros* of Candomblé of Bahia (Tall 2012; Tromboni 2012). *Caboclos* are sometimes associated in Candomblé with the *orixá* Oxossi or with the morally ambivalent, trickster figure of Exu (Santos 1995, 135–146). They play a prominent role in the Afro-esoteric religion Umbanda (Engler 2016c).

In Candomblé, the rituals that work with *caboclo* spirits are marginalized, hidden and often unacknowledged, reserved for core members in private sessions, often in a separate ritual space within the house. Maintaining the perceived purity of African roots is a basic strategy of legitimizing status relative to other groups in the same community. Candomblé de Caboclo is a diffuse sub-type of Candomblé that emphasizes rituals with *caboclo* spirits, and it pays the price of lower status for this explicit admission of *syncretic* impurity (Prandi, Vallado and Souza 2001; Engler and Brito 2016, 154–158). Nagô nations resist acknowledging their own rituals of *caboclos* (Tromboni 2012, 98–99; see Santos 1995; Tall 2012).

This difference between ritual types is an issue of *pure/authentic* vs. *impure/syncretic* as a strategic binary. When scholars take Nagocracy as an index of the true, historical or essential nature of Candomblé, it is seen as a religion where a certain vision of pure African roots defines *normal* and where syncretic divergence is a watering down of that authenticity.

The situation looks quite different if we accept all self-identified Candomblés as types of the religion, and if we bracket claims of authentic Africanness as part of strategies of legitimation. This approach reveals a complex space of Candomblés. If Candomblé, as a

> 'religion' is defined by a single set of beliefs, rituals, religious experiences, and social organization ... [then] such a 'religion' doesn't exist. What exists is a field of variants that resemble one another to varying degrees. ... Candomblé ... [is] a field of variants organized by family resemblances. This might be characterized as a syncretic continuum, where the variants vary syncretically in relation to the prototypical exemplar of the 'Candomblé' category, the Nagô Candomblé. ... [T]his [descriptive] argument ... must be distinguished from what is characterized as an 'Afrocentrist' bias in the classical studies of the Candomblés: that the Nagô Candomblés are of the most value, morally and academically, because they are 'the purest African.' (Giesler 1998, 1005, 1030, 1068)

If we follow fieldwork where it leads, we find a descriptive plurality and ideological polarity in Candomblé (Engler 2022). We find a range of ritual forms, and the fact that a majority of scholars accept normative Nagocracy has made this harder to see: 'one result of the valuing of the more "purely" African Candomblés was that the more syncretic Angola-Congo Candomblés and Candomblés de Caboclo received much less ethnographic attention' (Giesler 1998, 1071). We also find a discourse that asserts that one end of this range is most authentic. The ideological discourse of authentic African roots structures both emic and etic (insider and outsider) perceptions of the tradition, throughout the field of Candomblés. This is based in invented traditions, but it has become academic truth. Candomblé has become characterized, over the last century, by a dominant discourse of *tradition*.

When a majority of scholars accept the valorization of a particular sub-group as authentic, as happens in the case of the 'nagoization' or 'Nigerianization' of Candomblé, this itself is a discourse about *tradition* that must be assessed (Parés 2004, 185; Braga 1998, 85). We impose fewer presuppositions when we recognize and honour the ongoing, active, creative, improvisational and innovative re-inventions that constitute specific groups.

Chapter 4

Tradition and modernity

This chapter moves forward the book's goal of unpacking assumptions by looking at an important way in which *tradition* is seen as opposed to a certain set of other concepts (see Chapter 1.5). It asks a crucial question: what are the ideological implications of the fact that tradition is often seen as non-modern or pre-modern?

Tradition constructs or labels groups—us and them—in struggles for legitimacy, authority, power and resources. The idea that *traditional* and *modern* are somehow opposed to each other plays an important role in this. As discussed in the following chapter, scholars of post-coloniality, decoloniality and Indigeneity draw attention to harmful effects of this conceptual split. This chapter sets the context for that discussion of more dynamic conceptions of *tradition*.

4.1 Tradition and authority in European history

The erosion of tradition's role as a basis for authority is often seen as a central characteristic of modernity. Other ways of supporting authority emerged in the modern world, including rational bureaucratic techniques and the truth-claims of science. The erosion of religion's role as link between tradition and authority was crucial. This emerged in Europe and its settler colonies.

The link between tradition and authority was central in the ancient Roman Republic. From the beginning that link was already an invented tradition about *tradition*. In the Republic, we begin to see how *claimed* relations to the past are used as a strategy in struggles for authority:

> the characteristic Roman focus on ... continuity with the past need not mean that we have to accept their rhetoric at face value. By contrast, it seems evident that the dramatic changes Roman society was undergoing produced a discourse of tradition and an insistent claim to a timeless heritage, which should in itself be regarded as a cultural artifact created for a political purpose. (Flower 2010, 21)

The Republic went through radical social and political changes in the second century BCE, leading to the Empire. Cicero (106 BCE–43 BCE) lamented what he, like many, saw as a 'loss of tradition': 'What remains of those ancient customs on which ... the state of Rome stood firm? We see them so ruined by neglect that not only do they go unobserved, they are no longer known' (Furedi 2013, 57, citing Cicero at 51). Augustus (63 BCE–14 CE)—great-nephew, adopted son and heir of Julius Caesar, and the first Roman Emperor—claimed and maintained *auctoritas* by preserving and reinventing ancient customs: 'through this reinvention of tradition Augustus succeeded in constructing a multi-dimensional system of political authority' (Furedi 2013, 51). This underlines the strategic value of real or invented traditions for legitimizing authority. Niccolò Machiavelli (1469–1527) later used the Roman Republic as an example to illustrate his view that individuals and groups can draw on whatever stories of legitimation serve their purpose, seeing as there is no one true story of the basis of authority (Zambrano 2001, 979).

Modern critiques of the relation between tradition and authority emerged during the Renaissance, the Reformation, the Scientific Revolution and the Enlightenment. This was not entirely a good thing. Hannah Arendt saw the erosion of relations between religion, tradition and authority as problematic. Following Walter Benjamin, and rejecting the apolitical stance of philosophy, she argued that

> the thread of tradition is broken and we shall not be able to renew it. Historically speaking, what actually has broken down is the Roman trinity that for thousands of years united religion, authority, and tradition. The loss of this trinity does not destroy the past. ... What has been lost is the continuity of the past as it seemed to be handed down from generation to generation. ... What you then are left with is still the past, but a *fragmented* past, which has lost its certainty of evaluation. (Arendt 1978, 1:212, original italics; see Blumenthal-Barby 2013)

During the Renaissance, nostalgia for classical antiquity and the inertia of institutional forms was associated with the valuation of tradition, while humanism's growing emphasis on the individual was correlated with innovation and the devaluation of tradition in other contexts. For Arendt, this was a sign not of progress but of the loss of civilizational continuity: it was 'the error of the humanists to think it would be possible to remain within an unbroken tradition of Western civilization without religion and without authority' (1961, 128).

Two Renaissance developments marked changing views of tradition. First, techniques in the critical study of history, present to a lesser extent in the Middle Ages, were refined and used to criticize the authenticity of tradition. For example, Lorenzo Valla (1405–1457) argued—as did Erasmus (1466–1536)—that a set of mystical texts attributed to the first-century judge Dionysius the Areopagite (who is mentioned in the Christian New Testament in Acts 17:34) were written much later (Yates 1964, 160; Luscombe 2005). They are now attributed to the fifth- or sixth-century Pseudo-Dionysius. Historical studies of the Catholic Church also used the tools of historical criticism to chip away at tradition:

> When historians tried, as they did in the Renaissance, to reconstruct the early church, they often claimed to find that the bishop of Rome was but one bishop among many patriarchs, and that the early church did not in the least resemble the modern one, which had accumulated many institutions and practices unknown in fifth-century Antioch or Alexandria. (Emerson 2002)

Valla proved on philological grounds that the *Donation of Constantine* was a forgery. This document—granting authority in the Western Empire to the Pope—was alleged to have been written by the Emperor Constantine (272–337). Valla concluded that

> only by casting off a tradition that had come to dogmatize the 'Donation of Constantine' as the basis of Papal power ... would it be possible for the bishop of Rome positively and effectively to resume his authentic role as '*vicarius Christi et ... pater ecclesie*' [Vicar of Christ and Father of the Church]. (Camporeale 1996, 14)

The second Renaissance development was the rekindling of perennial views of tradition, which had the effect of criticizing other modes of appealing to traditions. This occurred in the Hermetic tradition that spread after the translation of portions of the *Corpus Hermeticum* (ancient texts of Hermeticism, and founding sources for western esoteric schools and streams) by Marcilio Ficino (1433–1499): 'Ficino was one of the first Renaissance authors to champion the notion of a secret, esoteric, and ... perennial wisdom that preceded and prepared the way for Christianity as the climactic Platonic revelation' (Allen 2005, 361; see Yates 1964, 12–17). This promoted a distinction between public and occult lineages of tradition, with only the latter being true and authoritative.

Tradition became a negative term during the Protestant Reformation. The Reformation unsettled authority by sacralizing individual conscience. The two main principles of the Reformation were *faith alone* (which undermined the sanctifying role of ritual) and *scripture alone* (which undermined the Church's role as the guardian of tradition):

> In the critical discourse of the Lutheran Reformation, tradition was used primarily in a negative sense. According to Luther, the Roman church was burdened with a multitude of human traditions that were defended in the name of God by the pope and his bishops as holy traditions; and according to Luther, nothing was more dangerous for the church than this confusion of human and divine. (Rasmussen 2005)

For Luther, Catholic *traditiones* were human attempts to turn believers away from God; and these false traditions fulfilled the biblical prophecy of the Antichrist. The only true tradition was found in God's promise, which had been given in the garden of Eden, echoed and renewed in the Old Testament, and fulfilled in Christ. Calvin and Zwingli also rejected Roman ecclesiastical *traditiones* and emphasized the absolute authority of the Bible. Protestant denominations soon began to develop their own traditions, as their confessional texts became normative. The Roman Catholic Council of Trent (1545–1563) addressed the issue of tradition but failed to come to any consensus, thus avoiding two thorny issues: relations between apostolic tradition and church *traditiones*; and relations between the authority of the Pope and that of the bishops.

The Scientific Revolution rejected tradition as a source of authority. It emphasized empirical evidence as a source of an expanding domain of verified claims about the world. It promised to weigh all traditional knowledge in the scale of scientific method: if that knowledge could not be tested and proven, it could be ignored. This shifted the emphasis from past to future:

> The men of the Renaissance and Reformation had not called into question the presumed authority of the past; they had merely wanted to return to its pure ancient wisdom and religion. The men of the seventeenth-century scientific revolution generally knew there was no such thing to be found in the natural philosophies of Aristotle or most other ancient thinkers. Real knowledge was yet to be found, and it should be sought in every field. (Emerson 2002)

The legacy of these developments, at the beginning of the so-called modern world, was a dramatic erosion of the legitimacy, naturalness and general acceptance of the idea that tradition was a basic source of authority. However, as this chapter underlines, this is not a reason to suggest that tradition (or religion) is a dying leftover from the past. That view must be qualified on both sides, before and after the rise of the modern. On the one hand, as noted above, since at least the Roman Republic, tradition was often far more than unthinking repetition of the past. The discourse of *tradition* had been an ideological tool for almost two millennia before modernity arrived on the European scene. On the other hand, tradition remains alive and well in the modern, late modern or post-modern world.

4.2 Tradition vs. modernity

Tradition and modernity are often *seen* as opposites. The reality is more complex. To understand *tradition* we need to understand the ideological effects of this misleading opposition. Drop the idea that tradition and modernity are opposed *in fact*; what matters are the conditions under which they are *held* to be opposed.

Modernity refers to whatever it is that makes the modern world modern. The modern period is often divided into three phases: early

(1500–1800), classical (1800–1900) and late (1900–?). (The question mark in the latter points to ongoing debates about whether the last 30 years or so mark a new phase of history, as globalization has facilitated the emergence of economic forces more powerful than nation states.) Scholars point to many causes or symptoms of modernity: colonization, capitalism, nationalism, globalization, industrialization, specialization of work, urbanization, the growing importance of science and technology and of mass literacy and communications media, individualization and the erosion of local community- and family-centred social relations. Three *modern* developments are relevant here: the (alleged) decline of religion, the (alleged) move from traditional to rational factors in the organization of society, and the separation of distinct social spheres (for Max Weber: political, economic, aesthetic, erotic, intellectual and religious; Terpe 2020).

From this *great-divide* perspective, *tradition* (like *religion*) names something left behind by modernity. The modern is valued because dynamic and tradition devalued because static: '*traditionalism* ... [has become] a description of habits or beliefs inconvenient to virtually any innovation, and traditionalist is almost always dismissive' (Williams 1983, 319–320). On this view, traditions are pre-modern survivals; and religious traditions are even more extreme cases of the sort of non-rational, unthinking obedience to habit that stands in tension with reason, science and progress.

This tension is rooted in Enlightenment thinking. The Age of Enlightenment or Age of Reason was a period (in western Europe, 1685–1815) that brought together ideas about reason, science, progress, nature and humanity in a broad intellectual movement. At its heart, the Enlightenment rejected *irrational* reliance on tradition and traditional religion. Its slogan was that rational humanity can think its way to a brighter future, instead of blindly retracing the shadowy past.

The Enlightenment was not just a reaction against a specific pre-existing historical condition—as if it was clear what *tradition back-then* was. It constructed a certain *modern* conception of tradition as the target of its selective rejection. This was clear in the Haskalah, the Jewish Enlightenment:

many of the Maskilim [Enlighteners] intended to counteract the traditional rabbinical culture. In their attempt to revive the Jewish people and its culture, the Maskilim, in general, desired to create a new Jewish identity, cultivating a modern and updated Jewish orientation. ... Their efforts followed the ideals advocated by the European Enlightenment in counter distinction to the traditional Jewish identity as adhered to by the rabbinic dictates and practices. (Pelli 2010, 19–20)

Counter-Enlightenment reactions arose almost immediately, as philosophical, artistic, religious and esoteric movements swung the pendulum back to emphasize emotion, spirituality and beauty, not just reason. Examples include the Romantic movement in literature, the Anglican Oxford Movement's return to ornate ritual and church decoration, and esoteric currents like high-degree ritual magic. The Counter-Enlightenment invoked a return to *tradition* as a path to a more balanced future. But these views of tradition were often more romanticized (note the word) than accurate.

Modern senses of *tradition*, as a selective construction of the past to be rejected, often take a dialectical trajectory, where the new stands over against the old, and a new third thing emerges through these tensions. In 1903, a key post-Haskalah thinker, Mordechai Ehrenpreis (1869–1951), made this explicit:

> The new generation will not waste its strength on negative war; it wants a positive endeavor; it does not fight against the old, but for the new. ... We freed ourselves of the shackles of sickly, rotting, dying tradition. ... We freed ourselves from the rabbinic culture, that encased us in a narrow cage of legal decrees, restrictions and prohibitions. ... In as much as we removed ourselves from tradition, we also removed ourselves from its opponent, the Haskalah. (Cited in Pelli 2010, 237–238)

This rejects both tradition and the dominant mode of rejecting it. Enlightenment and counter-enlightenment views of *tradition* involved *selective* ideas about past and future, and they both took for granted a sharp ideological contrast between traditional and modern.

This contrast played a central role in colonialism and its aftermaths. The idea of modernity, as the result of a unified historical trajectory of tradition, is Eurocentric (Sakai 2022, 109–110). The conceptual opposition between *traditional* and *modern* is a modern and European development. The attempt to push tradition into the (pre-modern) past—in order to create space for a modern (post-traditional) future—is ideological. The relevant historical fact is not that a real division between two periods occurred (traditional vs. modern) but that this conceptual contrast began to do important work.

We can make sense of this by looking at developments in specific contexts. Politics provides one of the clearest examples. *Democratization* is considered a characteristic of *modernity*—but so was the rise of totalitarianism. It was a modern anti-modern and pro-tradition development:

> fascism had and arguably still has a popular cultural appeal as an ostensibly anti-modern movement. As a promise of release not only from the great political and economic disasters of modern times but from both the relentless pace of change and the mundanity of modern everyday life, fascism shares a reactionary cultural impulse with nativist movements around the world that idealize whatever 'traditions' they can cast as not-modern or non-Western—thereby reaffirming the latter's primacy. (Morris and Sakai 2005, 222)

The connection pointed to here between fascism and nativism (the reassertion of Indigenous identities and interests in a post-colonial world) underlines that the Enlightenment emphasis on reason (and rejection of tradition) was a European and often colonial development.

Ideological uses of *tradition* can cut both ways. On the one hand, the tension between tradition and modernity is tied to the colonial project—to the fact that European countries took over much of the world. In this context, tradition is the mark of backward, non-rational, non-scientific- non-modern cultures. On the other hand, *tradition* is used by those at the margins of the modernity project—by Indigenous, African, Asian and Latin America cultures etc.—as a tool for reaffirmation and critique:

> the idea of traditional cultural entities which lies behind anthropological and nationalistic discourse is not the exclusive property of Westerners. It has become an important concept adopted by people throughout the world to constitute themselves culturally, and thus aspire to equality within the Western dominated world. (Olwig 1993, 90)

Traditions and religions are alive and well in modern twenty-first-century societies. Just look at the rise of fundamentalist movements and the prominence of *religion and spirituality* sections in bookstores. Given this obvious fact, we need to ask why so many people have suggested that *God is dead* or that religion is dying out. Is this just prejudice, as western Europe and its settler cultures project their own experience onto the rest of the world? Or has religion been changing in ways that challenge our usual ways of understanding it?

Asking whether religion has changed in the modern world is a distorting question. Why wouldn't religions change? If we find ourselves assuming that they are traditional in a pure sense, that *authentic* religious beliefs and practices are echoes of the past (or if we make the related mistake of assuming that medieval and ancient societies were themselves not dynamic, even if the pace of change was less), then we remain trapped in the ideological discourse of modernity.

4.3 Multiple modernities

The distinction between tradition and modernity is one of the *great divides* that scholars argue about. When, where and how do we draw the line? Is it a sharp division or a spectrum? Is it real or an ideological artefact? Did modernity cause imperialism and colonialism or is it a result of them?

There is some truth to the view that pre-modern and small-scale societies are often traditional in ways that reflect their relative stability: for example,

> the expectations cultivated in this peasant-artisan world (and no other expectations could be cultivated) subsisted entirely on the experiences of their predecessors, experiences which in turn became those of their successors. If anything changed, then it changed so slowly and over so long a time that the breach separating previous experience and an expectation to be newly disclosed did not undermine the traditional world. (Koselleck 2004, 264)

But it would be a mistake to hold that this sort of tradition and the resulting understanding of *tradition* apply to all contexts, when social, intellectual and technological change are so fast-paced. We cannot just assume that the ideas of *traditional* and *modern* are opposites (see Case Study 3).

Great divide theories are found in Karl Marx's identification of tradition with feudalism, in Ferdinand Tönnies's distinction between *Gemeinschaft* and *Gesellschaft* (community and society), in Max Weber's distinction between traditional and rational-legal authority, in Émile Durkheim's distinction between organic and mechanical solidarity, and in Lucien Lévy-Bruhl's distinction between primitive (mystical/participatory) and modern (logical) thought (Noyes 2009, 240–241). Claude Lévi-Strauss distinguished between 'cold' and 'hot' societies: 'the first, using the institutions they give themselves, seek to cancel almost automatically the potential effects that historical factors might have on their equilibrium and continuity; the second resolutely internalize historical development in order to make it the motor of their development' (1962, 309–310). These views almost always assign religion to the traditional side of the divide. They define the modern as post-traditional in a way that often means post-religious.

More recent scholarship moves past this broad distinction. Pascal Boyer points to three problems with great divide theories:

- their essentialist stance gets in the way of empirical studies that reveal more nuanced stories (the idea that *there just are* two kinds of societies doesn't fit the evidence);

- their asymmetry imposes a biased *us vs. them* viewpoint (there is one unified modernity over *here* and a bunch of traditional societies over *there*);

- the assumed passivity ignores the issue of agency, of how and why people *choose* different stances (the assumption that people stick to old ways until some external factor forces them to change undermines the idea that people actively shape their social worlds) (Boyer 1990, 113–114).

Sharp distinctions between tradition and modernity assume that all societies follow a single path of historical development toward a single type of modernity, with some societies seen as further along that path. It is assumed that the great variety of traditional paths all—at least theoretically—converge on a single modernity. According to this outdated view, modernity is the fulfilment of a universal historical trajectory, with its end point of mature modernity exemplified by (surprise!) the USA and western Europe.

In recent decades, this assumption has been rejected in favour of an emphasis on *multiple, entangled* and *fragmented* modernities: 'actual developments in modernizing societies have refuted the homogenizing and hegemonic assumptions of this Western program of modernity' (Eisenstadt 2000, 1; see Therborn 2003). Focus has shifted from universal processes (rationalization, disenchantment, secularization, de-traditionalization etc.) to transnationalization, glocalization (a balance of globalizing and local forces), boundary-work and identity formation, and to issues of dependency and peripherality in non-Western, postcolonial societies (Spohn 2006; Roudomet 2016).

Throughout the trajectory of these complex modernizing processes, religion has been and continues to be a key place for dynamic and evolving work with *tradition*. Appeals to tradition can be creative and selective as they appropriate the past. In the USA, Hasidic journalist Joshua (Samuel) Rocker (1864-1936) innovated within his very conservative Jewish tradition by reframing relations between tradition and modernity:

> Rocker ... understood that the Jews who constituted his audience had detached themselves from an immediate connection with the Jewish tradition of yesteryear, but might yet be reached through innovative literature emanating from that tradition. Joshua Rocker attempted to use the power of the Hasidic tradition, not to oppose modernization as such, but to show his readers that there were different paths available to them as Jews other than a lockstep acculturation into an American 'melting pot.' (Robinson 2005, 294)

Multiple modernities are found even in self-consciously modern nations.

The flip-side of this plurality of modernities is the need to move past a monolithic view of *tradition*. (The following chapter develops this insight.) Revivalist thinking in Africa argues that 'the key to effectively addressing contemporary problems lies in reclaiming and revitalizing indigenous traditions that have been degraded and suppressed in the wake of colonialism' (Ciaffa 2008, 121). As Paulin Hountondji suggests, this leads us to also look at *tradition* (not just *modernity*) in nuanced, polyvalent ways:

> the adjective 'traditional' may be misleading because it flattens the cultural legacy and favors the illusion that all its components are both contemporary to and convergent with one another. It would be better to retain the noun and, instead of 'African traditional thought', consider 'African traditions of thought.' (Hountondji 1996, xxiv)

The importance of witchcraft in many African cultures illustrates this:

> Occult forces are ... a true obsession—and a highly conspicuous one—to people in postcolonial Africa, most notably in the modern sectors of society. ... This resilience of tradition in modern contexts is hardly exceptional ... [and it] should be studied not only from an economic or technical angle but also with attention to culture. ... The modern world ... is marked by increasing cultural heterogeneity ...: 'traditional', more often 'pseudotraditional', traits are reproduced in new forms and on a wider scale. (Geschiere 1997, 215, 8)

The case of *anti-witchcraft* shrines in Ghana illustrates the complexity of modern views of *tradition*:

> A sense of tradition can evolve out of a cosmopolitan knowledge that embraces an orientation towards the future but that nevertheless goes along with a concern for building respect for the past and past generations. A further twist in this contested terrain concerns the fact that in spite of the views of the old and new elite, the young *abosom-brafo* [anti-witchcraft] priests at the shrines popular with the marketeers actually see their shrines as representing the most contemporary powers of their gods as opposed to the demonized ways of the past. (Parish 2001, 129)

In the face of this sort of anti-traditionalist tradition, we keep recalibrating our understanding of *tradition*.

Tradition and *modernity* are polyvalent concepts with far more complex relations to each other than historical and conceptual opposition. As Japanese-American comparativist Naoki Sakai underlines, the idea of a single modernity has always been an ideological facade for *the West*:

> The relationship between the West and the non-West seems to follow the old and familiar formula of master/slave. ... There is no inherent reason why the West/non-West opposition should determine the geographic perspective of modernity, except for the fact that it definitely serves to establish the putative unity of the West, ... a name always associating itself with those regions, communities, and peoples that appear politically or economically superior to other regions, communities, and peoples. ... In this regard, the West thinks itself to be ubiquitous. (Sakai 1997, 163, 154–155)

Western cultures think of themselves as *uniquely* modern. The idea of multiple modernities undermines this view.

4.4 Chapter summary

The concepts of *tradition* and *modernity* (i.e., whatever it is that makes the modern world *modern*) are often opposed to each other. Over the past five hundred years or so, tradition's status as an important source of authority was eroded in Europe. But this does not mean that, before that time, everyone accepted tradition as authoritative. Self-serving uses of invented traditions as strategies for claiming political and religious authority were already prominent in ancient Rome.

The idea that history is divided into two different periods (traditional and modern) is called a *great-divide* theory. If this view is true, then any traditions still left in the modern world are just survivals and hang-ons, doomed to die out. What does this tell us, when the words *traditions* and *religions* are often used as if they mean the same thing?

The *tradition vs. modernity* binary is itself a modern invention. Counter-Enlightenment reactions (trying to reclaim aspects of pre-modern, traditional worlds) started appearing at the same time that this binary began to have great influence. That is, some of the most important meanings of *tradition* were invented at the same time that *modernity* and *anti-modernity* were invented. This is a sign that we are in the realm of ideology.

Great-divide theories have been criticized. Scholars now talk more of multiple, entangled and fragmented modernities. These views often see religion as an important element in the differences between modernities. And, if there are multiple modernities, there are multiple traditions. The idea of one modernity opposed to one tradition made sense when Europe was held up as a model of *the* modern world. Not anymore.

The power of the *tradition vs. modernity* binary can cut both ways. If groups turn their back on the modern idea of *tradition*, then, in a sense, they remain defined by it. However, many Indigenous groups resist, critique and reject colonial structures and ways of thinking by reframing the idea of *tradition* for their own purposes. *Tradition* is used in differing, creative and unpredictable ways by many marginalized groups. This goes beyond rejecting, denying and inverting colonial discourses to blaze a path of creative re-appropriation. In this light, the shattering of one modernity into many modernities and many traditions results in a wide variety of modernizing moves defined by local interests. Scholars of religion/s have been slower than anthropologists to note these dynamic uses of *tradition*.

Key take-home points—*The sharp opposition between* traditional *and* modern *is a modern invention, often used to marginalize colonized peoples by portraying them as backwards. Some Indigenous groups reject this modern concept of* tradition. *Others re-think* tradition *for their own purposes. SoR should pay more attention to these dynamic views of* tradition.

Case Study 3: Great and little traditions

The distinction between *great and little traditions* is a variant of the *tradition/modernity* binary that has had significant impact in SoR, especially the study of south Asian religions. Based on anthropological studies of Mayan culture(s), anthropologist Robert Redfield distinguished between 'great tradition' and 'little tradition' (1956). Great traditions tend to be elite, urban, universal, textual, 'religious', orthodox, scholarly, refined, central and, above all, 'consciously cultivated and handed down'; little traditions tend to be popular, peasant-based, local, oral, 'superstitious', heterodox, folk, unrefined, peripheral and unreflective (Redfield 1956, 70). Redfield stressed the need to study mutual interactions between the two: 'Great and little tradition can be thought of as two currents of thought and action, distinguishable, yet ever flowing into and out of each other' (1956, 72).

Later scholars developed Redfield's idea in debates about Hindu cultures. McKim Marriott suggested that processes of *universalization* and *parochialization* were responsible for the slow two-way movement between village and more global levels (1955). Foreshadowing Hobsbawm and Ranger's discussion of *invented traditions* (1983), Milton Singer emphasized the strategic use of public ritual to manage portrayals of India's 'great tradition' (1972). He criticized Redfield by pointing out that great vs. little does not correspond to modern vs. traditional, because much that is called *modern* is old and many things called *traditional* are recent developments.

Redfield's distinction has been criticized as over-generalized and under-theorized, as colonialist and orientalist (reflecting biased outsider discourses) and as elitist and fundamentalist (reflecting biased insider discourses). His distinction has two main problems: it hides value judgments behind a descriptive tool; and it turns attention to the two extremes (e.g., village-level micro-analyses and global generalizations that privilege sacred texts). It has led many scholars to ignore the mutual influences between these levels of analysis and the ideological dimensions of the distinction itself.

As a result, this distinction has often been used to prop up vague, problematic concepts like *Hinduism* or *the* (single) *Hindu tradition*, along with superficial contrasts between elite and popular religion.

This ignores the need to pay attention to specific contexts, and it fails to consider the academic history of these ideas (see Sontheimer and Kulke 1989; Fitzgerald 1990; 2000). For example, Talal Asad argues that the great vs. little-tradition distinction leads scholars to link religion to a rigid split between social types, ignoring the complexities of social contexts:

> One way in which anthropologists have attempted to resolve the problem of diversity [within Islam] is to adapt the Orientalist distinction between orthodox and non-orthodox Islam to the categories of Great and Little Traditions, and thus to set up the seemingly more acceptable distinction between the scripturalist, puritanical faith of the towns and the saint-worshiping, ritualistic religion of the countryside. ... [This view] rests on false conceptual oppositions and equivalences, which often lead writers into making ill-founded assertions about motives, meanings, and effects relating to 'religion.' ... If the anthropologist seeks to understand religion by placing it conceptually in its social context, then the way in which that social context is described must affect the understanding of religion. If one rejects the schema of an unchanging dualistic structure of Islam promoted by some anthropologists, if one decides to write about the social structures of Muslim societies in terms of overlapping spaces and times, so that the Middle East becomes a focus of convergences (and therefore of many possible histories), then the dual typology of Islam will surely seem less plausible. ... No coherent anthropology of Islam can be founded on the notion of a determinate social blueprint, or on the idea of an integrated social totality in which social structure and religious ideology interact. (Asad 2009, 8, 18, 16, 19–20)

The great- vs. little-tradition distinction draws attention to important phenomena, but it should not be over-generalized or reified. It bundles many distinctions into one: urban vs. rural; impersonal vs. personal; elite vs. folk; religion vs superstition, etc. These distinctions differ, and none are sharp. Each is in some ways a spectrum, different in different contexts, and linked in complex ways with other flexible, conceptual binaries.

The great vs. little distinction can serve as a general frame for a contrast between types of traditional societies if and only if the contrast is spelled out in more specific terms. Eisenstadt, for example, argues that the transition to great tradition is characterized by 'a tendency for tradition to become differentiated in layers ... [which is] usually connected with growing structural differentiation between the various spheres of social life ... [and to] a growing "partialization" and privatization of various traditions, especially of the older existing traditions' (2003, 141–142). This is more useful because it is more specific and because it presents a spectrum of social forms, not a sharp distinction between two types. (Of course, the spectrum should not be seen as universal, a path that all societies do or must follow.) This underlines that the great vs. little-tradition distinction is a shorthand way of pointing to a whole set of issues that need to be studied in their contexts.

Chapter 5

Agency and reason

The previous chapter looked at ideological implications of the *traditional* vs. *modern* contrast, and this one looks at a related theme. The way that traditional is *received* is often seen as the opposite of rational action: tradition is adopted and imitated mindlessly, unquestioningly; it makes people into passive subjects; and this means that it is not assessed *rationally*. Along these lines, this chapter looks in particular at colonial uses of this *traditional* vs. *rational* contrast, as it works together with the *traditional* vs. *modern* binary.

Mark Twain wrote, 'Often, the less there is to justify a traditional custom, the harder it is to get rid of it' (2003 [1876], 46). As often happens, humour tells a deeper truth. Lack of clarity regarding a tradition's origin and function often helps us understand its power—and its relation to religion. A key concept here is *agency*, which refers to *the capacity for, nature of and constraints on intentional action*.

Pure tradition is seen as a matter of receiving and passing on what came to us from our predecessors. This obscures the fact that those who receive tradition—the current holders of the torch that is being passed along in this multi-generational relay—have an active role to play: 'The application of the customs and traditions of the past always involves an element of reinterpretation and innovation' (Furedi 2013, 98). The historical continuity of tradition requires human action. Because people die, past things are left without anyone to possess them 'unless the newly born, who did not begin by possessing them, are induced to take them up' (Shils 1981, 35). There is a gap here between the view that tradition is obligatory and the active work of selecting, interpreting and inventing it.

If we ask, *what reason do people have to follow tradition?* then we are asking about rationality. The *tradition vs. modernity* binary often frames tradition as irrational, as lacking the kind of instrumental or means-end rationality that is often seen as modern. The question that lurks in the background here is *what sort of rationality can tradition manifest*? If tradition is the result of quasi-automatic social forces, and if those who receive it did not create it, then who is doing anything? If a tradition *just happens*, how can we say that anyone is doing anything *rational* if they follow it?

This chapter makes a case that the study of religion/s (SoR) should start by thinking of tradition as always involving intentional human action. Tradition is a site for both hiding and affirming human agency. This will lead to a recognition that dynamic uses of tradition—among Indigenous and subaltern communities—reclaim agency in the case of static views of tradition (see Case Study 4). These more dynamic and creative views of tradition are sometimes seen as threats to be contained.

5.1 Who enacts tradition?

The view of *tradition* as *received-and-not-created* denies agency in one context and exaggerates it in another. Seeing tradition as something fixed and given—external to and imposed on us—implies that we have no choice in how it affects us or even to walk away from it. The concept of *innovation* emphasizes the opposite, i.e., freely chosen acts of creativity. If traditional societies are defined by receiving and passing on things handed down from previous generations, then this defines them in terms of a lack of creativity and agency. If tradition is invented, then this turns even innovation into a game of follow the leader. The innovator creates, but those who accept the innovation as tradition lose their agency. But there are many positions between the conceptual extremes of the forced repetition of allegedly pure tradition and the free innovation of non-traditional action.

Various ideas come together in the issue of agency. In social theory, agency is often opposed to structure: *agency* flags our freedom to act, and *structure* the constraints (social, cultural, economic, political etc.) that limit this freedom. Scholars tend to focus on whether we have intentional agency (freely willed) or whether our actions are structurally determined (forced on us). They argue over which side of this polarity offers the best account of relations between individual and society, and various middle ground positions try to have it both ways, e.g., the work of Pierre Bourdieu and Anthony Giddens.

This *agency-structure debate* has been with us for at least 80 years with no resolution in sight. *Agency* seems to be a bit of a red herring (Loyal and Barnes 2001). My focus is not on which side is right. *Agency* and *structure* are both 'devices or frames [that] different observers ... use to perform different sorts of cultural work' (Fuchs 2001, 24). We can start by noting that insider accounts tend to emphasize agency, where academic accounts tend to emphasize structural issues. This help us see how tradition de-emphasizes agency. And this in turn tells us a lot about how religions work.

Let's start with the word *tradition*. Like many languages, English has a noun, *tradition*, an adjective, *traditional,* and an adverb, *traditionally*. Why is there no verb?

Consider the comparable word *extradition*, which refers to an official process of handing over a legal suspect from one jurisdiction to another. Extradition is what happens when an extraditer—that is, an extraditing agent, usually a State—*extradites* a person accused of a crime. There is the verb. By analogy, the missing transitive verb would be *to tradite*. What might it mean to say, *X tradites Y*? When tradition happens, who is making it happen? The lack of the verb *tradite* suggests that tradition has no agent. What happens in the shadows of this action that has no verb and so no subject? We should smell ideology at work. There is something hidden here, a blind spot or a form of misrecognition without which tradition could not do its work. There is something central to religion/s here.

With no verb, the idea that some person or group *makes* tradition becomes less sayable, less thinkable. Some might say that this is to be expected, because that is the very nature of tradition. But to hold this view would be to just accept *pure tradition* as the truth of the matter. We cannot start by assuming this.

An obsolete word that comes closest to the missing verb, *tradite*, underlines this point. The *OED* tells us that *traditor* referred to both 'a person who transmits or sustains a tradition' and 'a traitor'. This places the act of passing on tradition under the same heading as its betrayal: the agency of the latter reflects on the former. *Traditor* flagged the possibility of *failing* to hand over tradition's content correctly. In other words, in the case of tradition, people could *choose and act* one way or another. That lost meaning suggests that tradition is not an automatic process of repetition:

> Like everything that results from human effort, transmission can fail. It can fail for two very different kinds of reasons: because of a bug in transmission (we get misunderstood, we fail to imitate others accurately, etc.) or (more commonly...) because of a lack of motivation to transmit. (Morin 2016, 50)

Individuals and groups do make tradition. But its agents often capitalize on the fact that innovation is more powerful if its origin is denied.

5.2 Ritual and deference

Pure tradition is similar to ritual: both *displace, translocate* or *dissociate* human agency (Engler 2009c, 469). Ritual and tradition often work together, of course. Tradition is a key source of ritual, passing down and defining orthopraxis (correct ritual). On the flip side, ritual is central to the transmission and elaboration of tradition. Hobsbawm notes, for example, that the invention of tradition is 'essentially a process of formalization and ritualization, characterized by reference to the past, if only by imposing repetition' (2012, 4).

But there is a deeper similarity. Both tradition and ritual constrain human agents by unhooking actions from intentions. In both ritual and tradition, we follow a script, not our own inclinations or desires; we follow the plan of action that we are given, not one we choose. According to Caroline Humphrey and James Laidlaw, the comparison of 'ritualized action with action which is not ritualized' plays out mainly in terms of intentionality and meaning: rituals are learned purely as sequences of actions, and meanings are added later (1994, 2). The ritualization of action 'consists in it becoming non-intentional, stipulated, and elemental or archetypal' (Humphrey and Laidlaw 2006, 278).

Maurice Bloch argues something similar: 'any act ... that appears to originate fully from the actor cannot properly be called ritual' (2006, 496). He distinguishes three other characteristics of ritual. The first is *deference* ('reliance on the authority of others to guarantee the value of what is said or done'; Bloch 2006, 497). The second is that ritual *explicitly* involves deference: 'deference is a common aspect of human life', but ritual is distinctive because it 'involves high degrees of deference'; 'Rituals are orgies of conscious deference' (2006, 505–506). Up to this point, Bloch covers much the same ground as Humphrey and Laidlaw: ritual action is non-intentional, stipulated and archetypal.

Bloch's third criterion does more. It spells out a crucial aspect of the non-intentionality of ritual, i.e., 'lack of clarity on the person to whom one is deferring' (Bloch 2006, 500; see also Bloch 2005). The origins of a ritual are almost always obscure. Its given-ness reminds us that ritual is not ours to control or modify. So who owns ritual?

> In the case of ritual actions ... the search for intentional meaning is inevitably frustrated because the actions in question do not originate in the intentions of the ritual actor. If there is an intentional agent behind it all, then who is it? And why did he or she insist on these particular procedures rather than any other? (Whitehouse 2006, 662–663)

It is clear that those who receive and follow do not create their rituals. It is seldom clear just who did. Even where a human or supernatural origin is (believed to be) known, the concept of deference highlights not the alleged agency of a founder but the *normative lack of agency* of those who follow.

Bloch notes in passing that these same ideas apply to tradition:

> The secret to the problem of wanting to locate meaning without having normal originators of that meaning is to merge all the shadowy transparent figures into one phantasmagoric quasi-person who may be called something like 'tradition', 'the ancestors as a group', 'our way of doing things', our 'spirit', our 'religion', perhaps even 'God.' (Bloch 2006, 502, 504)

The point is worth dwelling on. The idea of *deference* highlights how agency is shifted away from the people who participate in traditions today. Tevye, in *Fiddler on the Roof*, does not know where his traditions come from, but he follows them anyway. Here is a key point: both ritual and tradition can translocate or dissociate agency from current actors *onto mythological or supernatural agents*.

Tradition's displacement of agency is a relative mode of transcendence. Tradition and ritual are situated beyond a *horizon of intentionality*, beyond the zone of actions that are perceived or described as being caused by the members of a given group. They are independent of the intentional agency of any particular social group. Coming from beyond that horizon, they unify those who suspend their own agency by following the script. Tradition and ritual create a *we* by fostering the illusion that none of *us* are acting in a self-interested manner: we are all following the same script together.[1]

This is a big part of how ritual and pure tradition subsume human action under perceived authority: 'when one is in trouble and does not know what to do, one allows oneself to be taken over by the knowledge and the authority of others' (Bloch 2006, 506). *Pure tradition* creates an *agency vacuum* by displacing the origin or formal cause of present belief and practice into the distant past. Then appeals to founders, deities and other (relatively) transcendent beings can serve as bases of authority by occupying this vacuum.

At the same time, there is an important sense in which ritual and tradition are not *completely* independent of people's intentions and plans. People *choose to follow* tradition, to accept their membership in a community, to participate and to move their bodies in certain ways and to say certain words in rituals. The primary intent is to follow the script, but this presumes a choice to *not* invent or innovate—unless that is part of the script.

---

1. In this sense, tradition works like 'Gift exchange[which] is one of the social games that cannot be played unless the players refuse to acknowledge the objective truth of the game ... Gift exchange is the paradigm of all the operations through which symbolic alchemy produces the reality-denying reality ... [of] a collectively produced ... misrecognition of the "objective" truth' (Bourdieu 1990, 105, 110; see Engler 2005a).

5.3 Reason and excess

This logic of displaced agency lurks at the heart of the colonial *tradition vs. modernity* binary. The modern agent acts for individual, rational reasons. Only non-moderns unthinkingly follow tradition (see Latour 2010, 2–7, 34, 133 n.38).

Displacement of intentional agency in tradition and ritual is often read as displacement of rational agency. The ideological work of *tradition* is similar in both cases. The first creates an agency vacuum that can be appropriated by a certain mode of authority. The logic goes like this: 'You people did not make this tradition or ritual. This founder or deity did make it. Their authority is vested in me. So, you owe me the same obedience that you give to the traditional/ritual script.' In a similar light, this section looks at a colonial logic that justifies the policing of the *rationality vacuum* created by tradition and ritual: 'You people follow tradition or ritual out of habit. That is not a good rational reason to act: tradition and ritual are irrational. The guidance of a rational authority is needed to control your irrational traditional behaviour.'

Weber writes of 'inviolably sacred but irrational tradition'; he contrasts the 'rationally trained expert' to procedures that are 'bound to tradition or to irrational presuppositions'; the latter were 'in part tradition-bound, in part patriarchally, that means, irrationally oriented' (Weber 1978, 1395, 975, 1401). But his view of tradition is ambivalent. He points to the core of *pure tradition*: 'tradition: the belief in the inviolability of that which has existed from time out of mind'; 'valid is that which has always been' (1978, 1006, 36). Yet, he underlines that cases of pure tradition are rare because unstable (1978, 263). That means he needs another, more dynamic, view of tradition in order to make sense of the majority of cases. To do this, he distinguishes between (i) traditional actions as unthinking habit and (ii) as self-conscious convention (granted that 'at least some of those who act according to the "norms" are totally unaware of them'):

> It is by way of conventional rules that merely factual regularities of action, i.e., usages, are frequently transformed into binding norms, guaranteed primarily by psychological coercion. Convention thus

makes tradition. ... Whenever the regularities of action have become conventionalized, i.e., whenever a statistically frequent action ... has become a consensually oriented action ... we shall speak of 'tradition.' (Weber 1978, 326–327)

This view is incoherent. On the one hand, Weber distinguishes rational non-traditional behaviour (done for a good reason) from irrational traditional behaviour (done just because that is how things have always been done). So, tradition is irrational. This is pure tradition, and Weber says it is rare and unstable. On the other hand, he emphasizes a different sense of *tradition* in terms of consensually oriented convention, as what people *agree* on the best way to act. So, tradition is rational. This is the most important sense of tradition in Weber's work, but it escapes the *irrational tradition* vs. *rational modernity* binary.

Weber emphasized methodological individualism, which sees individual actions (and so the intentional states that motivate individuals) as the basis of social explanations. He viewed both reason and tradition from the perspective of the individual: 'The ... revolutionary force of "reason" works from *without*: by altering the situations of life and hence its problems, finally in this way changing ... [people's] attitudes toward them; or it intellectualizes the individual'; 'individuals are still markedly influenced by convention and custom even today' (Weber 1978, 245, 337, original emphasis).

From this perspective, tradition and ritual are irrational because they displace individual intentionality, undermining both agency and reason. How can you claim to act for rational reasons when you are just following a script or someone else's orders? The answer, of course, is that there are both habitual (unthinking) and rational (goal-directed or principled) reasons for doing so. Given Weber's emphasis on *ideal types* (generalized models used to analyse types of social action), he starts with a view of tradition similar to that of *pure tradition*. But that model is only a first step. In itself, it has little value for analysing the work of tradition, as we have seen. It helps us understand why some people in some circumstances blindly follow tradition. It also helps us understand that pure tradition can be used as a strategy for claiming authority over others. This points to the value of a flexible analysis that looks at overlapping types of authority: for example, where charismatic authority is *presented as* traditional or revelatory authority. Beliefs in and about pure tradition should be analysed in specific contexts (as in the discussions of post/decolonial and Indigeneity studies below). In the end, Weber's sharp line between pre-modern (traditional) and modern (post-traditional) societies prevents him from appreciating dynamic appeals to tradition. That is, he fails to recognize the instrumental rationality of dynamic—often eminently modern—uses of *tradition*.

If tradition is seen, by definition, as outside of modernity and reason, then it is a threat to be controlled. It is a source of excess, of emotional, spiritual, uncontrollable behaviour. This view is central to orientalist and colonial discourses: eastern and Indigenous cultures, being traditional, are more prone to such excess; and modern, western cultures, being rational, are the obvious choice for models of control and progress in this regard.[2] As discussed in Chapter 4, separating *tradition* and *modernity* like this prevents us from seeing the important work that tradition does, both oppressive and liberating: totalitarianism—a modern development—appeals to *tradition* in its call for unquestioning obedience; but Indigenous peoples around the world appeal to *tradition* in their ongoing struggle against the legacy of colonialism.

Piyel Haldar argues that colonialist discourse in India saw excess enjoyment as the transgressive other of reason, especially in the legal and political spheres. The contrast between modern rationality and pre-modern tradition supported this view: 'Indigenous custom has to surrender to the logic of reason. ... The 'civilising mission' rested upon the very image and symptoms of despotic excess which it sought to eradicate' (Haldar 2007, 11, 14, 138, 142). This is the view that tradition is passive and irrational. It is useful to flip things around and suggest that the many ideological implications of the *tradition vs. modernity* binary should lead us to reject the whole contrast.

---

2. Georges Bataille's view of religion as related to the *uncalculating* expenditure of excess energy and value can extend the link between *religion* and *tradition* here (1988, 1989).

The forms of misrecognition discussed in the previous section—which results in the failure to see creative agency in tradition—deny and obscure the rationality of dynamic uses of *tradition*. These dynamic views avoid both extremes of pure tradition and a colonial view of the *tradition* vs. *modernity* binary. They are examples of instrumental rationality in action: what could be more *modern* than attacks on the legacy of colonial systems, as Indigenous people attack those systems by strategically using the systems' own concepts? The separation of *tradition* from its conceptual opposites rejects binary thinking, emptying out this middle space where dynamic work with *tradition* takes place. Real work with *tradition* becomes invisible if we let ideological views rule it out of bounds. If tradition is defined as backward-looking, irrational, unintentional, habitual, repetitive, scripted, conservative, static and constraining—i.e., if all tradition is reduced to the ideological caricature of *pure tradition*—then how can it be used as an improvised tool of activism? If we turn things around and start by noticing that that *tradition* is used in this and other dynamic ways, then the pressing question is 'why did we ever see tradition in such a limited way?'

5.4 Post-colonial and decolonial critiques

Postcolonial and Decoloniality studies are related perspectives that analyse and historicize the ongoing effects of colonization. Despite many differences, they offer convergent views of tradition as the invented other of modernity, and they argue that the concept of tradition has been used to occlude the agency and rationality of colonized peoples. They read it as, in part, a tool used to label—and so to marginalize and oppress—the colonized. The ideological split between *traditional* and *modern* has both a descriptive and a normative dimension (see the discussion of orientalism in Text Box 4). Seeing tradition as impure and polluting is part of the game of *modern* power. From a colonial perspective, there is a radical (allegedly factual) difference between the colonizers' modern ways and the traditional ways of the colonized. Those (alleged) differences mark *the modern* as both superior to and threatened by *the traditional*: 'Values are ...

irreversibly poisoned and infected as soon as they come into contact with the colonized. The customs of the colonized, their traditions, their myths ... are the very mark of this indigence and innate depravity' (Fanon 1965, 7). This recognition is a symptom of the complex work of *tradition* in colonial contexts.

Postcolonial studies, along with the related field of Subaltern studies, looks at many inter-related issues: e.g., the history, impacts and legacy of European colonial conquests; the modes of discourse and of institutional subjugation that constructed colonizers and subjects in different ways; the forms of resistance of colonial subjects; the hybrid subjectivities that result from lives lived at and across colonial boundaries/borders; the intersectionality of gender, race and class in these contexts; and the range of responses to these processes, responses and processes that continue to shape societies and cultures around the world today. Postcolonialism is more than anti-colonialism (Ashcroft, Griffiths and Tiffin 2013, 204–209). It is a complex set of critiques by a wide range of scholars, looking at the ideological roles of discourse, influenced by such thinkers as critical historian and philosopher Michel Foucault, Marxist philosopher Louis Althusser, post-structuralist psychoanalyst Jacques Lacan, and deconstructionist philosopher Jacques Derrida. Postcolonial theory emphasizes British colonies in the nineteenth and twentieth centuries, with a huge impact on literary theory and critique.

Decoloniality studies—or the modernity/coloniality/decoloniality project—consists of the work of a smaller, more integrated group of scholars. The themes they address overlap in many ways with those of postcolonial studies, but with important differences. Decoloniality scholars foreground Latin America, which is often neglected in postcolonial studies. They hold that Eurocentric modernity—the modern world-system—began with the conquest of the Americas in the 1500s, and that this system continues to obscure the plurality and specificity of gender, race and class differences by presenting a distorted view of history and modernity. *Modern* Europe became the measure of all things: 'societies around the planet began to be measured and classified according to their similarity or dissimilarity with the natural order offered by cosmo-polis' (Mignolo 2012, 151). The 'coloniality of power' silences the multiple ways of knowing and being of those who live at the borders and margins of colonial modernity (Quijano 2000). The response of those at the margins has been and should be to reclaim repressed forms of 'border thinking', by transforming 'the rigidity of epistemic and territorial *frontiers* established and controlled by the coloniality of power' (Mignolo 2012, 12, original emphasis; see Martín Alcoff 2007).

Postcolonial studies sees tradition as an ideological construct, part of the colonizers' ideological toolbox. The modern idea of tradition was invented by the colonizers, and then projected onto the colonized:

> It was during the modernist regime (in collusion with colonialism) that traditions were invented by the colonizer on behalf of the colonized and ... that the so-called authority of Indigenous traditions was created and constructed by the colonizer to legitimate and inferiorize Indigenous traditions, all in one move. (Radhakrishnan 2000, 51)

Lata Mani's analysis of debates over *sati* (Hindu widow-burning in India) underlined the relation between *tradition* and *religion* in this ideological project:

> The women who burned were ... the ground for a complex and competing set of struggles over Indian society and definitions of Hindu tradition. ... [T]he discourse on *sati* was ... underwritten and framed by a modern discourse on tradition. ... [W]hat we have here is not ... a situation in which preexisting traditions are challenged by an emergent modern consciousness, but one in which both tradition and modernity as we know them are contemporaneously produced. (Mani 1998, 2, 77–78)

There are several key points in this passage: tradition is equated with religion; it is *seen as* timeless, ancient and unchanging; this view is modern; it is ideological (it is seen as just *how things are*, and it props up power differences); and it erases the agency of the colonized, in this case of women.

Saba Mahmood makes a similar point in the Islamic context: 'continuity between Islamism and nationalism would appear to be all the more pronounced in regard to the question of gender, insomuch as both ideologies seem to cast women as the repositories of tradition and culture, their bodies made the potent symbols of collective identity' (2005, 118).

There are clear ideological effects when identity is pinned to a *traditional* context above and beyond individuals or even beyond particular social groups (e.g., *society* lies beyond individual women, and *women* is a category that dictates the identity of individual women). Individual choices that diverge from this tradition-grounded identity are seen as a social problem of moral divergence, not a simple matter of individual preference.

Decoloniality studies see tradition in a similar light:

> modernity was imagined in contradistinction with tradition. Modernity and tradition are two modern concepts, not two ontologies, one modern and the other premodern. ... Tradition is construed as a period preceding the advent of modernity. In these narratives, coloniality is always absent and therefore 'tradition' materializes the hidden logic of coloniality, which is how the rhetoric of modernity operates. ... Seeing modernity through the logic of coloniality—tradition appears in all its clarity as a term invented in the process of building the very idea and the imaginary of modernity. (Mignolo and Walsh 2018, 118)

From both postcolonial and decolonial perspectives, *tradition* is applied by colonizers to the colonized, framing them as the *other* of the modern. The ideology of pure tradition justifies forced integration into modern history because *tradition is a problem* to be solved by the colonizers' rationality, science and progress.

However, there is another, more dynamic, side to this story. Traditions and *tradition* can be wielded as counter-ideological tools. Frantz Fanon (1925–1961) moved beyond his early focus on Blackness to insist on the strategic and tactical value of traditions. He analysed *tradition*'s use as a form of revolutionary resistance, as he defended women's central role in maintaining and transmitting social values (Fanon 1965, 37–38, 63, 42).

Post/decolonial critique underlines the possibility of appropriating and re-framing *tradition* as a tool for criticizing the legacy of colonialism. This is not a passive acceptance of the colonial *traditional vs. modern* binary nor a simple rejection of it: it is a creative, and very rational, strategy for attacking the foundations of unjust structures that were built on the basis of that binary.

This strategy can require the rejection of superficial versions of identity politics:

> projects of return to one's own traditions have become epistemologically unfashionable, thanks to the postmodern insistence on identity deconstruction. ... [However,] revisionist return projects are characterized not necessarily by nostalgia or by a fundamentalist impulse but by the need to separate the truth of one's own traditions from the significances attributed to them by the colonizer. (Radhakrishnan 2000, 59)

Naive identity politics can be a tool of oppression. Fluid, rootless views of traditional identity can mirror, and so reproduce, the colonialist essentialism of pure tradition by insisting on its absolute rejection. Seeing *tradition* as a toxic idea that must be abandoned is a path that still reflects colonial binaries: defining yourself by rejecting the other leaves you defined by the other. Rejecting *all* traditions because they are traditional retains a monolithic colonialist view of *tradition*. Extreme critique of tradition risks dismissing the agency and rationality of Indigenous and subaltern groups. It can reproduce European/northern theory and rule out the possibility of people's creative re-appropriation and re-purposing of their traditions. It invalidates *the choice to make tradition work* against colonialism's legacy. The fact that *tradition* plays an ideological role in modernity must not disqualify the option of using the same concept to fight *against* these same ideological uses.

The key step is to recognize the plurality of traditions, along with the closer relation between religions and this plurality (Smith and Vaidyanathan 2010). There is no one view of modernity and no one right view of tradition: 'traditions should not be regarded as essentially homogenous [sic]. ... [W]idespread homogeneity is a function, not of tradition, but of the development and control of communication techniques ... [in] modern industrial societies' (Asad 2009, 23). Traditions are part of, not opposed to, modernities: 'Modernity must not be described in monolithic terms and the ambiguities inherent in the project must be recognized. There were earlier modernities and there are other modernities. And each of these modernities accommodates traditions, often invented traditions' (Arts 2000, 10).

As developed in the following section, a first step away from colonial or settler discourses and institutions is to pay attention to the pragmatic, tactical and improvisatory agency of Indigenous and subaltern groups. Tradition is an active process, not just passive reception or rigid imitation, and not just colonial invention to be rejected. Fanon put it this way: 'Tradition ... is not solely a combination of automatic gestures and archaic beliefs. At the most elementary level, there are values, and the need for justification' (1965, 100).

5.5 Toward active senses of *tradition*

Strategic and tactical uses of *tradition* offer symmetrical tools for the creative agency of Indigenous and subaltern people. Not seeing this is a problem, and scholars are a big part of it. By using the *tradition vs. modernity* binary, the social and human sciences 'helped to justify colonial domination at particular moments in the power encounter between the West and the Third World' (Asad 1973, 274). Divergences from pure tradition are still often seen as inventions and, as a result, inauthentic. This deauthorizes and marginalizes Indigenous and subaltern people.

Drawing too sharp a distinction between *authentic* and *invented* tradition echoes the exclusionary effects of colonial and settler discourses:

> the demand for a rejection of the influence of the colonial period in programmes of decolonization has invoked the idea that certain forms and practices are 'inauthentic', some decolonizing states arguing for a recuperation of authentic pre-colonial traditions and customs. The problem with such claims to cultural authenticity is that they often become entangled in an essentialist cultural position in which fixed practices become iconized as authentically indigenous and others are excluded as hybridized or contaminated. This has as its corollary the danger of ignoring the possibility that cultures may develop and change as their conditions change. (Ashcroft, Griffiths and Tiffin 2013, 22)

The view that tradition is *static* is linked to its conceptual opposition to modernity. Dynamic views of tradition undermine this ideology. Australian anthropologist Nicholas Thomas points to 'the inversion of tradition' and he asks a key question: '*Against what* are traditions invented?' (1992, 216, original emphasis).

The concept of *tradition* itself becomes a tool of critique, liberation and asserting identity in this context. It is oriented by strategic and tactical interests, sometimes in continuity with the real or mythical past, and sometimes independent of it, and with an emphasis on local values and social forms (Thomas 1992). Modern counter-ideological uses of *tradition* make perfect, rational sense:

> A more or less self-conscious fabrication of culture in response to imperious outside 'pressures' is a normal process. ... Rather than the overthrow of the World System, which is now an irreversible fact of their existence, the local peoples' inventions and inversions of tradition can be understood as attempts to create a differentiated cultural space within it. ... How else can the people respond to what has been inflicted on them except by devising on their own heritage, acting according to their own categories, logics, understandings? I say 'devising' because the response may be totally improvised, something never seen or imagined before, not just a knee-jerk repetition of ancient custom. (Sahlins 1993, 16, 20, 18–19)

The value of dynamic views of *tradition* is clear in the anthropological and Indigeneity literatures. Like anthropologists, scholars of religion/s should acknowledge dynamic Indigenous views of *tradition*.

We have seen that the meaning of *tradition* is not unified or stable. It can unhook from certain ideas over here and engage with others over there. Meanings shift when a culture imports and appropriates *tradition* or similar terms. After Australian colonial law introduced the term *custom* as a legal category in Papua New Guinea (PNG), the neologism *kastam* (like *kastom* in other parts of the South Pacific region) began to spread among PNG peoples in the 1970s (Filer 2006). Originally associated with government- and school-organized festivities, with their displays of traditional cultural elements, *kastam* shifted its meaning to mean less a relationship to the past than an authoritative mode of public ceremony (T. Schwartz 1993, 519; Filer

2006, 77–79). It is a dynamic concept. It does not mean repetition of or adherence to a model of the past:

> It is apparent that the Manus [a PNG people] do not mean, when they speak of retaining or reviving *kastam*, that everything their ancestors did or believed is to be preserved. What they value or identify as *kastam* is selective and in part figmentary. They also may ignore or be unaware of extensive continuities in Manus culture, among them some of the very things of their present lives that they wish to replace with *kastam*. *Kastam* is not, however, a free construction; it serves contemporary functions and wishes, yet it also bears positive or negative relations to past and present Manus culture. (T. Schwartz 1993, 515–516)

Strategic appeals to tradition are different than religious and academic ideas of pure, static tradition. (We will see something similar in the discussion of Halbwachs in Chapter 6.1). Anthropology has a better track-record of seeing this than SoR: 'In sociocultural anthropology there have been two major views of tradition: the first is the passive idea of tradition borrowed from the theoretical literature of the social sciences; the second is the active, indigenous use of tradition recorded in the ethnographic literature' (Shanklin 1981, 71).

This second sense is active, interested, innovative, rational, strategic and tactical: it is used as a tool for leverage on both sides of many different social boundaries. Views of pure tradition can be part of this mix. This is clear in *kastam*'s relation to the newer Melanesian concept of *kalsa* (from *culture*):

> *kastam* as a value and identity marker in the present has a strong orientation towards the past, where the proper standard of knowledge and performance is to be found. As a result *kastam* is considered as continuous with the past; ideologically it may not be changed, although in practice it does—like all forms of culture. *Kalsa* also refers to the past as the source of the specific cultural heritage of the islands, but its orientation is as much towards the future where its relevance is considered to be. (Otto 2014, 126)

Indigenous appropriations, redefinitions and reinventions of *tradition* and related words prompted many scholars to stop pretending that *tradition* is theirs to define:

anthropologists maintained a duty of care towards 'native custom' that set them apart from all the other agents of the colonial enterprise. But they could treat it as the generic object of their own actions and reflections only so long as its native owners did not think and talk about it as one of the many things that occupied their own cultural landscape. Once 'custom' became a topic of village conversation, anthropologists began to treat it as a symbolic tool applied to the destruction of the colonial legacy or the reconstruction of an ethnic identity. (Filer 2006, 67)

A key lesson from the peoples of the south Pacific is this more dynamic view of tradition:

> Rather than viewing tradition as a passively accepted legacy of the past, it is useful to think of it as continually reemerging in transmuted form from the crucible of history. That is, practices and institutions are continually reevaluated and reinterpreted in relation to changing circumstances that include other peoples. (Turner 1997, 372)

5.6 Indigeneity and *tradition*'s dynamism

The word *Indigenous* itself encapsulates this chapter's key point about *tradition*. That idea is often used to homogenize and marginalize allegedly non-*western*, non-*modern* peoples, but it cuts both ways. It can be rejected or re-appropriated. Colonial discourses can become tools for tactical counter-ideological critique.

Colonial concepts of *Indigenous* and *tradition* do similar ideological work. This is clear in discussions of global migration:

> In the discourse of the West and the Rest, it is postulated that there is a fundamental difference in life attitude toward knowledge production between Westerners and non-Westerners. ... It is assumed that non-Westerners are destined to be stationary, reactive, and traditional, whereas Westerners are dynamic, active, and restless by nature. Hence, the adjective 'Indigenous' is rarely attributed to Westerners ... even though the vast majority of the European or Western population, in fact, do not participate in global migratory movement. (Sakai 2022, 20)

This highlights the fact that settler attitudes to Indigenous cultures are orientalist (see Text Box 4).

Colonialist attitudes to Indigenous traditions embody both modes of orientalist distortion: accusations of traditionality and backwardness; and romantic exaltations of spiritual depth and oneness with nature. Both modes have the effect of distancing Indigenous people and nations from current material, political, legal and economic realities. The ideological work of *tradition* is central to this process.

Here is a concrete example, reflecting the fact that the collection of *authentic* artefacts for museum collections has often manifested this bias. French ethnographer Marcel Griaule commented in the 1930s on the case of an African drum that was rejected as inauthentic because it showed a man with a rifle:

> The height of absurdity is reached ... when the ... [European] refuses the African the right to 'make art' with a European motif, claiming first that it is European—a somewhat amusingly self-castrating remark—and, secondly, that it looks 'modern.' ... As for the argument of antiquity, only ... [a wine connoisseur] could give it any value whatsoever, confusing ... antiquity with ethnography. (Griaule 1995, 98)

This is a toxic double-bind. If Indigenous people stick to their tradition (as defined by the colonizers) they are backward; if they move beyond it, they are no longer authentic members of their culture. If tradition is defined as a survival from the past, then *traditional* people sacrifice their identity if they change, innovate or create.

Tradition, however, can critique as well as prop up orientalist contrasts between Indigenous and settler cultures. *Kanien'kehá:ka* (Mohawk) author and activist Taiaiake Alfred argues that the path of seeking Indigenous recognition from settler governments is linked to problematic programs of assimilation (2005). As an alternative, he proposes an active turn toward *tradition* as a more effective form of Indigenous revitalization:

> people can begin to free themselves from colonialism by thinking as traditionalists. ... We have a responsibility to recover, understand, and preserve these values, not only because they represent a unique contribution to the history of ideas, but because renewal of respect for traditional values is the only lasting solution to the political,

economic, and social problems that beset our people. To bring those roots to new fruition, we must reinvigorate the principles embedded in the ancient teachings, and use them to address our contemporary problems. (Alfred 1999, 81, 5)

For Indigenous nations, a *traditional solution* focuses 'on actualizing their own power and preserving their intellectual independence. This is an Indigenous approach to empowerment'; a 'process of self-conscious reflection and *selective* re-adoption of traditional values' can 'begin to make traditional values and principles the foundations for governance' (Alfred 1999, 48, 81, emphasis added). The word *selective* marks the path: this traditionalism is strategic, dynamic and contextualized; it is not automatic reception or repetition of the past. This approach undermines the distinction between static tradition and dynamic modernity: 'when the people we [scholars] speak of speak for themselves, their sovereignty interrupts anthropological portraits of timelessness, procedure, and function that dominate representations of their past and, sometimes, their present' (Simpson 2014, 97).

The concept of *authenticity* is often used to draw a colonialist distinction between *true* Indigenous traditions and the beliefs and action of people who, though Indigenous by birth, are not *properly* or culturally Indigenous: 'the demand for alterity and its containment within the terms of tradition is inherent in liberal multiculturalism. ... Traditionality is a test of entitlement' (Merlan 2006, 86). When settler governments frame recognition and rights in terms of this link between static tradition and Indigenous identity, this imposes a form of 'repressive authenticity':

> To understand repressive authenticity, we have to attend to the consequences for those whom it renders inauthentic—historical Indigenous people who do not embody the construction. ... Since the feature most crucially shared by Indigenous people and colonizers is an economic interest in the same land, it is only to be expected that the symbols of Aboriginality that figure most prominently in repressive authenticity are precisely those that least conflict with settler-colonial economics. Though the official rhetoric of land rights ... is ostensibly benign, the rarefied traditional Aboriginality that it dispenses perpetuates the logic of elimination. (Wolfe 1999, 179–180)

By defining *authentic, traditional* Indigenous culture in terms of a mythical past of pre-colonial beliefs and rituals, settler governments define Indigenous identity in ways that keep Indigenous groups at arm's length from present political, legal and economic issues, above all the full ownership of land: 'what is being coded as culture is in fact a theory of jurisdictional authority and legitimacy' (Simpson 2014, 92).

Tradition plays a central role in legal discussions of Indigenous rights (see Case Study 4). Canadian courts have tended to base decisions on a 'frozen rights' view, according to which 'traditional present-day indigenous practices are those that are substantially similar to pre-colonial indigenous practices'; and this limits the ability of First Nations to enact and perform their traditions in more dynamic ways:

> The concept of tradition in an aboriginal rights claim serves to enable judicial choices while also providing a basis for denying the making of choices. ... The concept of tradition in Canadian aboriginal rights law *mystifies*—perhaps unconsciously, perhaps not—the exercise of power by the courts over indigenous claimants. (Connolly 2006, 28–30)

More dynamic views of *tradition* and *authenticity* are not just a possible alternative to colonial views of tradition. They are active threats to colonial structures:

> The battleground of repressive authenticity is that of Indigenous 'post'-colonial identities, which strive to historicize the mythical duality that the discourse propounds [to expose the ideological work of the *tradition vs. modernity* distinction]. The further from the pole of mythic authenticity that an Indigenous identity can be asserted or reclaimed, the greater the ideological danger that it presents. (Wolfe 1999, 183)

Historicizing *mythic authenticity* involves rejecting any sharp distinction between tradition and modernity; but it also rejects the forced choice between accepting a colonial view of *tradition* or none at all. The *ideological danger* that threatens colonial structures is the possibility of more dynamic, flexible, creative and tactical views of *tradition*, which threaten to allow groups displaced by settler cultures to reclaim autonomy. This is a reminder that, as scholars of religion/s, we need to pay close attention both to our own tendencies to see *tradition* as static and unchanging pure tradition and to the dangers of rejecting the concept of *tradition* entirely.

At the same time, dynamic Indigenous views of tradition can also be repressive. For example, both static colonial views of *tradition* and dynamic Indigenous appropriations of the concept have resulted in the oppression of women in some contexts. On the one hand, the erosion of inclusive Indigenous views of tradition, in part through the imposition of a colonial view of pure tradition, attacked women and Indigenous conceptions of family. Domestic relations ground cultural and individual agency, and here the struggle over tradition remains crucial:

> The labor that the colonizers were least able to control was that of reproducing, provisioning, and caring for Indigenous children and other household members: reproducing the colonized kinship group, its culture and practices. Additionally, without such control, Indigenous domestic relations remained intact and thus a source of support for Indigenous resistance. Thus appropriating control of women's sexuality and domestic labor reduced the power of Indigenous men and of Indigenous communities. Households were the last sites of resistance to the colonizers ... (Harding 2017, 628)

On the other hand, women's attempts to draw on modern, western discourses of rights and equality has placed them in tension with an Indigenous traditionalist stance:

> The oppression faced by Indigenous women in Canada cannot be adequately understood when separated from the other axes of oppression that have converged to sustain it over time. Gender equality claims and individual rights of reinstated women and children are pitted against the collective right of First Nations to determine their own membership. The result ... has been a dismissal of Native women's concerns as 'untraditional and, by extension, as deleterious to indigenous liberation.' ... [This results from] a zero-sum contest pitting the individual human right of Indigenous women to sex equality against the collective human right of Indigenous peoples to self-determination. (Coulthard 2014, 96, 88, 91; citing Joyce Green)

The concept of *tradition* can be used as a tool of both oppression and resistance, and it pulls in different ways within Indigenous communities. Some Indigenous groups reject tradition and its discourses as a tactical response to their situations: 'they invert, rather than transcend, the identities and narratives created by colonialists, traditionalists, and nation states' (Thomas 1992, 228). Others use *tradition* in more contextualized, strategic ways. Uses of *tradition* reflect specific contexts and agendas, and scholarship should reflect this. Yellowknives Dene scholar Glen Coulthard calls for a contextualized approach:

> we have to be cautious that our appeals to 'culture' and 'tradition' in our contemporary struggles for recognition do not replicate the racist and sexist misrecognitions of the Indian Act and in the process unwittingly reproduce the structure of dispossession we originally set out to challenge. ... No discourse on identity should be prematurely cast as either inherently productive or repressive prior to an engaged consideration of the historical, political, and socioeconomic contexts and actors involved. ... This is particularly relevant from the perspective of Indigenous peoples' struggles, where *activists may sometimes employ what appear to outsiders as essentialist notions of culture and tradition* in their efforts to transcend, not reinforce, oppressive structures and practices. (Coulthard 2014, 103, emphasis added)

It is racist and colonialist to portray Indigenous cultures as repositories of *pure, authentic tradition* and to portray white settler cultures as modern. It is also problematic to reject tactical Indigenous appropriations of essentialist concepts of tradition. Indigenous people, living across imposed cultural boundaries, can choose to engage in 'self-conscious attempts ... to learn traditional ways', and these can result in 'reconstructed versions of those traditions' and 'reconstructed traditional values' (Fleming Mathur 1975, 458). This *self-conscious traditionalism* should be assessed in terms of its pragmatic value, not judged by ideological binaries of *tradition* vs. *modernity* and *authentic* vs. *invented* (Alfred 1999). Sharp, static binaries are often orientalist. But dynamic appropriations of such binaries can be a powerful tool for social change: strategic, dynamic, tactical, flexible, contextualized and pragmatic. Coulthard's emphasis on the tactical and contextual nature of appeals to tradition has three key implications: the past need neither be accepted nor rejected in absolute terms; it provides materials for re-invigorating and re-inventing tradition on the fly; and essentialist views of tradition can be both a tool of oppression and a tool for rejecting and resisting it. Once again, context is crucial.

5.7 Chapter summary

The *pure tradition* vs. *modernity* binary is not just modern, it is colonialist. Scholars of religion/s risk falling into these ideological traps if we use the *pure tradition* vs. *modernity* binary and related conceptual contrasts to define cultures and religions.

There is no verb to go with *tradition* (as *extradite* goes with *extradition*). This makes it hard to even talk about people *making tradition happen*. Our language has a built-in assumption that tradition is *passive* reception. In this light, tradition is related to ritual. In both, people follow a script. Supposedly, no one who has ever *received and followed* a given tradition played any role in *creating* it. This obscures the ways in which people creatively *work* with tradition.

This logic of displaced agency lurks at the heart of the colonial *tradition vs. modernity* binary. On this view, the modern agent acts for their own individual *reasons*; only non-moderns unthinkingly follow tradition. When tradition is defined as irrational (because received without thinking), it can be seen as a threat that must be contained and policed. This rules out of bounds dynamic uses of tradition, which are central to the strategies and tactics of Indigenous and other subaltern groups: a mix of respect for the past and tactical innovation in response to present circumstances. Denying this active, creative work with tradition can be a colonial tool of oppression: if we define Indigenous communities as unchanging (*authentically* traditional), this hinders their ability to defend their interests in current political, legal and economic debates.

Postcolonial and decoloniality studies have made important contributions to the counter-ideological critique of modern and colonial views of *tradition*. From these academic perspectives, the modern idea of *tradition* was invented by colonizers and projected onto the colonized. It was used as a tool for dismissing non-European cultures. It was also used by elite groups among the colonized for positions of power *within colonial power structures*, over who would have authority over tradition. Women were often oppressed and marginalized by these discourses, which portrayed their actions and bodies as repositories of tradition.

At the same time, dynamic views of tradition can also be oppressive, for example, limiting Indigenous women's attempts to claim autonomy. The concept of *tradition* can be used as a tool of both marginalization and resistance, contributing to either the erosion or the enabling of Indigenous agency, and it pulls in different ways within Indigenous communities.

Key take-home points—*If none of its followers created a tradition, then its origin can be projected onto mythological founders or supernatural beings. The flip side of this religious point is colonialist: this logic of displaced agency lurks at the heart of the colonial tradition vs. modernity binary. On this view, the modern agent acts for rational reasons; only non-moderns, including Indigenous people, blindly follow tradition. This ideological reduction of all tradition to pure tradition rules out of bounds the kinds of dynamic uses of tradition that often characterize the tactics of Indigenous and other subaltern groups.*

Case Study 4: Indigenous tradition and Canadian law

In 1992, Former National Chief of the Assembly of First Nations in Canada, Ovide Mercredi, said,

> One of the things we have to do as First Nations peoples is to create a balance in our relationships with the other governments and the Canadian people. We cannot find balance if we are dominated by the other society. We cannot find harmony when we are threatened with choices like 'take this policy or nothing else.' (Cited in Turpel 1993, 117)

Who decides whether a practice is traditional or authentic? Who weighs a tradition's normative force against other moral claims? If traditions give 'rights', then who balances these rights against others? If Indigenous communities and settler governments have different answers to these questions, who decides which answers are right?

Canadian courts are one place where these questions are asked and answered. Legal decisions in Canada have yet to deal with the relation between Canadian constitutional rights and Indigenous traditions. Section 35(1) of the Canadian Charter of Rights and Freedoms reads, 'The existing aboriginal and treaty rights of the aboriginal peoples of Canada are hereby recognized and affirmed.' Section 25 reads, 'The guarantee in this Charter of certain rights and freedoms shall not be construed so as to abrogate or derogate from any aboriginal, treaty or other rights or freedoms that pertain to the aboriginal peoples of Canada ...'. What implications does this have for *tradition*?

In 1988, an Indigenous man was initiated into a tradition, against his will, by several members of the Coast Salish nation, guided by an Elder. He sued the men who did this. In his 1992 decision, Justice Hood of the Supreme Court of British Columbia summed up the defence's argument:

> The aboriginal right claimed by the defendants is their right to carry on and exercise the Tradition, which is called the Coast Salish Spirit Dance. ... The defendants admit that they 'grabbed' the plaintiff in order to initiate him into the Coast Salish Big House Tradition. ... [One of one of the defendants explained, 'It's called grabbing, when

someone is grabbed for the big house. ... Every winter people are grabbed and put in the big house for dancing.' Asked about harsh conditions of the ritual, one of the defendants said, 'we all go through it'.] ... The defendants say that their right to traditional practices is an aboriginal right ... In performing the Spirit Dance Tradition they are not bound by the common law, and the plaintiff's civil rights ... must give way, to the collective right of the aboriginal nation to which he belongs, and which is protected by s. 35(1) [of the Charter]. (*Thomas vs. Norris*, 1992)

The judge decided in favour of the plaintiff:

The assumed aboriginal right, which I perceive to be more a freedom than a right, is not absolute. ... Civil rights ... protect citizens from the wrongful conduct of others, including those who engage in such conduct while purporting to be exercising their religious practices or other freedoms or rights. ... If such conduct cannot be separated from the spirit dancing, and thus is an integral part of it, then in my opinion spirit dancing is not an aboriginal right recognized or protected by the law. ... Assuming that spirit dancing was an aboriginal right, and that it existed and was practiced prior to ... the imposition of English law, in my opinion those aspects of it which were contrary to English common law ... did not survive the coming into force of that law ... (*Thomas vs. Norris*, 1992)

There are different possible views of this judgment. First, the defence did not provide evidence to support the claim that the Spirit Dance was a traditional ritual, nor did they make an argument on the basis of s. 25 of the Charter. Those were missed opportunities. Second, 'Hood J. failed to take sufficient account of the fact that Aboriginal rights are constitutionalized, whereas common law rights generally are not. So Aboriginal rights should prevail in the event of conflict' (McNeil 1996, 76 n.44). Third,

The decision and this discussion possess an inherent problem in relation to Aboriginal peoples and their many cultures. The Canadian legal system is based in part on the protection of rights, whereas many Aboriginal peoples conduct themselves according to duty or responsibility. Further to the point, from an Aboriginal perspective, the fact that Hood J. held that s. 35(1) provided no protection to spirit dancing (practiced against unwilling participants) underscores the ethnocentricity inherent in the Canadian legal system. Individual rights are supreme. (Isaac 1992, 630)

A basic background issue is whether s. 25 of the Charter is to be read as constructive (serving as a basis for elaborating the "other rights or freedoms" mentioned there) or as merely protective (shielding existing rights from Charter infringement) (Swiffen 2019). The former view is consistent with granting maximal autonomy to Canada's First Nations; the second frames Indigenous rights as a contingent bubble within a space dominated by the Charter. The deck seems stacked in favour of the latter view: 'given the current constitutional framework it seems hard to imagine a way of applying section 25 that does not create a hierarchy between legal cultures' (Swiffen 2019, 116). The Government of Canada sees the Charter as preeminent: 'Self-government agreements, including treaties, will ... have to provide that the Canadian Charter of Rights and Freedoms *applies* to Aboriginal governments and institutions in relation to all matters within their respective jurisdictions and authorities' (Government of Canada 2023).

As I write this, a relevant case has been heard by the Supreme Court of Canada, and the judgment is currently reserved. Ms Cindy Dickson—a member of Vuntut Gwitchi, a small First Nation in the northern Yukon—was blocked from running for election to the Council, because she was unwilling to move, if elected, to the traditional community of Old Crow, about 800 km north of Whitehorse. She gave family medical and financial reasons for her decision. She sued the Vuntut Gwitchi nation. The case is now being considered by the Supreme Court, which sees a number of issues in play. For example:

> [whether] s. 25 of Charter operates so as to shield requirement from review—Whether scope of "other rights and freedoms" that "pertain to aboriginal peoples of Canada" set out in s. 25 of Charter includes residency requirement—... whether application of s. 25 means collective rights need not be balanced with other interests—Whether Charter applies to residency requirement in constitution of self-governing First Nation. (Supreme Court of Canada 2023)

The fact that a self-governing First Nation awaits the decision of the court appears to answer the question of where power lies.

There is a different lesson in how the Vuntut Gwitchi First Nation itself defines *tradition*. The Vuntut Gwitchin Heritage Act sees tradition as flexible and dynamic, and it adds openness and depth with related ideas of *heritage, customs, practices, values* and *laws*:

> In our way 'tradition' includes 'openness to new things.' ... You don't know traditional knowledge, you have to live it. ... The oral, cultural, experience-on-the-land basis of our heritage makes it flexible, adaptive and evolving. It is a dynamic, living heritage and culture based on traditions which are shaped by our history in a harsh environment. Balancing tradition and adaptability has ensured our survival. In our way, change and adaptation are aspects of our laws, practices and values ... Heritage is our way of life. The stories about creation and how we learn from the animals and the land teach us about how to take care of ourselves and to survive on the land and to do it 'in a good way.' And I guess that 'in a good way' means respect. That is our biggest law. ... The supreme value of respect pervades our traditional laws, customs and practices. (Vuntut Gwitchin 2016)

This dynamic view of tradition escapes the colonial *pure tradition* vs. *modernity* binary (see Chapters 1.5, 4.2 and 5.6). It does not see tradition as locked in by the past, and it completely ignores *modern* as a contrasting label. The Act begins by distinguishing 'what our Elders call "our way" from the "western" or "English way"'. It speaks of respect, not rights.

Dynamic views of *tradition* like this face an uphill battle to be granted legal, political and economic respect. But the lesson for students and scholars of religion/s is clear: let's stop defining *tradition* as *pure tradition*; let's read uses of *tradition* in their contexts.

Chapter 6

Key thinkers of *tradition*

This chapter looks at some important academic views of *tradition*. The main point is that all such views are limited due to their choice of examples, conceptual presuppositions, definitions of related terms and theoretical agendas. This is not a problem; it is an unavoidable result of *tradition*'s complexity. As such, it illustrates the value of this book's approach: looking at how *tradition* relates to other concepts.

Here are two examples not featured in the chapter. Scottish-American philosopher Alasdair MacIntyre uses *tradition* as part of his critique of the dysfunctional and incoherent nature of modern moral discourse:

> all reasoning takes place within the context of some traditional mode of thought, transcending through criticism and invention the limitations of what had hitherto been reasoned in that tradition; this is as true of modern physics as of medieval logic. Moreover when a tradition is in good order it is always partially constituted by an argument about the goods the pursuit of which gives to that tradition its particular point and purpose. ... A living tradition then is an historically extended, socially embodied argument, and an argument precisely in part about the goods which constitute that tradition. (MacIntyre 2007 [1981], 222)

Is it surprising that a philosopher who argues that moral discourse has been cut free from distinct communities of value would define *tradition* in terms of distinct communities of value?

French sociologist Danièle Hervieu-Léger tries to make sense of the persistence and revival of religion in modern French society. She sees the contemporary religious landscape as manifesting a complex interrelation of tradition and modernity. Its symptoms include individual religious or spiritual seeking (as opposed to fixed belonging), flexible adoption of belief (rather than obligatory ritual practice) and voluntary association (rather than identity formation by being born into a religion).

With its stark rejection of secularization theory, this research focus rules out a simple contrast between *religion* and *tradition*, on the one hand, and *modernity*, on the other. Instead Hervieu-Léger proposes 'to rearticulate the core relationship between tradition and religion within modernity' (2000 [1993], 84). This signals a presentist position, i.e., seeing the past in light of present interests (see the section on Halbwachs just below):

> One cannot ... make tradition encompass the ... whole stock of representations, images, theoretical and practical knowledge, behaviour and attitudes which is inherited, received from the past. All that constitute tradition in the proper meaning of the term are the parts of this stock ... that a group or society accepts in the name of the *necessary* continuity between the past and the present. (Hervieu-Léger 2000 [1993], 87, original emphasis)

For Hervieu-Léger, the premodern view of tradition as guarantor of continuity has changed to this view of tradition as a selective bridge to visions of the past as shaped by the present:

> There is de-structuring and re-structuring, disorganization but also re-development and re-employment of elements deriving from the earlier order in the fluid system of modern society. Religion, as total expression of the former order in the register of symbolism and ritual, has become caught in the same dialectic of change. In choosing a definition that stresses its being anchored in the world of tradition, it is not thereby excluded from the world of modernity. Its place there is signalled from the outset but in the reconstructed form of tradition within modernity. (Hervieu-Léger 2000 [1993], 97)

In this light, Hervieu-Léger defines *religion* in terms of 'the expression of believing, the memory of continuity, and the legitimizing reference to an authorized version of such memory, that is to say to a tradition' (2000 [1993], 97). Is it a surprise that her definition of *tradition* as 'reference to a chain of belief' fits with this view of religion (2000 [1993], 123)?

The question to ask when comparing academic views, with their inherent limitations, is not *which one best captures the nature of tradition itself?* but *which is most useful?* What other concepts are connected to *tradition*, for what reasons, and to what effect? What insights might different approaches to *tradition* offer for your own particular work: your substantive case and materials in their contexts, your research methods, your emerging theoretical frame? All are useful in some ways and all leave out certain things. This final chapter illustrates that tradition is not a *thing* to be found out there in history, culture or the world; rather, *tradition* is a concept so fundamental yet so broad that it forces us to be clear about which other concepts we bring along with it.

6.1 Maurice Halbwachs: cultural memory

In the 1920s, French sociologist Maurice Halbwachs (1877–1945) introduced the concept of *mémoire collective* (cultural, collective or social memory). His teacher, Émile Durkheim (1858–1917) had limited his own discussion of memory to small-scale societies. Halbwachs saw memory as central to all societies, and he saw it as social. He had started by researching individual memory, and his work with aphasia (inability to speak) led him to emphasize social meaning in both remembering and forgetting: 'Halbwachs's work shows that people act according to the meaning they ascribe to their own and other people's behavior ... [and] the content of those meanings is provided, originally, by the conventions of the community to which the individual belongs' (Marcel and Mucchielli 2008, 143–144). An isolated individual would be unable to develop any memory at all: 'Every collective memory requires the support of a group. ... It is in society that people normally acquire their memories. It is also in society that they recall, recognize, and localize their memories' (Halbwachs 1992 [1952], 84, 38).

For Halbwachs, groups collectively reconstruct their past experiences. Individuals may have distinct perspectives on this group reconstruction of the past, but they do not have independent memories of it. Halbwachs suggested that the lived memory (*mémoire vécue*) of present individuals is transcribed into two different sorts of written archives, i.e., history and tradition: 'The former consists in the critical overview and impartial archiving of events stored in the memory, and the latter in the ever-present process of capturing and keeping by all means possible the live impressions made by a remorselessly receding past' (J. Assmann 2011, 48).

The idea that memory varies by group shifts focus from the content of memory to processes of remembering and to the make-up of different groups as sites of cultural memory. This de-emphasis of the individual reflects Halbwachs's Durkheimian allegiances: 'almost everywhere that Durkheim speaks of "Society" with a capital S, Halbwachs speaks of "groups"' (Coser 1992, 22; see Olick 2008, 156–157). More recent scholars, like those drawing on the cognitive psychology of memory, insist on the importance of individual experience as an element of cultural memory.

In the same decade, art historian Aby Warburg (1866–1929) worked with the idea of *social memory*. His theory of response insisted on the 'social mediation of images', the need to study the content of traditions (artistic representations, texts, events) in detailed historical context (Forster 1976). He also underlined the close relationship between the social and the political in the history of memory, a balance that shifted with later scholars' growing emphasis on the political in cultural memory studies (Confino 1997). The work of Jan Assmann and Aleida Assmann (discussed in the following section) re-emphasizes the social, and it foregrounds the role of religion.

Prior to the work of Halbwachs and Warburg, ideas of collective memory were prominent by other names: they emphasized both things remembered and the personal legacy or 'immortality' of outstanding people or actions; but there was no attention to groups as agents of remembering (Russell 2006). The idea of *racial memory* had been prominent, before being rejected in favour of a cultural approach: 'both Warburg and Halbwachs shift the discourse concerning collective knowledge out of a biological framework into a cultural one' (J. Assmann 1995, 125).

The resulting cluster of issues has led to an important trans- and inter-disciplinary subfield of *cultural memory studies*, held together by a broad emphasis on 'the interplay of present and past in socio-cultural contexts':

> 'cultural memory' can serve as an umbrella term which comprises 'social memory' (the starting point for memory research in the social sciences), 'material or medial memory' (the focus of interest in literary and media studies), and 'mental or cognitive memory' (the field of expertise in psychology and the neurosciences). (Erll 2008, 2, 4)

The idea of a dynamic interplay between past and present is central to this recent work, but it is obscured in Halbwachs.

Halbwachs had an important influence on later work,[1] but his views have various problems (Connerton 1989, 36–38; Misztal 2003, 54–55). He does not explain how memory is passed on from generation to generation within groups. His idea of *collective memory* is never defined clearly. He has been critiqued for prioritizing groups at the expense of the individual, reflecting his Durkheimian emphasis on collective representations.[2]

Halbwachs has also been criticized for seeing the past as a construction that is shaped *entirely* by present concerns: 'history does not limit itself to reproducing a tale told by people contemporary with events of the past, but rather refashions it from period to period ... to adapt it to the mental habits and the type of representation of the past common among contemporaries' (1992, 75). More recent work on cultural memory finds his extreme *presentism* unable to account for the central role of cultural memory in maintaining cultural continuity (Coser 1992, 30; see B. Schwartz 1982). This is an important point, but the past does have effects of its own: structures that we inherit

---

1. For example, his emphasis on episodic (detailed, personal, contextualized) memory—a shift from earlier scholars' implicit work with semantic (general, decontextualized) memory—prefigured developments in memory studies and cognitive science (Russell 2006, 798–799).

2. American philosopher George Herbert Mead had a similar view: 'The significant content which historical research reveals ... [is not] the past object as implied in the present ... History is trying to restate the past so as to make our present situation intelligible. ... The community wants to bring up the past so it can state the present situation and bring out what the actual issues themselves are' (Mead 1938, 94, 81).

from the past narrow our field of choices, and we are limited in our ability to redefine the past in the face of clashing reconstructions made by others (Schudson 1989). These processes themselves are in part socially constructed, which underlines the dynamic nature of tradition, its tug-of-war between reception and invention (see Text Box 8).

> **Text Box 8** Dynamic relations between past and present
>
> Masada was an ancient palace and fortress in south Israel, enlarged (if not built) by Herod the Great (c.72 BCE–4 or 1 BCE). It sits on a stark-walled mesa overlooking the Dead Sea. Masada exemplifies how the present shapes the past but is also shaped by it. Flavius Josephus (c.37 CE–c.100 CE), a near-contemporary Jewish-Roman historian, is the sole source of non-archaeological information on the site and the events that took place there. The Roman garrison stationed at Masada was overrun by a group of Jewish rebels in 66 CE, at the start of the first Jewish-Roman War. The Zealots of Masada were the last significant group of rebels conquered by the Romans, who built a ramp and breached the wall in 73 CE, discovering that the Jewish rebels had committed suicide.
>
> These events were ignored until the twentieth century. In 1927, Israeli journalist and poet Yitzhak Lamdan published an epic poem in Hebrew, 'Masada: A Historical Epic'. The poem was for the most part a pessimistic assessment of a lack of options for Jewish immigrants to Palestine, given difficulties in their new home, exclusionary immigration quotas in the USA, and ongoing violence in Eastern Europe: in 1927 almost twice as many Jews were leaving Palestine as were entering (Schwartz et al. 1986).
>
> After the Second World War, Israeli emphasis shifted to a middle portion of the poem, with its defiant affirmation, 'Never again shall Masada fall!' A largely forgotten past—Masada—was reclaimed because it resonated with sentiments during a changed time of national autonomy and external military threats. Masada

> became 'a symbol of military valor and national commitment. ... Most Israelis ... interpret the mass suicide at Masada as a heroic affirmation of national dignity' (Schwartz et al. 1986, 151). The Israeli government website for Masada National Park says, 'In the days of the Great Revolt, the last of the rebels against Rome entrenched themselves at Masada, and turned their desperate fight into a symbol of the struggle for freedom' (Israel 2019). This illustrates how the past is reinterpreted, reframed and revalued by present concerns. But it is not just invented. History, like tradition, is a dynamic relation between present and past.

Halbwachs's focus is on the concept of memory, not *tradition*. He is more interested in group construction of history in light of the present than in the ongoing work of lived memory, and he limits tradition to the latter. He does recognize that something much more interesting is going on with tradition, but he fails to develop the point, because he sees it as a phenomenon limited to religion. He comes very close to making a pioneering statement of the ideological role of the idea of pure tradition—with its denial of history—but his narrow focus on institutional Christianity as the prototype of religion gets in the way of a more general analysis. He sees the issue clearly:

> If ... the object of religion seems exempt from the law of change, if religious *representations* are fixed—while all the other notions and traditions that form the content of social thought evolve and become transformed—this is not because they are outside of time but rather because the time to which they refer is detached, if not from all that preceded it, at least from all that follows. In other words, the totality of religious remembrances subsists in a state of isolation and is all the more separated from other social remembrances to the degree that the epoch in which they were formed is more remote. (Halbwachs 1992, 91, emphasis added)

This is problematic because, as we have seen, pure tradition (received and invented) is found outside of religion, and it is found in only some religious discourses.

He also recognizes the power of invented tradition, decades before Hobsbawm and Ranger (see Chapter 3.1):

> The Church can ... allow without apparent contradiction that new revelations occur. But it tries nevertheless to link these new data to the ancient data and to place them within the body of *its doctrine, that is, of its tradition*. In other words, the Church does not acknowledge that these data are really new; it prefers to conjecture that the full content of the early revelation was not immediately perceived. ... Although religious memory attempts to isolate itself from temporal society, it obeys the same laws as every collective memory: it does not preserve the past but reconstructs it with the aid of the material traces, rites, texts, and traditions left behind by that past ... (Halbwachs 1992, 119, emphasis added)

Halbwachs's view has two nested problems. By linking pure tradition to religion, he misses the chance to see how ideological (invented) uses of pure tradition play roles in many non-religious contexts. And by defining religion in terms of pure tradition and institutional context, he makes it difficult to explain other religious phenomena, especially religious innovation. His isolation of religion from his broader analysis expresses itself in a *sui generis* view, that religion is fundamentally different from other social phenomena: 'Since all the rest of social life is developed within the passage of time or duration, it stands to reason that religion withdraws itself from this' (1992, 93). The resulting inability to make sense of religion leads Halbwachs to frame 'mystics and heretics [prophetic innovators]' as irrational sources of false memories: 'Should we say that the dogmatic tradition alone possesses the attributes of a collective memory, and that a religious tradition that gathers together and deals with the revelations of mystics as testimony resembles a memory that is encumbered with residues of paramnesia [memory errors, e.g., *déjà vu* or recalling a dream as real]?' (1992, 118).

The more dynamic views that we have been exploring in this book allow us to extend Halbwachs's partial insights, in part because they refuse to separate religion out as a special sphere. Once we relativize the distinction between pure and invented tradition (see Chapter 3.1), and once we see the resulting dynamics as general social (not just religious) processes, we resolve these tensions in Halbwachs's account.

Durkheim's contemporary—and frequent theoretical opponent—Gabriel Tarde (1843-1904), critiqued the idea of collective representations for drawing an indefensible line between individual and collective (Karsenti 2010, 54-56; see Némedi 1995). Tarde emphasized the dynamic nature of tradition's 'fixing and perpetuating its new acquisitions and consolidating its increments' (1903, 369). He emphasized the overlap of old and new meanings—along with the necessity for 'points of likeness' and 'the possession of a common foundation of ideas and traditions, of a common language'—in the elaboration of new social forms (1903, 62): 'the traditional and customary element is always ... preponderant in social life, and this preponderance is forcibly revealed in the way in which the most radical and revolutionary innovations spread abroad; for their supporters can further them only through ... the old and antique language of the people' (1903, 246). Tarde points to one path of moving past Halbwachs's Durkheimian constraints on views of tradition.

6.2 Hans-Georg Gadamer and Paul Ricoeur: hermeneutics and ideology

For Hans-Georg Gadamer (1900-2002), 'understanding is determined by tradition' (2004 [1960], 559). Tradition is open-ended and always under development: understanding is 'the interplay of the movement of tradition and the movement of the interpreter' (2004, 293). Tradition is the site of a dynamic interplay between past and present:

> Understanding is to be thought of less as a subjective act than as participating in an event of tradition, a process of transmission in which past and present are constantly mediated. ... Tradition is not simply a permanent precondition; rather, we produce it ourselves inasmuch as we understand, [and] participate in the evolution of tradition ... Historical understanding always implies that the tradition reaching us speaks into the present and must be understood in this mediation—indeed, as this mediation. (Gadamer 2004, 291, 293, 325)

This grounds Gadamer's rejection of an 'unconditional antithesis between tradition and reason': 'both the Enlightenment's critique of tradition and the romantic rehabilitation of it' objectify the past; they both undermine the 'living relationship to tradition' that is required for understanding (2004, 282, 283, 354). (This undermines the opposition between *tradition* and *modernity*: see Chapter 4.) This relationship is *living* because it does not consist in passive or habitual repetition or copying: 'For Gadamer, ... tradition involves the past in its potentiality as a process of transformation and transmission that is ongoing and unfinished' (Brogan 2020, 11). Where most discussions make the similarity or continuity of past and present central to *tradition*, Gadamer underlines difference. He is interested

> not so much with the continuance of the existing tradition as with the temporal distance that, despite the continuing effect of tradition, separates us from our historical past and thus brings an element of strangeness and unfamiliarity to the process of understanding. ... Tradition is therefore inexhaustibly open to new interpretations and additional dimensions of meaning. (Leiviskä 2015, 589)

This makes *tradition* a prime example of the hermeneutic circle:[3] 'The anticipation of meaning that governs our understanding of a text is not an act of subjectivity, but proceeds from the commonality that binds us to the tradition. But this commonality is constantly being formed in our relation to tradition' (Gadamer 2004, 293).

Jürgen Habermas (b. 1929) argues that Gadamer is too optimistic, because he leaves no room for criticizing tradition. For Habermas, Gadamer's view leaves no place outside of the dynamic dance of past and present that would allow *reflection* to engage in ideological critique:

> Gadamer's prejudice in favor of the legitimacy of prejudices (or prejudgments) validated by tradition is in conflict with the power of reflection, which proves itself in its ability to reject the claim of traditions. ... The right of reflection requires that the hermeneutic

---

3. This *circle* metaphor points to the way that interpretive experience has a dynamic spiral character: we go deeper through a back-and-forth movement between making sense of parts and wholes of a text, and between ideas that we bring to the table and those we take away. As we move back and forth, all sides shift.

approach limit itself. It requires a system of reference that transcends the context of tradition as such. Only then can tradition be criticized as well. (Habermas 1988, 170)

Paul Ricoeur (1913–2005) agrees with Gadamer that interpretation and understanding are always situated within an 'interconnecting historical succession' (Ricoeur 1988, 219). His dynamic view of tradition is very similar to Gadamer's:

> Tradition means transmission, transmission of things said, of beliefs professed, of norms accepted, etc. Now such a transmission is a living one only if tradition continues to form a partnership with innovation. Tradition represents the aspect of debt which concerns the past and reminds us that nothing comes from nothing. A tradition remains living, however, only if it continues to be held in an unbroken process of reinterpretation. (Ricoeur 1995, 8)

However, Ricoeur also agrees with Habermas that views of *tradition* must leave room for ideological critique. He tries to find a middle ground by distinguishing between *traditionality* (form), *traditions* (content) and *tradition* (normative authority). *Traditionality* is about *how* we understand the past: it refers to the 'primordial signification of transmitted tradition', and to the way it mediates present and past, through 'the chain of interpretations and reinterpretations': 'Traditionality designates a formal style of interconnectedness that assures the continuity of the reception of the past' (1988, 219–221, 227). *Traditions* refers to the 'transmitted contents' that we receive from the past, in the form of many distinct traditions (1988, 223). *Tradition* marks the shift from descriptive to normative views, from the multiplicity of traditions to the acceptance that one particular tradition is authentic and authoritative: 'passing from 'traditions' to 'tradition' is ... to introduce a question of legitimacy' (1988, 224). For Ricoeur, Gadamer is right about traditionality, and Habermas is right to point to the tension between the descriptive plurality of *traditions* and the normative exclusivity of (any single) *tradition*. He suggests that, hermeneutics can appropriate 'the weapons of a critique of ideologies ... by setting language ... into a much broader constellation, which also includes labor and domination', and that, to do this, it must 'renounce its universalist claim' (1988, 225).

Ricoeur's distinction between the form (traditionality) and content (traditions) of tradition is more than just a useful conceptual tool (as it is in this book). He describes it in far more general and ambitious terms as 'a material dialectic of the contents' versus 'the formal dialectic of temporal distance' (1988, 223). This raises a problem:

> Ricoeur insists that traditionality is something *universal*—that there is a single form of human understanding to be found at all times and all places. ... *What* we receive from the past varies according to our historical and cultural context; *that* we receive things from the past, and *how* we receive them, do not vary. ... [However,] there is good reason to think that traditionality *cannot* be defined without making reference to particular traditions, and that the form of human understanding is intelligible only if reference is made to its contents. (Piercey 2004, 273-274, original emphasis)

Robert Piercey concludes that 'the concept of tradition is much more complicated than even Ricoeur recognizes' (2004, 278).

This critique recognizes that Ricoeur and Gadamer also constrain their definitions of *tradition* in ways that reflect their theoretical agendas. Both develop far more dynamic views of tradition than Halbwachs. However, Gadamer rules out ideological dimensions of the concept, with his universalization of the hermeneutic (interpretive) circle. Ricoeur, trying to avoid the same conceptual limitation, ends up making a similar move, by universalizing the form vs. content distinction. This also constrains *tradition*. The lesson is that tradition's flexibility undermines the idea that there is anything universal about its forms, processes, contents or the relation between these.

6.3 Jan and Aleida Assmann: communicative memory

Jan and Aleida Assmann place tradition and religion within a broader context, by developing Halbwachs's views of cultural, collective or social memory. Aleida Assmann distinguishes three levels of memory: individual, social (intergenerational) and cultural/political (transgenerational) (2006). The first two are embodied and grounded in lived experience; the third is mediated by texts, artefacts, symbols etc. Individual memory—the unreliable, fallible, fragmented memory of individual human beings—has three types: procedural (habitual body skills and movements), semantic (what we learn consciously) and episodic (personal experiences). Social memory is the memory shared with one's group. A prominent type is generational memory, which shifts after about thirty years (as a new generation becomes senior) and last about 80 years (three generations).[4] Collective national memory is a core example of political memory, diverging from individual and social memory: a more unified collective account emerges through such devices as narratives, monuments, symbols and commemorations. (See Chapter 3.3 on folklore as an example of the invention of tradition.) Cultural memory, more generally, has two dimensions, canon (active remembering) and archive (passive remembering):

> Cultural memory … is based on two separate functions: the presentation of a narrow selection of sacred texts, artistic masterpieces, or historic key events in a timeless framework; and the storing of documents and artifacts of the past that do not at all meet these standards but are nevertheless deemed interesting or important enough to not let them vanish on the highway to total oblivion. (A. Assmann 2008, 101)

Jan Assmann frames the distinction as one between communicative (social) and cultural memory: 'Cultural memory is a kind of institution. It is exteriorized, objectified, and stored away in symbolic forms that … may be transferred from one situation to another and transmitted from one generation to another' (J. Assmann 2008, 110–111).

The Assmanns see religion, especially the canonization of sacred texts, as central to the historical evolution of cultural memory. (Canon is 'a text or a body of texts that is decreed to be sacred and must not be changed nor exchanged for any other text'; A. Assmann 2008, 100.) The study of oral traditions shows that, in the absence of

---

4. Studies of oral tradition show the time frame for generational memory varies by culture, from one to five generations (Vansina 1985). On generations as concrete social groups, see Mannheim (1959).

cultural memory, the limit of generational memory is quite constant across cultures, and it is separated by a temporal break from earlier traditions:

> For recent times there is plenty of information which tapers off as one moves back through time. For earlier periods one finds either a hiatus or just one or a few names, given with some hesitation. There is a gap in the accounts, which I will call the floating gap [because it is always relative to the current generation]. For still earlier periods one finds again a wealth of information and one deals here with traditions of origin. (Vansina 1985, 23)

This underlines the distinction between intergenerational oral tradition and transgenerational tradition, which is based on the textual and artefactual supports of cultural memory.

What does *tradition* mean in relation to these types of memory? There are conflicting accounts in the Assmanns's work. On the one hand, tradition is cultural memory:

> the passing of the generation of contemporary witnesses ... [requires] the transition from the lived, embodied memory to a tradition that is to be handed down from generation to generation. ... To make sure that this memory does not die with them, it has to be transmuted into tradition, into the symbolic forms of cultural memory. (J. Assmann 2006, 17)

On the other hand, tradition is not quite cultural memory:

> some of those elements described by the terms 'memory culture' or 'cultural memory' may also be called tradition, but this leaves out the aspect of reception, the bridging of the gap, and also the negative factors of oblivion and suppression. This is why we need a concept that embraces both aspects. Dead people and memories of dead people cannot be handed down. ... These are the elements that characterize cultural memory and take it far beyond the reaches of tradition. (J. Assmann 2011, 20)

Tradition is also not canon: 'The decisive criterion for the distinction between tradition and canon is the [latter's] exclusion of alternatives and the "fencing-in" of what has been selected' (J. Assmann 2011, 102). Yet, at other places, Jan Assmann seems to treat *tradition* and *canon* as synonymous: 'instead of constantly having to reconstruct events anew, there are fixed traditions. These become separated from communicative, everyday references and take on a canonical, commemorative substance' (2011, 48).

Jan Assmann reads tradition in static terms, saving more dynamic issues—like invented traditions and forgetting—for work under the heading of *cultural memory*. Tradition is framed as raw material for the dynamic work of cultural memory: 'What communication is for communicative memory, tradition is for cultural memory' (2011, 8).

The academic literature on *tradition* does not limit the concept in these ways. *Tradition* can and does encompass religious canons and the memories of the dead. It can bridge the floating gap. Analyses of *tradition* take on the topics of reception, canonization, forgetting and suppression. Assman writes that cultural memory is the 'externalization of social tradition and communication' and 'a cultural sphere that combines tradition, awareness of history, myth in action, and self-definition' (J. Assmann 2011, 9–10). In other words, he *defines* the concept of *tradition* as not exteriorized in his sense and as not encompassing historical awareness, the pragmatics of myth, and issues of identity and self-definition. But published work on *tradition* includes all these things.

As noted in Chapter 1.4, we can distinguish between three levels of *tradition* (similar to Ricoeur's distinction, discussed in the previous section, but here just a contingent heuristic tool): zero-order (examples of traditions); first-order (talk about traditions: i.e., *tradition* as the characteristics that traditions have in common, whatever it is that makes them *traditional*); and second-order (talk about talk about traditions: e.g., critical academic discussions of the nature, scope, functions and ideological effects of uses of *tradition*). The Assmanns limit *tradition* to the first two and reserve the third for their preferred concepts of *communicative* and *cultural memory*, *canon*, *archive* etc. They define *tradition* in an idiosyncratic way that fits their agenda.

We can see the effects of this strategy in the Assmann's most pointed argument for their choice to work with *cultural memory* and not *tradition*:

> 'Tradition' refers to the business of handing down and receiving, as well as the continued existence of what has been received. The only dynamics conceivable in terms of this concept are those which are released in cultural work in a controlled and conscious fashion; every interaction with the dynamics of identity and memory is cut off. The concept of tradition leaves no space for the unconscious. (J. Assmann 2011, 25)

This illustrates their static view of *tradition* and its impact on their other conceptual work. The argument is a vicious circle: it defines *tradition* as a static concept in order to conclude that it cannot serve as a dynamic concept. As previous chapters of this book have shown, there is no justification for defining *tradition* so narrowly: second-order discussions of *tradition* explore the dynamics of the concept in many insightful ways, grounding various lines of ideological critique. The Assmanns *stipulate* the value of *cultural memory* over *tradition* by *defining* critical discussions of the latter as out-of-bounds. However, critical work with *tradition* leaves plenty of space for the unconscious. The best example is Richard J. Bernstein's book-length analysis of 'Freud's rethinking of what a religious tradition involves, and of the unconscious dynamics of the transmission of a religious tradition' (1998, xi).

What we see here is not a fatal flaw in conceptual work but a choice to go a different direction. It is unfortunate, but understandable, that comparable critical work on *tradition* was ignored in order to make a case for the value of *cultural memory*. In the end, both concepts, *tradition* and *cultural memory*, can guide scholarship. The key question is not the choice of term but how each is used.

6.4 Pascal Boyer: truth and cognition

Pascal Boyer was the first scholar to develop an extended cognitive analysis of tradition (1986a; 1986b; 1987; 1990; 1992). He returned to the theme in passing more recently, as part of a broader cognitive analysis of selected social issues (2018). Both books are oriented by cognitive theory: the earlier view was narrow, where the later treats *tradition* as a broad umbrella category. In each case, Boyer defines *tradition* in a way that reflects and supports his basic assumptions and his theoretical agenda. The result is not contradiction or incoherence but a pragmatic use of second-order discourse (talk about talk about tradition aimed at a specific goal). If we drop the idea that there is one *right* definition because there is just one *thing* that *tradition* truly signifies, then Boyer's divergent definitions are a strength, not a weakness. We can assess the role that they play in their separate argumentative contexts, as opposed to asking which captures the single truth of tradition itself. We can also consider the possibility that an alternative account might be more useful.

In his more recent book, *Minds Make Societies*, Boyer defines *tradition* as 'sets of mental representations and associated behaviours that have some stability in a particular social group'; and he underlines his pragmatic focus: 'this is a very broad and extensive understanding of traditions, but it should be sufficient to point to many problems with our common assumptions about information and transmission' (2018, 248–249). His definition is presented not as true but as useful for a specific analytic purpose.

Boyer's earlier book—*Tradition as Truth and Communication: A Cognitive Description of Traditional Discourse* (*TTC*: 1990)—is more ambitious. *TTC*'s goal is to offer a 'more empirically plausible account of the acquisition of cultural ideas', and not 'a comprehensive alternative to the inadequate "explanations"' that he critiques (1990, 117). (I refer to *TTC* rather than *Boyer*, because this work is a bit of an outlier relative to Boyer's other work.) Most of the book elaborates a complex alternative account. The cognitive approach sets out a starting point: ('there is no theory of what happens in cultural interaction without some strong hypotheses about what is happening in actors' minds') and a focus of research (cognitive processes involved in traditional interaction and discourse). Tradition is defined as 'a specific type of *communication*, not in the restricted sense of a transmission of information but rather as a type of interaction which modifies people's representations in a relatively organised way' (1990, 109, original emphasis; see 1990, 23).

At the most general level of analysis, *TTC* does two separate things: it critiques common views of tradition; and it develops an alternative view. The critiques are powerful: they make a strong case that most published views of *tradition* are on the wrong track. The book is must-read for that reason alone.

In terms of its focus, *TTC* looks at oral communication, not written traditions, because the former are unexceptional examples of traditions. Though *TTC* uses only examples from pre-literate societies (e.g., divination rituals in sub-Saharan Africa), it claims that its view of tradition is also found in literate societies, on the basis of the twentieth-century example of English practitioners of witchcraft (1990, viii, 111–112, drawing on Luhrmann 1986). This modern group is an example of tradition because 'the guarantee that these persons make true statements is ... to be found in the fact that their utterances are caused by the forces they are talking about' (Boyer 1990, 112).

This is a narrow and odd view of *tradition*. Like the other works discussed in this chapter, *TTC* limits *tradition* in light of certain assumptions and a particular theoretical agenda. The scaffolding of the argument, like the ground it stands on, reflects one set of possible views. The result is a claim that *traditional* discourse is *a specific manner of organizing claims to truth*. This is so contextualized and limited that its links to most things called *traditional* are cut.

Here is a brief sketch of *TTC*'s conceptual trajectory. With a series of persuasive arguments, it rejects

> the 'common assumptions' about tradition, namely (i) that traditions are conserved because people want to transmit them unchanged, and (ii) that they are held together by some underlying ideas which constitute a general description of the world ... [e.g.,] 'world-views', 'cultural models', 'local theories', 'collective representations' etc. (Boyer 1990, 3–4)

Drawing on ethnographic cases and cognitive psychology's distinction between episodic and semantic memory (roughly: experiential memories tied to specific events, times or locations vs. learned knowledge not linked to particular contexts),[5] *TTC* argues that, where

---

5. Noting resonances between rituals forms and types of memory, cognitive anthropologist Harvey Whitehouse proposes two contrasting 'modes of religiosity', imagistic and doctrinal (1995; 2000; 2004; 2021). The resulting theory has direct implications for tradition. It implies two modes of passing on beliefs and practices: rituals in the imagistic mode 'tend to produce intense cohesion within

normal categories use semantic memory, most representations of traditions are episodic.

As a result, the idea that tradition works through *intentional* processes of communication is rejected: people focus on, conserve and transmit superficial aspects of interactions, not deeper underlying aspects. *TTC* also rejects the idea that 'the cause of traditional repetition is people's conservatism about the surface properties of interaction' (1990, 14). The idea of conscious conservatism grants us too much control over memories: psychology has shown the lack of a direct relationship between wanting to remember and remembering. It follows that tradition is automatic, not intentional: people are not conservative in the sense that they *want* to repeat relevant surface features; they conserve certain things because we think in certain ways (1990, 15-18).

Local cultural categories are analysed as a key type of mental *representation*; these tend to be thought of in terms of shared definitions, but traditional categories are undefinable (vague, ambiguous, vacuous) (1990, 24-25, 27-30). The proposed alternative is to distinguish *registers of discourse*: gossip and common discourse that offer standard evidence that people speak the truth; and expert discourse which does not. Where most anthropologists look at these issues in terms of *conceptions* of truth, *TTC*'s proposed alternative to focus on 'specific criteria of truth ... [i.e.,] common properties, specific to traditional interaction, in the reasoning whereby statements produced in various cultures and contexts are judged true' (1990, 56, 60).

Turning to the example of divination rituals, *TTC* argues that 'traditional truths are created by 'customising speech', and by initiation rituals that produce 'customised persons': ritual 'utterances are supposed to convey truth not in spite of but *because of* their formalization'; and initiation becomes 'a condition of truth', because 'truth seems a privilege of certain social positions' (1990, 91, 94, 81, 99, 105).[6]

---

small communities of participants, but are difficult to spread to wider populations'; whereas rituals in the doctrinal mode facilitate 'the rapid spread of standardized versions of both orthopraxy and orthodoxy, and thus the homogenization of a regional tradition' (Whitehouse 2006, 665).

6. Anne Brydon asks an insightful question in a review of Boyer's book: 'Is he speaking of truth or the authority to speak?' (1994, 209). Is it possible that Boyer

This distinguishes normal and traditional discourse in terms of two views of the truth of representations. In normal discourse, all people are held to speak the truth when what they say is believed to match up with reality. In traditional discourse, *certain experts* are held to speak the truth because formal, ritual frames point beyond them to a deeper warrant of truth, i.e., to the realities that *cause their utterances*. In normal discourse, language is believed to *represent* reality; in traditional discourse language is believed to be *caused* by that reality: 'An utterance is judged true, not because the speaker has the appropriate picture of the world in his or her mind, but because a causal link is assumed to exist between the state of affairs described and the event of the person making the utterance' (1990, 100, see 111–112). And that is how we get to the idea that the English witchcraft practitioners studied by Tanya Luhrmann are *traditional*, because 'their utterances are caused by the forces they are talking about' (Boyer 1990, 112).

To get my head around *TTC*'s labyrinthine argument, I made a schematic overview. It included over 40 distinct steps. The argument is convoluted, but it often has a distinctive shape. At many points, it makes a three-step conceptual move: (i) critiquing a particular view of tradition; (ii) presenting only one viable alternative; and (ii) moving forward with the latter on the assumption that no other option exists. This logic guides us step-by-step to Boyer's insightful but narrow definition of *tradition*. This would work with a chain of valid deductive arguments, but that is not what we have here. *TTC*'s path is paved with ideas like tradition, truth, representation, communication, intentionality, concepts, categories, discourse, definitions, social positions, institutions, formalization, ritual etc. A theoretical

---

may have started out with the idea of truth that he ends up with, and that the vagaries of his argument could be read as rationalizing this desired endpoint? In a 1986 article (prefiguring much of *TTC*'s argument but not cited in the book), he writes 'We might be tempted to see ... [M. Detienne's] work on archaic (pre-"philosophical") Greek conceptions of truth ... as an intermediary figure between our "philosophical" conception of truth and a traditional usage in which truth is implicitly understood as deriving from a causal relationship between the real world and certain people' (Boyer 1986a, 326; see Stewart 2002, 116; Detienne 1999 [1967]).

stance in this thicket of multivalent ideas requires robust multi-sided discussion, not a single progression of mutually exclusive conceptual dichotomies.

The result of *TTC*'s conceptual strategy is the legitimation or reification of a whole series of distinctions, some built into assumptions and others emerging as tactical responses to contingencies of the argument: e.g., normal vs. religious language, normal vs. ritualized actions, natural vs. traditional categories, representational and causal accounts, literal vs. metaphorical language, conceptions vs. criteria of truth, surface vs. deep features, common vs. expert registers of discourse, explicit vs. implicit causal notions, normal vs. artificial mechanisms of producing discourses, etc. Some are more defensible than others. Some would make better sense if discussed in more nuanced ways. Overall, this expanding, cumulative series of dichotomies raises many difficult questions regarding how they would play out in other contexts. This argumentative strategy threatens to create more problems than it is worth: is all this conceptual fragmentation a price worth paying for such a limited view of *tradition*?

This expanding series of conceptual rifts splits traditional from normal discourses. This results in an inability to explain important aspects of tradition: for example, *TTC* is able to address the issue of transmission, but not the ways that traditional discourse comes to form part of normal discourse, infiltrating and shaping it, eventually becoming normalized (Parmentier 1993). At points, Boyer seems to recognize the value of tempering his dichotomizing approach, holding that traditional categories are part of a spectrum, with key examples serving as 'a limiting-case, in which these features of the traditional process are especially visible' (1990, 42).

We can only trust *TTC*'s intricate trail of conceptual moves if the conceptual divisions that it relies upon to develop its view of tradition are solid. At several points, this is not the case. Boyer's choice to add philosophical argumentation to his cognitive anthropology is valuable, and it requires a response in a philosophical register. I will make two critical comments from this perspective.

First, as noted above, *TTC* affirms that the nature of tradition 'cannot be a question of conceptions of truth and *therefore* has to be explained by specific criteria of truth' (1990, 56, emphasis added). The word 'therefore' implies that we face a hard choice between mutually exclusive options: we must choose one, because there are no others. Conceptions of truth are defined as 'sets of general propositions about the relationships between sentences and states of affairs in general, or about the meaning of truth-terms' and criteria of truth as 'reasons for finding specific statements true or false' (1990, 56–57). This definition of *conceptions of truth* is inadequate because 'relationships between sentences and states of affairs' are an aspect of one specific conception of truth—the correspondence view—not a characteristic of the broader category. More generally, *conceptions of truth* is ambiguous here, applying both to general theories of truth and to accounts of more specific epistemological concepts (*truth-terms*). As a result, *conceptions of truth* encompasses *criteria of truth*, given that the latter unpacks into a subset of epistemological concepts, centring on ideas of justification and warrant. If *conception of truth* is an over-arching umbrella category, then *criteria of truth* flags just one set of issues falling under it. There is no mutually exclusive choice between the two: the argument here rests on a category mistake. Instead, we would need to spell out the relation between a particular conception of truth and particular accounts of epistemological concepts from a specific perspective in a specific context. *TTC* rejects the idea that 'different cultures have different "concepts" of truth' (1990, 48). But there *are* different concepts of truth: philosophers argue endlessly over them. Whether or not these vary by culture, they have profound implications for complex epistemological arguments, like *TTC*'s elaboration of *tradition*. Too much is taken for granted here.

Other forced conceptual moves in *TTC*'s argument rely on a second problematic assumption. The book assumes that there is just one way to think about definition: 'To have a definition, if this term has any meaning, is to have a set of necessary and sufficient conditions for an object to be a member of the class [in question]' (1990, 37–38). For example, *TTC* rejects the idea that cultural categories are represented by shared definitions because traditional categories cannot be defined *in this way*: they are, by contrast, empty notions; and this motivates the move to an alternative account in terms of registers of discourse (1990, 25–26, 32–39). Note the false dichotomy: either a concept can be defined in this narrow, rigid way; or it is empty.

For the same reason, *TTC* rejects the idea that social/ritual positions are thought of in terms of typical activities: 'the representation of activities cannot be the mental definition of the positions, since it provides neither necessary nor sufficient conditions for membership of the category' (1990, 103). This motivates the move to an account of *customized persons*, given that the usual account has been rejected.

This is not the only view of definition, and it is not the best option for analysing complex cultural concepts like *tradition* (Stausberg and Gardiner 2016; Engler and Gardiner 2024). The rigid idea of definition—providing a list of individually necessary and jointly sufficient conditions for inclusion in a category—reflects an essentialism that scholars in the human and social sciences have been trying to move past for decades. The medieval Aristotelian contrast between essentialist and nominalist positions focused on tensions between ontology and semantics. Many scholars still echo this with a false dichotomy: complex cultural concepts either refer to ontologically real things or they are relativist discursive constructs. The more general point is semantic: 'Disregarding all the talk about essences, what Aristotle was advocating in modern terms is definition by properties connected conjunctively which are severally necessary and jointly sufficient' (Hull cited in Winsor 2003, 390). (We end up with essentialist definitions of even discursive constructs if we insist on framing *definition* in terms of necessary and sufficient conditions.) *TTC*'s rigid, essentialist view of definition focuses on identity conditions, and it regards proposed definitions as being either true or false, as either correctly capturing what words refer to or not. There are other—pragmatic and lexical—approaches to definition that focus on defining words not things, and that are assessed in terms of usefulness not truth. The latter approach to definition would be more appropriate for an analysis of discourses of *tradition*. Once we drop a rigid, essentialist view of definition, then key aspects of *TTC*'s rejection of standard views of tradition fail, and its case for an alternative account is undermined.

In sum, *TTC*'s overall result is a strong critique of standard conceptions of *tradition*, along with one possible, if problematic, alternative account. This makes the book an excellent example of the main point of this chapter: academic views of *tradition* are limited by their particular meta-theoretical premises, theoretical agendas, disciplinary discourses/literatures, conceptual assumptions and analytical trajectories. This tells us more about how complex cultural concepts work than about actual traditions. Another way to assess *TTC*'s view of tradition is to note that—being the result of problematic and *ad hoc* conceptual work at many points—it fails as a rigid, essentialist definition that is meant to tell the truth of the thing called *tradition*. But it is useful, and so successful, as a pragmatic lexical definition of the concept of *tradition* in a specific context.

6.5 Olivier Morin: transmission as reconstruction

French cognitive scientist Olivier Morin argues that traditions are more than the trans-generational imitation of customs. They are complex adaptive systems characterized by repetition, redundancy and a balance between transmission and invention. As with the other authors discussed in this chapter, Morin's view of tradition reflects his theoretical commitments. As with those other views, this is not a problem in itself. The kaleidoscopic nature of *tradition* makes it necessary to focus on selected facets or cross-sections. This highlights the question of what is lost and what gained when adopting specific perspectives.

Like Boyer, Morin sets out his position as he criticizes standard views. He rejects the idea that cultural transmission is a form of teaching or imitation. Instead, he emphasizes ostensive (voluntary and overt) communication, which results in the reconstruction of what is transmitted by those who receive it.

His argument reflects some conceptual constraints. He defines *tradition* as

> anything that is widely distributed in a population. Distributed, or rather, diffused; when traditions are concerned the words 'diffusion' and 'distribution' will be used interchangeably. ... This way of seeing traditions accommodates many widely shared intuitions, but not all of our intuitions. Our traditions, for instance, will not have to be long-lived: their diffusion chains have to be extended, but not necessarily in time. ... Transmission inside a generation matters as much as transmission between generations. (Morin 2016, 37, 1)

Transmission is also central to his definition of *culture*. Not everything that is transmitted is culture: only cases in which a diffusion chain reaches well out in space or time.

His shift away from a focus on imitation and repetition underlines cognitive capacities for and constraints on action in tradition's diffusion. He notes the value of accounts that see tradition as reconstructions on the basis of incomplete cues (i.e., later generations receive just a sketch of tradition's content, filling in the details, guided in part by their cognitive capacities). Those who receive tradition reconstruct much of it from those clues. This relates to his view that the transmission of tradition is neither faithful nor compulsive: tradition involves selective choices: 'We lack both the desire and the capacity to imitate everything that circulates around us. Instead we transform, we customize, we reinvent, we forget, we select. ... Traditions ... are never completely copied without a share of reinvention' (2016, 6, 252, 4).

Morin's overall claim is that 'there is something extraordinary about information exchange in our species—what might be called the human public domain. ... Humans ... go beyond mere assisted development: they engage in cooperative learning on a massive scale' (2016, 228, 231).

The core claims set out an evolutionary view of tradition. Natural selection favoured cognitive traits that allow people to reconstruct traditions from the clues provided: 'ours is a doubly cultural species: because our social learning skills were originally fit for transmitting cultural traditions with fidelity and precision; and because natural selection has strengthened this gift, making human social learning better adapted to culture' (2016, 237).

As a result, the task of explaining tradition involves relating two things: cognitive and communicative capacities of humans; and the resulting tendency for *some* cases of cultural transmission ('extreme traditions'; Morin 2016, 233) to spread widely. This leads to

> a quantitative view of culture [which] demands that we study the traditions themselves, instead of their bearers. This means abstracting away a great many social ties, and retaining only the links that make up long transmission chains. Such chains may bring together people who are connected in no other way: generations or societies that

never come into contact but through cultural transmission. (Morin 2016, 21)

This approach emphasizes human action in one sense (the role of ostensive communication in the continual reinvention and diffusion of traditions) and de-emphasizes it in another (the place of social ties and roles). This is just what we would expect of a cognitive, as opposed to social, theory of tradition. But this frame brings its limitations, above all a blind spot regarding issues of power, including the many ideological, political and economic factors that shape the persistence and domination of certain traditions.[7]

Like Boyer, Morin uses philosophy to buttress his cognitive anthropology, which requires a response in the same register. He sees tradition in terms of the transmission of representations, a stance developed by Dan Sperber:[8]

> Widely distributed, long-lasting representations are what we are primarily referring to when we talk about culture. ... So, to explain culture is to answer the following question: why are some representations more successful in a human population, more 'catching' than others? In order to answer this question, the distribution of representations in general has to be considered. (Sperber 1996, 57–58)

Morin, like Boyer, rejects the idea that tradition itself is a sort of representational content that is passed on: 'the transmission of a tradition need not entail the reproduction of one enduring mental representation' (2016, 42). He goes beyond Boyer in rejecting the idea that tradition *consists of* transferred representations:

> Cultural transmission is an exchange of mental representations. This is indeed the standard definition of cultural transmission for the new approaches of culture ... [which] take it for granted that culture is a set of socially transmitted representations (or bits of information). Not all of them mean to say that cultural transmission can be reduced to an information transfer, but little effort is made to dispel that impression. (Morin 2016, 47)

---

7. See Carrette (2005), for a related ideological critique of cognitive approaches to the study of religion.

8. Morin's book is a revised version of his 2010 dissertation, supervised by Sperber.

This results in what seems a convoluted view of tradition: it is the transmission of representations; but it is not these representations; and it is also not the process of transmission, because it is a different sort of content, i.e. *anything widely distributed in a population*. Also like Boyer, Morin turns to a certain sort of social interaction to support this view:

> Does a tradition's transmission necessarily imply an exchange of representations? Yes; otherwise a virus hopping from a tree to another would count as a case of cultural transmission. Transmission as discussed here implies that at least one of the partners in the interaction acts upon the other's cognition, in a broad sense of that word (including emotions and motivations in addition to reasoning, perception, etc.). Can traditions be identified with the information that is passed on when they are transmitted? No, not always. Just because cultural transmission involves an exchange of ideas does not mean that traditions themselves are the ideas that their proliferation relies on. Complex cultural forms can subsist through rudimentary interactions. ... the means that permit a behavior to be reproduced in a transmission chain do not themselves need to be passed on along the chain. Culture often differs from the ideas whose exchange allows it to get diffused. (Morin 2016, 48–49)

A philosophical argument carries the weight here. Tradition does not consist of representations that are transferred, but of cognition that is influenced. Morin uses the idea of ostensive communication to justify this move. This idea's impact on cognitive views of communication is being worked out in parallel with Thom Scott-Phillips, a fellow member of Le Groupe NaSH [Naturalisme et Sciences Humaines] at the institution where Morin works (Morin 2016, xv; Scott-Phillips 2014).

Morin and Scott-Phillips appropriate this idea from the work of philosopher Paul Grice (1913–1988). Grice distinguished between (1) literal and (2) intended, implied or implicated meaning: 'intensionality is embedded in the very foundations of the theory of language' (Grice 1991, 133). Literal meaning is what can be read from vocabulary, grammar and syntax *independent of the contexts* of communication. Intended meaning adds something crucial to this: the contextualized intention that one's words will cause other people to do or believe certain things. For Grice, words in action go beyond words on a page, because they include the intended and potential effect of influencing how other people think and act. Morin and Scott-Phillips find just what they need here: a view of communication that centers not on transfer of literal information (the standard view of tradition) but on cognitive influence.

This emphasis on intentionality is a valuable approach to tradition. It moves beyond views that see tradition as an external force or structure that automatically shapes how people think and act: e.g., 'the transmission of things, practices and collective representations happens by itself' (Mauss 1931, 63). However, Grice's distinction between two types of meaning raises problems. Perhaps surprisingly, these stem not from the concept of intentionality but from that of literal meaning. Grice sees literal meaning as fixed by social convention, which establishes stable correlations between words and their meanings. On this view, our attempt to make sense of language always take place against this external structure, a set of normative standards: word meanings, grammatic rules and syntactical guidelines. (Halbwachs saw conventions as the basis of collective memory; see Chapter 6.1.)

Donald Davidson (1917–2003) makes an influential argument that conventional theories of meaning cannot account for the constant ability of speakers to interpret each other with success, given the instability and variability of language: we have an 'ability to interpret words we have never heard before, to correct slips of the tongue, or to cope with new idiolects [the distinct linguistic systems of individual speakers]. These phenomena threaten standard descriptions of linguistic competence' (Davidson 1986, 437). For example, we understand malapropisms (mistaken uses of an incorrect word in place of a word with a similar sound) even though they break conventions. A student of mine once wrote that 'we are all prawns in a game of chess'; I got the point with no problem. Davidson's own article tells us that 'most of *"The Jabberwock" is intelligble* [sic] on first hearing': we understand him despite the typographical error and the fact that Lewis Carroll's poem is called 'Jabberwocky' (1986, 434, emphasis added). The fact that we understand such things—even though they break linguistic conventions—tells us that there must be more to the idea of literal meaning than norms or conventions. If the idea of convention serves as the basis of a theory of meaning, then meaning must *always* be conventional: if we can make sense of meaning when the conventions are broken, then the theory fails: exceptions could only be explained by a more basic theory of meaning. Grice's—and so Morin's and Scott-Phillips'—account of meaning seems inadequate: social agreement cannot be the means or precondition of literal interpretation (though it may be the result of it).

If we accept this critique, then ostensive communication loses the comparative framework that allows us to make sense of the idea that tradition involves the 'reconstruction of what is transmitted' (Morin 2016, 6).

Ironically, Morin's emphasis on representations runs counter to his own theoretical agenda (as is the case with Boyer). An interpretational (not necessarily Davidsonian) view of meaning would suit his purposes better than a Gricean conventional account. An interpretational view acknowledges that 'Grice has ... shown why it is essential to distinguish between the literal meaning ... of words and what is often implied (or implicated) by someone who uses those words' (Davidson 1986, 437). It emphasizes, 'following Grice, the central importance of intention in communication' (Davidson 2001, 112). But it rejects the idea that we arrive at meanings by working on the basis of conventions. It re-thinks literal meaning not as the measure of *how-words-should-be-used*, but as a context-dependent opening gambit that sparks a particular game of mutual interpretation.

On an interpretational view, successful interpretation does not require conventions or standards shared by speakers: it relies on a series of best-guess hypotheses (what Davidson calls *passing theories*) that allow speakers to converge on mutual understanding, despite inevitable variability in meaning. Far from being a barrier to communication, this variability makes interpretation possible by spurring dynamic imaginative theorizing about *the-state-of-communication-in-play* at each given moment. Success depends on innovative, improvisational interpretation, not fixed conventions. We do not follow rules; we muddle through, with the crucial proviso that we are looking for best-possible pragmatic interpretive results. Success is not speaking-by-the-book. *Success* is a retrospective label for getting somewhere useful, for making sense, for attaining meaning.

This would work to ground Morin's view of tradition, and it would make better sense of the status of reinvention as part of cultural transmission. Where a conventional view of meaning insists that 'you cannot change what words mean ... merely by intending to', an interpretational view holds that 'you can change the meaning provided you believe ... that the interpreter has adequate clues for the new interpretation. You may deliberately provide those clues' (Davidson 1986, 439). Doesn't this offer a better basis for Morin's view that, in tradition, 'a small set of cues can trigger the formation of a much more elaborate representation' (2016, 27)? Morin uses Grice to support his view that 'to communicate with someone in an overt way is to try to change their mental life (instruct them, arouse feelings, orient attention, etc.) by making a communicative intention manifest' (2016, 60). Interpretationism gets us to the same place, with a greater symmetry between speakers and interpreters.

6.6 Chapter summary

This chapter looks at some important views of tradition, noting that each is limited, because it reflects its conceptual work and theoretical agenda. That is less a problem than a fact about complex conceptual work: the lesson is the value of reading in context.

Maurice Halbwachs's work marked a crucial shift toward seeing memory, and so tradition, as inherently social. The past is always a group reconstruction. He over-emphasized the group over the individual and the influence of present interests on views of the past. He also reduced tradition too much to pure tradition and religion too much to Christianity.

Hans-Georg Gadamer sees tradition in terms of a hermeneutic circle: we make sense of past and present as part of a dynamic, open-ended mutual interpretational relation. His view leaves no place to stand, outside the circle, for finding problems with tradition. Paul Ricoeur tries to develop Gadamer's view by building in a viewpoint for ideological critique: a universal idea of traditionality (the form of tradition, as opposed to its content). Where Gadamer universalizes one thing (the hermeneutic circle), Ricoeur universalizes another (the form vs. content distinction). Both give us limited views of *tradition*.

Jan and Aleida Assmann develop Halbwachs's emphasis on cultural memory. They distinguish between the living dynamics of communicative memory and the institutional memory of on-line canon (key texts, artefacts etc. that many people are aware of) and off-line archives (accessible with some effort). They define *tradition* in limited ways, leaving space for their preferred concepts to do the critical work. But *tradition* does comparable critical work in the hands of other authors. Their delimited view of *tradition* serves and reflects their theoretical agenda. This reminds us that *tradition* is just one concept among many: the important thing is the level of critical analysis, not the particular concepts used to frame it. After all, related concepts are all networked together, no matter where we start.

Pascal Boyer's cognitive analysis sees tradition as a type of social interaction that structures people's representations. His conceptual work makes some unjustified assumptions, and the result is a radical split between traditional and normal discourse. This seems a high price to pay for the resulting narrow view of tradition: a social situation where experts' utterances are seen as true because the things they talk about are seen as causing the talk about them.

Olivier Morin offers a different but related cognitive view. He sees tradition not as the transmission of content but of cues that allow people to reconstruct something very like that content, using their evolved cognitive abilities. He draws on philosophy to support this view, and this defines meaning as a matter of following linguistic conventions. Philosophical critiques of this assumption, along with the centrality of representations (the latter also a problematic aspect of Halbwachs's and Boyer's views) suggest that a move to emphasizing an interpretational view of meaning might better suit Morin's agenda.

Key take-home points—*Academic views of tradition are bound to vary because making sense of such a complex concept requires taking a certain perspective. This forces us to ask not which view is true (which captures the reality of tradition) but which is more useful for a particular purpose.*

Conclusion

Tradition is often assumed to be pre-modern or even the opposite of modernity, but it is also a synonym for *religion*. This implies that religion, like tradition, is an out-of-date holdover, irrelevant for the modern world. But most scholars of religion/s reject this view, for various reasons. The result is a messy tangle of views of *tradition*.

This book suggests that the best way to make sense of this is to think of the word *tradition* not as referring to some singular thing (tradition itself) but as meaning different things in different contexts, depending on how that concept is connected to others: e.g., agency, authority, collective memory, communication, habit, identity, ideology, innovation, legitimization, (post)modernity, origins, ritual, transmission etc. These semantic (meaning-related) links shape what *tradition* means.

Here are some of the connections that we looked at:

- Tradition informs *identity*. People that follow a traditional path together distinguish themselves from other groups because of the pragmatic pay-offs.

- Tradition is seen as having normative *authority* (it *should* be followed), but only selected things are taken as worthy of respect and duty.

- Traditions remain faithful to their *origins*. But they often have weight in part because we are unclear about just when they started.

- Tradition is like and unlike other types of cultural *transmission*. It changes even when (or perhaps because) it is seen as unchanging.

Throughout the book, we looked at tensions between the (alleged) reality of traditions and (different groups') perceptions of them. This contrast means that *tradition* is ideological: we must look beyond *facts* about tradition to ask how *beliefs* about tradition can be used in struggles for authority, legitimacy and power.

Jacques Derrida sees tradition as a process of iterative citation, of repeating and alternating original sources, of inserting difference and deferring fixed meaning. This leaves alleged origins and their legacies always unstable. As Michael Naas puts it, Derrida situates us within 'a particular tradition of thinking tradition':

> We are signed into a tradition and a history not only by agreeing with those who have come before us, that is, by explicitly taking on their tradition or their history, but simply by recognizing or receiving … a certain way of either accepting or rejecting it and its authority. … Each time we receive the tradition, each time we take it on, we are offered a chance to receive something unforeseeable and unprecedented within it. Although all our thinking, all our receptions, are illuminated in advance by the horizon of our tradition, our turning toward that horizon is not. … For although there may indeed be nothing new under the sun, there is no tradition, no sun even, before we have received it. (Naas 2003, xvii–xviii)

This is an insightful view of the way that the past conditions the present and the present conditions the past. But it seems to apply to *all* aspects of culture; so, perhaps it includes too much. On the other hand, it also seems to exclude the continuity and stability that characterize *tradition*; so, perhaps it includes too little. This paradoxical symmetry suggests that Derrida has put his finger on a key point.

Traditions, tradition and *tradition* are always unstable. If this book's goal had been to answer the question of tradition's identity, it was doomed to fail: 'simple definitions dismiss tradition from serious consideration' (Glassie 1995, 405). My goal was different. I tried to sketch some of the concepts, distinctions and issues that cross, mesh, clash and knot with each other in the space of meanings called *tradition*: article of faith; foundation of identity; repository of shared values; link to the past; guide for the present; rallying cry for conservatives; target of reformers; and, for all sides, a source and tool of ideological distortion. To make some sense of this jumble of ideas, it helps to take a relational view of tradition: seeing what sorts of conceptual binaries and normative frames shape its roles in specific contexts.

Because this book is more interested in echoing *tradition*'s tangle than in telling a nice, neat story, there is no easy way to sum it up. I end by making some points that address the question that first motivated my thinking about *tradition*: 'What use is all this for the study of religion/s (SoR)?' I offer one line on this by looking at the intersection of three themes: (i) *tradition* and *religion* are often used as synonyms; (ii) pure tradition is an impossible ideal and an effective source of authority *because* of that; and (iii) the distinction between authentic and invented traditions applies just as much to what scholars say as it does to what they study. I will throw in a series of open-ended questions along the way, suggesting other implications.

We started with English-language meanings (recognizing that not all languages have an equivalent word) and a disciplinary location, SoR. As soon as we note that *tradition* and *religion* are used as synonyms, tough questions arise. Do we really want to define religion as something ancient, pre-modern, backward-looking, always scripted, blindly repetitive, conservative etc.? What are we saying if we distance religions from cultural innovation and novelty, from ritual improvisation and creative spontaneity, from progressive activism and liberation from oppressive structures?

These questions arise above all when we see religions in terms of *pure* tradition, the normative ideal that perfect repetition of the past is valuable or essential. If we take a more dynamic view, then *tradition* and *religion* include all these extremes and everything in between.

In Chapter 2.1, we saw that the idea of *pure tradition* is ideologically powerful and patently false. The meanings of ideas and practices always reflect their contexts, and contexts always change. However, denying tradition's dynamism is a powerful tactic for claiming authority. When a group insists that its (and only its) beliefs and practices are a pure tradition, they have a means of claiming absolute epistemic, moral and soteriological (salvational) authority. Pure tradition affirms positive vertical identity through continuity with the past (and often the supernatural), and negative horizontal identity by defining as false all competing traditions in the present. For SoR, pure tradition is best read, at least in part, as an ideological construct.

The *pure* vs. *historical tradition* distinction is relative. These are not opposed cultural options but endpoints on a spectrum that can play different roles, depending on how they overlap with other distinctions. For example, this spectrum does not line up with that between religious and secular traditions. Pure tradition—escaping from the entropic forces of time, change and history—is *more* religion-like than secular. But both views of tradition are often found in the same religion, and there are affinities between pure tradition and non-religious spheres like politics. For example, some conservatives in the USA see 'American constitutionalism as a tradition in the Burkean sense, in which meanings are passed down unchanged from one generation to the next' (Machacek and Fulco 2005, 338).

The lesson here is to pay attention to our own assumptions: not to accept pure tradition as a *fact* in one or more religions; but to pay attention to how *discourses* of tradition are used. SoR often goes too far in the direction of accepting pure tradition as the one right view of tradition, along with sharp versions of the related *tradition vs. modernity* binary, as discussed in Chapter 4.2. Where these ideas shape descriptions of religions and definitions of *religion*, scholars of religion/s echo and reinforce ideological views, instead of being critically aware of them.

A problematic aspect of many studies of *tradition* is their tendency to presume a sharp contrast between (i) natural or real pre-modern memory and (ii) invented traditions that forget the past and help fuel the modern motor of progress. For example, a key figure in cultural memory studies, Pierre Nora, leverages this contrast. His important and innovative work with *lieux de mémoire* (sites of memory) underlines the role of monuments and other artefacts/spaces in national memory. However, his emphasis on modern *memory without a past* presumes that a fundamentally different sort of relation to the past once existed:

> there is no [longer] spontaneous memory, ... we must deliberately create archives, maintain anniversaries, organize celebrations, pronounce eulogies, and notarize bills because such activities no longer occur naturally. ... The 'acceleration of history' ... confronts us with the brutal realization of the difference between real memory—social and unviolated, exemplified in but also retained as the secret of

so-called primitive or archaic societies—and history, which is how our hopelessly forgetful modern societies, propelled by change, organize the past. (Nora 1989, 12, 8)

This points to an important difference, but the overly stark contrast gets in the way of looking for processes of transition that lead from there, to here and on into the future. Recall how the first Roman Emperor Augustus propped up his authority through the self-conscious reinvention of tradition (see Chapter 4.1). We should be wary of sharp contrasts between *natural* and *artificial* memory and tradition. We should always focus, at least in part, on the work done by these and related ideas when scholars put them on the table.

Chapter 3 looked at the claim that some or all traditions are invented. If only some are invented, then others are authentic. This commits scholars to serving as judges of historical authenticity. And this risks complicity in colonial binaries: *authentic* vs. *invented*, *traditional* vs. *modern* etc. On the other hand, if all tradition is invented, this is because the past is always constructed in the light of present interests. This tells us something important about ideological uses of *tradition*. Halbwachs's exaggerated insistence that visions of the past are tools of present interests set an important agenda for later work. But this universalization of *invented tradition* goes too far: it denies ways in which the past does impose itself.

The case of invented traditions breaks apart the relation between *historical facts* about the origin and transmission of a tradition and what people *believe* about it. The work of *tradition* depends on the latter. If we want to head in the direction of scientific explanations, we could analyse religion and tradition in terms of empirical factors like evolved cognitive traits (see Chapters 6.4 and 6.5). But this can never be more than part of the story (Gardiner and Engler 2015; 2018). Where people *believe*, the issues of empirically and academically supported truth claims (not the same things) are often irrelevant. Even if scholars could all agree on a single account of what religion and tradition *really are*, that will always be a separate issue from what people and groups *make of* them. (And if we were to just *define* a tradition's reality and beliefs about it as the same, the resulting radical privileging of insider views would undermine SoR.) Traditions and religions are shaped by both historical and ideological processes, which blend together and pull in different directions.

Tradition has authority because people grant it authority. This lies behind Derrida's paradox: we change tradition as we receive it; and in doing so, we dissolve any possible original. Chapter 5 explored how denying the active participation of tradition's receivers is key to the *purification of tradition*. People and groups give agency and authority to tradition by the very act of denying their own agency, by seeing themselves as passive receivers. Tradition, like ritual, is a powerful agent of social cohesion and source of authority because it allegedly does not result from the intentional actions of those who receive it. Once we recognize tradition's and ritual's displacement of agency, we can ask where agency gets displaced to. The erasure of agency *here* (in the denial that tradition is invented as it is received) allows agency to be projected *there*. In many religious contexts, agency and authority are tied to the alleged sources of tradition and its continuity: e.g., mythological figures, supernatural beings and transcendent levels of reality.

In the end, as in the beginning, the implications of all this for SoR are questions more than answers. A useful first step back is to consider this possibility: 'the notion of "tradition" should not be taken as an analytic category of historiography. By contrast, scholars should apply it only with reference to its emic meaning and function' (von Stuckrad 2005, 211). The complication here is that academic uses of *tradition* are also an emic discourse. The idea of *tradition* seems most useful when we remain aware of the dangers of letting insider discourses define our categories (as discussed in Case Study 2), and if we remain open to dynamic uses and ideological effects of *tradition*, which means rejecting insider and academic emphasis on pure tradition as the one correct view.

What do we learn by reflecting on the overlap between *religion* and *tradition* in SoR? Here are a few among many questions we could ask, to assess whether that overlap presupposes a pure or a dynamic view of *tradition* in our disciplinary discourses. Does the use of *traditions* and *religions* as synonyms emphasize the past, or does it highlight current strategic uses and ideological effects? Religion is worth studying because it still influences the world today, but is this the focus of most graduate programs in SoR? Are there more job postings for new religious movements or for historical and *traditional* aspects of religions, especially those with ancient roots? Do textbooks and curricula emphasize recent developments, impacts and trends, or origins, pure tradition and history? Do scholars of religion/s see *tradition* as a sort of shorthand for core beliefs and practices of religious groups (which risks essentialism)? Or do we ask an open question: how does each group define, frame, use, encode, delimit, leverage or reject the concept of *tradition* for its own purposes (which calls for empirical research)?

Further reading

Chapter 1: Talking tradition

Stråth, B. (2013). 'Ideology and Conceptual History.' In *The Oxford Handbook of Political Ideologies*, edited by M. Freeden, L. T. Sargent and M. Stears, 3–19. Oxford: Oxford University Press. *(Valuable introduction to the concept of ideology.)*

The following offer useful entry points to the complexities of tradition.

Glassie, H. (1995). 'Tradition.' *Journal of American Folklore* 108(430): 395–412.
Hammer, O. (2016). 'Tradition and Innovation.' In *The Oxford Handbook of the Study of Religion*, edited by M. Stausberg and S. Engler, 718–738. Oxford: Oxford University Press.
Noyes, D. (2009). 'Tradition: Three Traditions.' *Journal of Folklore Research* 46(3): 233–268.
Shils, E. (1981). *Tradition*. Chicago: University of Chicago Press.

Chapter 2: Pure tradition vs. history

Hanegraaff, W. J. (2005). 'Tradition.' In *Dictionary of Gnosis and Western Esotericism*, edited by W. J. Hanegraaff, A. Faivre, R. van den Broek and J.-P. Brach, 1125–1135. Leiden: Brill. *(Essential historical context for tradition's European trajectory.)*
Krygier, M. (1986). 'Law as Tradition.' *Law and Philosophy* 5(2), 237–262. *(Valuable for its nuanced look at ideological effects of pure tradition.)*
Sedgwick, M. (2023). *Traditionalism: The Radical Project for Restoring Sacred Order*. Oxford: Oxford University Press. *(The best introduction to perennialism and Traditionalism, past and present.)*

Chapter 3: Invention and authority

Dorson, R. M. (1950). 'Folklore and Fake Lore.' *The American Mercury* 70: 335–343. (*The origin of this influential distinction.*)

Hobsbawm, E. and T. Ranger, eds. (2012 [1983]). *The Invention of Tradition*. Cambridge: Cambridge University Press. (*The classic collection that sparked the debate.*)

Linnekin, J. and R. Handler. (1984). 'Tradition, Genuine or Spurious.' *The Journal of American Folklore* 97(385): 273–290. (*An extreme statement that all traditions, even academic ones, are invented.*)

Matory, J. L. (2005). *Black Atlantic Religion: Tradition, Transnationalism, and Matriarchy in the Afro-Brazilian Candomblé*. Princeton: Princeton University Press. (*Essential reading on the trans-Atlantic nature of Afro-diasporic religions, and on normative* tradition *in Candomblé.*)

The following collections offer a wide variety of case studies on the invention of tradition in religious contexts:

Engler, S. and G. P. Grieve, eds. (2005). *Historicizing 'Tradition' in the Study of Religion*. Berlin: De Gruyter.

Lewis, J.R. and O. Hammer, eds. (2007). *The Invention of Sacred Tradition*. Cambridge: Cambridge University Press.

Chapter 4: Tradition and modernity

Eisenstadt, S. N. (2000). 'Multiple Modernities.' *Daedalus* 129(1): 1–29. (*The essay that launched discussion of this important idea.*)

Geschiere, P. (1997). *The Modernity of Witchcraft: Politics and the Occult in Postcolonial Africa*. Charlottesville: University Press of Virginia. (*An influential move beyond the modern vs. traditional divide and its relation to colonialism.*)

Smith, C. and Vaidyanathan, B. (2010). 'Multiple Modernities and Religion.' In *The Oxford Handbook of Religious Diversity*, edited by C. Meister, 250–265. Oxford: Oxford University Press. (*Bringing that discussion home to scholarship on religions.*)

Williams, R. (1983). *Keywords: A Vocabulary of Culture and Society*, rev. ed. New York: Oxford University Press. (*The chapters on 'Modern' and 'Tradition' set the context well.*)

Chapter 5: Agency and reason

Bloch, M. (2006). 'Deference.' In *Theorizing Rituals: Issues, Topics, Approaches, Concepts*, edited by J. Kreinath, J. Snoek and M. Stausberg, 495–506. Leiden: Brill. (*Sets out the idea that ritual and tradition distance the intentional actions of living participants.*)

Coulthard, G. S. (2014). *Red Skin, White Masks: Rejecting the Colonial Politics of Recognition*. Minneapolis: University of Minnesota Press. (*An essential work that—among other critical discussions and echoing Fanon—unmasks the role of tradition in the political and economic marginalization of Indigenous people.*)

King, R. (1999). *Orientalism and Religion: Postcolonial Theory, India and 'the Mystic East.'* London: Routledge. (*The best introduction to negative orientalism in the history and study of religion/s.*)

Mani, L. (1998). *Contentious Traditions: The Debate on Sati in Colonial India.* Berkeley: University of California Press. (*A powerful analysis of, among many other things, the inscription of tradition on women's bodies in colonial contexts.*)

Simpson, A. (2014). *Mohawk Interruptus: Political Life across the Borders of Settler States*. Durham: Duke University Press. (*A wide-ranging work on the politics of Indigenous identity in settler states, with important critiques of ideological uses of the concept of traditional culture.*)

Chapter 6: Key thinkers of *tradition*

The following are the key works discussed in this chapter (secondary works are cited in the chapter).

Assmann, J. (2011 [1992]). *Cultural Memory and Early Civilization: Writing, Remembrance, and Political Imagination*. Cambridge: Cambridge University Press.

Assmann, A. (2008). 'Canon and Archive.' In *Cultural Memory Studies: An International and Interdisciplinary Handbook*, edited by A. Erll and A. Nünning, 97–107. Berlin: de Gruyter.

Boyer, P. (1990). *Tradition as Truth and Communication: A Cognitive Description of Traditional Discourse*. Cambridge: Cambridge University Press.

Gadamer, H.-G. (2004 [1960]). *Truth and Method*, translated by J. Weinsheimer and D. G. Marshall, 2nd rev. ed. London: Continuum.

Halbwachs, M. (1992[1952]). *On Collective Memory*, translated by L. A. Coser. Chicago: University of Chicago Press.

Morin, O. (2016 [2011]). *How Traditions Live and Die.* Oxford: Oxford University Press.

Ricoeur, P. (1988 [1985]). *Time and Narrative, vol. 3*, translated by K. Blamey and D. Pellauer. Chicago: University of Chicago Press.

Bibliography

Abdel-Malek, A. (1963). 'Orientalism in Crisis.' *Diogenes* 11(44): 103–140.

Ackerman, S. (2007). 'Three Phases of Inventing Rosicrucian Tradition in the Seventeenth Century.' In *The Invention of Sacred Tradition*, edited by J. R. Lewis and O. Hammer, 158–176. Cambridge: Cambridge University Press.

Agier, M. (1995). 'Racism, Culture and Black Identity in Brazil.' *Bulletin of Latin American Research* 14(3): 245–264.

Åkerman, S. (2007). 'Three Phases of Inventing Rosicrucian Tradition in the Seventeenth Century.' In *The Invention of Sacred Tradition*, edited by J. R. Lewis and O. Hammer, 158–176. Cambridge: Cambridge University Press.

Alam, S. M. (1992). 'Evolution of Man: Qur'anic Concepts and Scientific Theories.' *Hamdard Islamicus* 15: 59–74.

Alfred, T. (1999). *Peace, Power, Righteousness: An Indigenous Manifesto*. Oxford: Oxford University Press.

Alfred, T. (2005). *Wasáse: Indigenous Pathways of Action and Freedom*, Peterborough: Broadview Press.

Allen, M. J. B. (2005). 'Ficino, Marcilio.' In *Dictionary of Gnosis and Western Esotericism*, edited by W. J. Hanegraaff, A. Faivre, R. v. d. Broek and J.-P. Brach, 360–367. Leiden: Brill.

Anonymous. (2016 [1614–1616]). *Rosicrucian Trilogy: Fama Fraternitatis, 1614; Confessio Fraternitatis, 1615; The Chemical Wedding of Christian Rosenkreuz, 1616*, translated by J. Godwin, C. McIntosh, and D. Pahnke McIntosh. Newburyport, MA: Weiser Books.

Arendt, H. (1961). 'What Is Authority?' In *Between Past and Future: Six Exercises in Political Thought*. New York: The Viking Press, 91–141.

Arendt, H. (1978). *The Life of the Mind*. New York: Harcourt.

Arts, W. (2000). 'Through a Glass, Darkly.' In *Through A Glass, Darkly: Blurred Images of Cultural Tradition and Modernity over Distance and Time*, edited by W. Arts, 1–11. Leiden: Brill.

Asad, T. (1973). 'Two European Images of Non-European Rule.' *Economy and Society* 2(3), 263–277.

Asad, T. (2009 [1986]). 'The Idea of an Anthropology of Islam.' *Qui Parle: Critical Humanities and Social Sciences* 17(2): 1–30.
Ashcroft, B., G. Griffiths, and H. Tiffin. (2013 [1998]). *Post-Colonial Studies: The Key Concepts*, 3rd ed. London: Routledge.
Asoya, M. (2006). 'Shinto and Its Tradition.' In *Tradition and Tradition Theories: An International Discussion*, edited by T. Larbig and S. Wiedenhofer, 49–63. Berlin: Lit Verlag.
Asprem, E. and K. Granholm. (2013). 'Constructing Esotericisms: Sociological, Historical and Critical Approaches to the Invention of Tradition.' In *Contemporary Esotericism*, edited by E. Asprem and K. Granholm, 25–48. London: Equinox.
Assmann, A. (2006). 'Memory, Individual and Collective.' In *The Oxford Handbook of Contextual Political Analysis*, edited by R. E. Goodin and C. Tilly, 210–224. Oxford: Oxford University Press.
Assmann, A. (2008). 'Canon and Archive.' In *Cultural Memory Studies: An International and Interdisciplinary Handbook*, edited by A. Erll and A. Nünning, 97–107. Berlin: de Gruyter.
Assmann, J. (1995). 'Memory and Cultural Identity.' *New German Critique* 65: 125-133.
Assmann, J. (2006 [2000]). *Religion and Cultural Memory: Ten Studies*, translated by R. Livingstone. Stanford: Stanford University Press.
Assmann, J. (2008). 'Communicative and Cultural Memory.' In *Cultural Memory Studies: An International and Interdisciplinary Handbook*, edited by A. Erll and A. Nünning, 109–118. Berlin: de Gruyter.
Assmann, J. (2011 [1992]). *Cultural Memory and Early Civilization: Writing, Remembrance, and Political Imagination*. Cambridge: Cambridge University Press.
Athanasius. (1951). *The Letters of Saint Athansius Concerning the Holy Spirit.* Trans. C.R.B. Shapland. London: The Epworth Press.
Bastide, R. (1973). 'Contribuição ao estudo do sincretismo católico-fetichista.' In *Estudos Afro-Brasileiros*, 159–191. São Paulo: Editora Perspectiva.
Bataille, G. (1988). *The Accursed Share: An Essay on General Economy. Vol. 1: Consumption*, translated by R. Hurley. New York: Zone Books.
Bataille, G. (1989). *Theory of Religion*, translated by R. Hurley. New York: Zone Books.
Baumann, G. (2015). 'Grammars of Identity/Alterity A Structural Approach.' In *Grammars of Identity/Alterity A Structural Approach*, edited by G. Baumann and A. Gingrich, 18–50. New York: Berghahn Books.
Bernstein, R. J. (1998). *Freud and the Legacy of Moses*. Cambridge: Cambridge University Press.
Bloch, M. (2005). 'Ritual and Deference.' In *Essays on Cultural Transmission*, 123–138. Oxford: Berg.

Bloch, M. (2006). 'Deference.' In *Theorizing Rituals: Issues, Topics, Approaches, Concepts*, edited by J. Kreinath, J. Snoek and M. Stausberg, 495–506. Leiden: Brill.
Blumenthal-Barby, M. (2013). '"The Odium of Doubtfulness": Or the Vicissitudes of Arendt's Metaphorical Thinking.' In *Inconceivable Effects: Ethics through Twentieth-Century German Literature, Thought, and Film*, 16–39. Ithaca: Cornell University Press.
Borella, J. (1992). 'René Guénon and the Traditionalist School.' In *Modern Esoteric Spirituality*, edited by A. Faivre and J. Needleman, 330–358. New York: Crossroad.
Borges, J. L. (1974 [1939]). 'Pierre Menard, autor del Quijote.' In *Obras completas*, 444–450. Buenos Aires: Emecé.
Boudon, R. and F. Bourricaud. (1989 [1982]). *A Critical Dictionary of Sociology*, translated by Peter Hamilton. London: Routledge.
Bourdieu, P. (1990 [1980]). *The Logic of Practice*, translated by R. Nice. Stanford: Stanford University Press.
Boyer, P. (1986a). 'Tradition et vérité.' *L'Homme* 26(97–98): 309–329.
Boyer, P. (1986b). 'The "Empty" Concepts of Traditional Thinking: A Semantic and Pragmatic Description.' *Man* (n.s.) 21(1): 50–64.
Boyer, P. (1987). 'The Stuff "Traditions" are Made of: On the Ontology of an Ethnographic Category.' *Philosophy of the Social Sciences* 17(1): 49–65.
Boyer, P. (1990). *Tradition as Truth and Communication: A Cognitive Description of Traditional Discourse*. Cambridge: Cambridge University Press.
Boyer, P. (1992). 'Causal Thinking and Its Anthropological Misrepresentation.' *Philosophy of the Social Sciences* 22(2): 187–213.
Boyer, P. (2018). *Minds Make Societies: How Cognition Explains the Worlds Humans Create*. New Haven: Yale University Press.
Braga, J. (1998). *Fuxico de Candomblé: estudos afro-brasileiros*. Feira de Santana: Universidade Estadual de Feira de Santana.
Briggs, C. L. (1996). 'The Politics of Discursive Authority in Research on the "Invention of Tradition".' *Cultural Anthropology* 11(4): 435–469.
Brogan, W. (2020). 'Basic Concepts of Hermeneutics: Gadamer on Tradition and Community.' *Duquesne Studies in Phenomenology* 1(1). https://dsc.duq.edu/dsp/vol1/iss1/3 (accessed 21 February 2023).
Brown J. E. (1989 [1953]). *The Sacred Pipe: Black Elk's Account of the Seven Rites of the Oglala Sioux*. Norman: University of Oklahoma Press.
Brydon, A. (1994). Review of P. Boyer *Tradition as Truth and Communication*. *Ethnologies* 16(1): 207–209.
Camporeale, S. I. (1996). 'Lorenzo Valla's "Oratio" on the Pseudo-Donation of Constantine: Dissent and Innovation in Early Renaissance Humanism.' *Journal of the History of Ideas* 57(1): 9–26.

Canadian Charter of Rights and Freedoms. 2023. https://is.gd/G05COA (accessed 3 August 2023).

Cantwell, C. and H. Kawanami. (2002). 'Buddhism.' In *Religions in the Modern World: Traditions and Transformations*, edited by L. Woodhead, P. Fletcher, H. Kawanami and D. Smith, 47–81. London: Routledge.

Carlyle, T. (1987 [1831]). *Sartor Resartus*. Oxford: Oxford University Press.

Carrette, J. (2005). 'Religion Out of Mind: The Ideology of Cognitive Science and Religion.' In *Soul, Psyche, Brain: New Directions in the Study of Religion and Brain-Mind Science*, edited by K. Bulkeley, 242–261. New York: Palgrave Macmillan.

Castaneda, C. (1972). *Journey to Ixtlan: The Lessons of Don Juan*. New York: Simon & Schuster.

Catechism of the Catholic Church. (1993). https://is.gd/qDTIAG (accessed 2 June 2024).

Chryssides, G. D. (2007). '"Heavenly Deception"? Sun Myung Moon and Divine Principle.' In *The Invention of Sacred Tradition*, edited by J. R. Lewis and O. Hammer, 118–140. Cambridge: Cambridge University Press.

Ciaffa, J. A. (2008). 'Tradition and Modernity in Postcolonial African Philosophy.' *Humanitas* 21 (1/2): 121–145.

Clifford, J. and G. E. Marcus, eds. (1986). *Writing Culture: The Poetics and Politics of Ethnography*. Berkeley: University of California Press.

Cohen, P. F. (2002). 'Orisha Journeys: The Role of Travel in the Birth of Yorùbá-Atlantic Religions.' *Archives de Sciences Sociales des Religions* 47(117): 17–36.

Cohn, B. S. (1983). 'Representing Authority in Colonial India.' In *The Invention of Tradition*, edited by E. Hobsbawm and T. Ranger, 165–209. Cambridge: Cambridge University Press.

Colby, F. S. (2005). 'The Rhetoric of Innovative Tradition in the Festival Commemorating the Night of Muhammad's Ascension.' In *Historicizing 'Tradition' in the Study of Religion*, edited by S. Engler and G. P. Grieve, 33–50. Berlin: De Gruyter.

Confino, A. (1997). 'Collective Memory and Cultural History: Problems of Method.' *The American Historical Review* 102(5): 1386–1403.

Connerton, P. (1989). *How Societies Remember*. Cambridge: Cambridge University Press.

Connolly, A. (2006). 'Judicial Conceptions of Tradition in Canadian Aboriginal Rights Law.' *The Asia Pacific Journal of Anthropology* 7(1): 27–44.

Corrigan, K. and M. Harrington. (2007). 'Pseudo-Dionysius: The Mediation of Sacred Traditions.' In *The Invention of Sacred Tradition*, edited by J. R. Lewis and O. Hammer, 241–257. Cambridge: Cambridge University Press.

Coser, L. A. (1992). 'Introduction: Maurice Halbwachs 1877–1945.' In *Maurice Halbwachs On Collective Memory*, 1–34. Chicago: The University of Chicago Press.

Costa, X. (2006). 'Sociability and the Transmission of Festive Traditions.' In *Tradition and Tradition Theories: An International Discussion*, edited by T. Larbig and S. Wiedenhofer, 26–48. Berlin: Lit Verlag.

Coulthard, G. S. (2014). *Red Skin, White Masks: Rejecting the Colonial Politics of Recognition*. Minneapolis: University of Minnesota Press.

DaMatta, R. A. (1987). *Relativizando: uma introdução à antropologia social*. Rio de Janeiro: Rocco.

Danner, V. (1991). 'Western Evolutionism in the Muslim World.' *The American Journal of Islamic Social Sciences* 8(1): 67–82.

Davidson, D. (1986). 'A Nice Derangement of Epitaphs.' In *Truth and Interpretation: Perspectives on the Philosophy of Donald Davidson*, edited by E. LePore, 433–446. Oxford: Blackwell.

Davidson, D. (2001). *Subjective, Intersubjective, Objective*. Oxford: Oxford University Press.

Davies, A. (1999). 'Tradition and Modernity in Protestant Christianity.' *Journal of Asian and African Studies* 34(1): 19–32.

Davies, D. J. (2007). 'The Invention of Sacred Tradition: Mormonism.' In *The Invention of Sacred Tradition*, edited by J. R. Lewis and O. Hammer, 56–74. Cambridge: Cambridge University Press.

Davies, P. R. (2007). 'Spurious Attribution in the Hebrew Bible.' In *The Invention of Sacred Tradition*, edited by J. R. Lewis and O. Hammer, 258–276. Cambridge: Cambridge University Press.

Despland, M. (2008). *Bastide on Religion: The Invention of Candomblé*. London: Equinox.

Detienne, M. (1999 [1967]). *The Masters of Truth in Archaic Greece*. New York: Zone Books.

de Vaan, M. (2008). *Etymological Dictionary of Latin and the Other Italic Languages*. Leiden: Brill.

Doniger, W. (1995 [1988]). *Other People's Myths: The Cave of Echoes*. Chicago: University of Chicago Press.

Dorson, R. M. (1950). 'Folklore and Fake Lore.' *The American Mercury* 70: 335–343.

Dorson, R. M. (1976). 'Folklore in the Modern World.' In *Folklore and Fakelore: Essays toward a Discipline of Folk Studies*, 33–73. Cambridge, MS: Harvard University Press.

Dorson, R. M. (1986 [1983]). 'Teaching Folklore to Graduate Students: The Introductory Proseminar.' In *Handbook of American Folklore*, edited by R. M. Dorson and I. G. Carpenter, 463–469. Bloomington: Midland Books.

Droge, A. J. (1989). *Homer or Moses? Early Christian Interpretations of the History of Culture*. Tübingen: Mohr Siebeck.

Dundes, A. (1989). 'The Fabrication of Fakelore.' In *Folklore Matters*, 40–56. Knoxville: The University of Tennessee Press.

Eckel, M. D. (2000). 'Buddhism in the World and in America.' In *World Religions in America: An Introduction*, edited by J. Neusner, 143–54. Louisville, KY: Westminster John Knox Press.

Eisenstadt, S. N. (2000). 'Multiple Modernities.' *Daedalus* 129(1): 1–29.

Eisenstadt, S. N. (2003). 'Some Observations on the Dynamics of Traditions.' In *Comparative Civilizations and Multiple Modernities*, 135–163. Leiden: Brill.

Emerson, R. L. (2002). 'Tradition.' In *Encyclopedia of the Enlightenment*, edited by A. C. Kors. Oxford: Oxford University Press. [on-line edition]

Engler, S. (2005a). 'Tradition's Legacy.' In *Historicizing 'Tradition' in the Study of Religion*, edited by S. Engler and G. P. Grieve, 357–378. Berlin: De Gruyter.

Engler, S. (2005b). 'Tradition.' In *The Brill Dictionary of Religion*, edited by K. von Stuckrad, C. Auffarth, J. Bernard and H. Mohr, 1907-1911. Leiden: Brill.

Engler, S. (2009a). 'Review of James R. Lewis and Olav Hammer, eds. *The Invention of Sacred Tradition*.' *Religion* 39(4): 395–396.

Engler, S. (2009b). 'Umbanda and Hybridity.' *Numen* 56(5): 545–577.

Engler, S. (2009c). 'Ritual Theory and Attitudes to Agency in Brazilian Spirit Possession.' *Method & Theory in the Study of Religion* 21(4): 460–492.

Engler, S. (2016a). 'Why Be Critical?: Introducing a Symposium on *Capitalizing Religion*.' *Religion* 46(3): 412–419.

Engler, S. (2016b). 'Dona Benta's Rosary: Managing Ambiguity in a Brazilian Women's Prayer Group.' *Journal of the American Academy of Religion* 84(3): 776–805.

Engler, S. (2016c). "Umbanda." In *Handbook of Contemporary Religions in Brazil*, edited by B. E. Schmidt and S. Engler, 204–224. Leiden: Brill.

Engler, S. (2022). 'Umbanda: Hybridity, Tradition and Semantic Plurality.' *Interdisciplinary Journal for Religion and Transformation in Contemporary Society* 2022: 1–24.

Engler, S. (2023). "Brazil." In, *Religious Minorities Online* edited by E. Baffelli, A. v. d. Haven and M. Stausberg. Berlin: De Gruyter. https://is.gd/1bzpTN (accessed 3 August 2023).

Engler, S. and Ê. Brito. (2016). 'Afro-Brazilian and Indigenous-Influenced Religions.' In *Handbook of Contemporary Religions in Brazil*, edited by B. E. Schmidt and S. Engler, 142–169. Leiden: Brill.

Engler, S. and M. Q. Gardiner. (2013). 'Lincoln's Clarion Call for Methodological Solipsism.' In *Twenty Five Years of Theory and Method*, edited by A. Hughes, 159–163. Leiden: Brill.

Engler, S. and M. Q. Gardiner. (2017). 'Semantics and the Sacred.' *Religion* 47(4): 616–640.

Engler, S. and M. Q. Gardiner. (2024). '(Re)defining Esotericism: Fluid Definitions, Property Clusters and the Cross-cultural Debate.' *Aries: Journal for the Study of Western Esotericism* 24(2): 151–207.

Engler, S. and G. P. Grieve, eds. (2005). *Historicizing 'Tradition' in the Study of Religion*. Berlin: De Gruyter.

Epega, S. M. (2006 [1999]). 'A volta à Africa: na contramão do Orixá.' In *Faces da tradição afro-brasileiro: religiosidade, sincretismo, anti-sincretismo, reafricanização, práticas terapêuticas, etnobotánica e comida*, edited by C. Caroso and J. Bacelar, 159–169. Rio de Janeiro/Salvador: Pallas/CNPq.

Erll, A. (2008). 'Cultural Memory Studies: An Introduction.' In *Cultural Memory Studies: An International and Interdisciplinary Handbook*, edited by A. Erll and A. Nünning, 1–15. Berlin: De Gruyter.

'Eucharist: A Lutheran-Roman Catholic Statement.' (1967). https://is.gd/FtFDQ6

Evola, J. (1994). *René Guénon: A Teacher for Modern Times*, translated by G. Stucco. Edmonds, WA: Sure Fire Press.

Faivre, A. (1999). 'Histoire de la notion moderne de Tradition dans ses rapports avec les courants ésotériques (XVe–XXe siècles).' In *Symboles et mythes dans les mouvements initiatiques et ésotériques (XVIIe–XXe siècles): Filiations et emprunts*, edited by R. Dachez, 7–48. Paris: Arché/La Table d'Émeraude.

Fanon, F. (1965 [1959]). *A Dying Colonialism*, translated by H. Chevalier. New York: Grove Press.

Fernandes, F. (2007 [1972]). *O negro no mundo dos brancos*, 2nd ed. São Paulo: Global Editora.

Ferraresi, F. (1987). 'Julius Evola: Tradition, Reaction, and the Radical Right.' *Archives Européennes de Sociologie* 28(1): 107–151.

Ferretti, S. F. (2001). 'Religious Syncretism in an Afro-Brazilian Cult House.' In *Reinventing Religions: Syncretism and Transformation in Africa and the Americas*, edited by S. M. Greenfield and A. Droogers, 87–97. Lanham, MD: Rowman & Littlefield.

Filer, C. (2006). 'Custom, Law and Ideology in Papua New Guinea.' *The Asia Pacific Journal of Anthropology* 7(1): 65–84.

Fitzgerald, T. (1990). 'Hinduism and the "World Religion" Fallacy.' *Religion* 20, 101–118.

Fitzgerald, T. (2000). *The Ideology of Religious Studies.* Oxford: Oxford University Press.

Fitzgerald, T. (2007). *Discourse on Civility and Barbarity: A Critical History of Religion and Related Categories.* Oxford: Oxford University Press.

Fleming Mathur, M. E. (1975). 'On Third-Generation Movements: Toward a Universal Model.' *Current Anthropology* 16(3): 457–461.

Florovsky, G. (1972). *Bible, Church, Tradition: An Eastern Orthodox View.* Belmont, MA: Nordland.

Flower, H.I. (2010). *Roman Republics.* Princeton: Princeton University Press.

Forster, K. (1976). 'Aby Warburg's History of Art: Collective Memory and the Social Mediation of Images.' *Daedalus* 105(1): 169–176.

Fuchs, S. (2001). 'Beyond Agency.' *Sociological Theory* 19(1), 24–40.

Furedi, F. (2013). *Authority: A Sociological History.* Cambridge: Cambridge University Press.

Gadamer, H.-G. (2004 [1960]). *Truth and Method*, translated by J. Weinsheimer and D. G. Marshall, 2nd rev. ed. London: Continuum.

Gardiner, M. Q. and S. Engler. (2012). 'Semantic Holism and the Insider-Outsider Problem.' *Religious Studies* 48(2): 239–255.

Gardiner, M. Q. and S. Engler. (2015). 'The Philosophy and Semantics of the Cognitive Science of Religion.' *Journal for the Cognitive Science of Religion* 3(1): 7–35.

Gardiner, M. Q. and S. Engler. (2018). 'Davidsonian Semantic Theory and Cognitive Science of Religion.' *Filosofia Unisinos* 19(3): 311–321.

Gayley, H. (2007). 'Ontology of the Past and Its Materialization in Tibetan Treasures.' In *The Invention of Sacred Tradition*, edited by J. R. Lewis and O. Hammer, 213–240. Cambridge: Cambridge University Press.

Geschiere, P. (1997). *The Modernity of Witchcraft: Politics and the Occult in Postcolonial Africa.* Charlottesville: University Press of Virginia.

Giesler, P. V. (1998). 'Conceptualizing Religion in Highly Syncretistic Fields: An Analog Ethnography of the Candomblés of Bahia, Brazil.' PhD dissertation in Anthropology. Brandeis University.

Gilbert, R. A. (2005). 'Hermetic Order of the Golden Dawn.' In *Dictionary of Gnosis and Western Esotericism*, edited by W. J. Hanegraaff, A. Faivre, R. van den Broek and J.-P. Brach, 544–550. Leiden: Brill.

Gisel, P. (2017). *Qu'est-ce qu'une tradition? Ce dont elle répond, son usage, sa pertinence.* Paris: Hermann.

Glassie, H. (1995). 'Tradition.' *Journal of American Folklore* 108(430): 395–412.

Government of Canada. (2023). 'The Government of Canada's Approach to Implementation of the Inherent Right and the Negotiation of Aboriginal Self-Government.' https://is.gd/oi2tHy (accessed 3 August 2023).

Granholm, K. (2014). 'Locating the West: Problematizing the Western in Western Esotericism and Occultism.' In *Occultism in a Global Perspective*, edited by H. Bogdan and G. Djurdjevic, 17–36. London: Routledge.
Griaule, M. (1995). 'Gunshot.' In *Encyclopaedia Acephalica*, edited by I. Waldeberg, 96–99. London: Atlas Press.
Grice, H. P. (1991 [1989]). *Studies in the Way of Words*. Cambridge MA: Harvard University Press.
Grieve, G. P. (2005). 'Histories of Tradition in Bhaktapur, Nepal: Or, How to Compile a Contemporary Hindu Medieval City.' In *Historicizing 'Tradition' in the Study of Religion*, edited by S. Engler and G. P. Grieve, 269–282. Berlin: De Gruyter.
Grieve, G. P., and R. Weiss. (2005). 'Illuminating the Half-Life of Tradition: Legitimation, Agency, and Counter-Hegemonies.' In *Historicizing 'Tradition' in the Study of Religion*, edited by S. Engler and G. P. Grieve, 1–15. Berlin: De Gruyter.
Guénon, R. (1994 [1927]). *La crise du monde moderne*. Paris: Folio Essais.
Guénon, R. (2009). *The Essential René Guénon: Metaphysics, Tradition and the Crisis of Modernity*. Bloomington: World Wisdom Inc.
Habermas, J. (1988). *On the Logic of the Social Sciences*, translated by S. W. Nicholsen and J. A. Stark. Cambridge, MA: MIT Press.
Halbwachs, M. (1992[1952]). *On Collective Memory*, translated by L. A. Coser. Chicago: University of Chicago Press.
Haldar, P. (2007). *Law, Orientalism and Postcolonialism: The Jurisdiction of the Lotus-Eaters*. London: Routledge.
Hall, C. W. (2002). 'When Orphans Became Heirs: J.R. Graves and the Landmark Baptists.' *Baptist History and Heritage* 37(1): 112–127.
Hammer, O. (2016). 'Tradition and Innovation.' In *The Oxford Handbook of the Study of Religion*, edited by M. Stausberg and S. Engler, 718–738. Oxford: Oxford University Press.
Hanegraaff, W. J. (2005). 'Tradition.' In *Dictionary of Gnosis and Western Esotericism*, edited by W. J. Hanegraaff, A. Faivre, R. van den Broek and J.-P. Brach, 1125–1135. Leiden: Brill.
Hanegraaff, W.J. (2012). *Esotericism and the Academy: Rejected Knowledge in Western Culture*. Cambridge: Cambridge University Press.
Harding, S. (2017). 'Latin American Decolonial Studies: Feminist Issues.' *Feminist Studies* 43(3): 624–636.
Hardman, C. E. (2007). '"He May be Lying but What He Says Is True": The Sacred Tradition of Don Juan as Reported by Carlos Castaneda, Anthropologist, Trickster, Guru, Allegorist.' In *The Invention of Sacred Tradition*, edited by J. R. Lewis and O. Hammer, 38–55. Cambridge: Cambridge University Press.

Hawley, M. (2005). 'Re-Orienting Tradition: Radhakrishnan's Hinduism.' In *Historicizing 'Tradition' in the Study of Religion*, edited by S. Engler and G. P. Grieve, 297–318. Berlin: De Gruyter.

Hervieu-Léger, D. (2000 [1993]). *Religion as a Chain of Memory*, translated by S. Lee. New Brunswick, NJ: Rutgers University Press.

Hjelm, T. (2005). 'Tradition as Legitimation in New Religious Movements.' In *Historicizing 'Tradition' in the Study of Religion*, edited by S. Engler and G. P. Grieve, 109–123. Berlin: De Gruyter.

Hobsbawm, E. (2012 [1983]). 'Introduction: Inventing Traditions.' In *The Invention of Tradition*, edited by E. Hobsbawm and T. Ranger, 1–14. Cambridge: Cambridge University Press.

Hobsbawm, E. and T. Ranger, eds. (2012 [1983]). *The Invention of Tradition*. Cambridge: Cambridge University Press.

Hofer, T. (1984). 'The Perception of Tradition in European Ethnology.' *Journal of Folklore Research* 21(2–3): 133–147.

Honko, L. (1990). 'The Kalevala: The Processual View.' In *Religion, Myth, and Folklore in the World's Epics: The Kalevala and its Predecessors*, edited by L. Honko, 181–230. Berlin: Mouton de Gruyter.

Hountondji, P. J. (1996 [1976]). *African Philosophy: Myth and Reality*. Trans. Henri Evans. 2nd ed. Bloomington: Indiana University Press.

Hughes, A. W. (2005). 'The "Golden Age" of Muslim Spain: Religious Identity and the Invention of a Tradition in Modern Jewish Studies.' In *Historicizing 'Tradition' in the Study of Religion*, edited by S. Engler and G. P. Grieve, 51–74. Berlin: De Gruyter.

Humphrey, C. and J. Laidlaw. (1994). *The Archetypal Actions of Ritual: A Theory of Ritual Illustrated by the Jain Rite of Worship*. Oxford: Oxford University Press.

Humphrey, C. and J. Laidlaw. (2006). 'Action.' In *Theorizing Rituals: Issues, Topics, Approaches, Concepts*, edited by J. Kreinath, J. Snoek and M. Stausberg, 265–284. Leiden: Brill.

Inden, R. B. (2000 [1990]). *Imagining India*. Bloomington: Indiana University Press.

Ingram, B. (2008). 'René Guénon and the Traditionalist Polemic.' In *Polemical Encounters: Esoteric Discourse and Its Others*, edited by O. Hammer and K. von Stuckrad, 201–226. Leiden: Brill.

Isaac, T. (1992). 'Individual versus Collective Rights: Aboriginal People and the Signficance of Thomas v. Norris.' *Manitoba Law Journal* 21(3): 618–630.

Johansen, B. (2004). 'Islamic Studies: The Intellectual and Political Conditions of a Discipline.' In *Penser l'Orient: Traditions et actualité des orientalismes français et allemand*, edited by Y. Courbage and M. Kropp, 65–93. Beirut: Institut français du Proche-Orient.

Johnson, G. (2005). 'Incarcerated Tradition: Native Hawaiian Identities and Religious Practice in Prison Contexts.' In *Historicizing 'Tradition' in the Study of Religion*, edited by S. Engler and G. P. Grieve, 195–210. Berlin: De Gruyter.

Johnson, P. C. (2002). *Secrets, Gossip, and Gods: The Transformation of Brazilian Candomblé*. Oxford: Oxford University Press.

Josephson Storm, J. A. (2021). *Metamodernism: The Future of Theory*. Chicago: University of Chicago Press.

Kamenetsky, C. (1992). *The Brothers Grimm and Their Critics: Folktales and the Quest for Meaning*. Athens: Ohio University Press.

Karsenti, B. (2010). 'Imitation: Returning to the Tarde–Durkheim Debate.' In *The Social after Gabriel Tarde: Debates and Assessments*, edited by M. Candea, 44–61. London: Routledge.

Keesing, R. M, and R. Tonkinson, eds. (1982). *Reinventing Traditional Culture: The Politics of Kastom in Island Melanesia*. Special issue of *Mankind* 13(4): 297–399.

King, R. (1999). *Orientalism and Religion: Postcolonial Theory, India and 'the Mystic East.'* London: Routledge.

Knox, R. A. (1950). *Enthusiasm: A Chapter in the History of Religion: With Special Reference to the XVII and XVIII Centuries*. Oxford: The Clarendon Press.

Koselleck, R. (2004). *Futures Past: On the Semantics of Historical Time*, translated by K. Tribe. New York: Columbia University Press.

Krygier, M. (1986). 'Law as Tradition.' *Law and Philosophy* 5(2), 237–262.

Latour, B. 2010 [2009]. *On the Modern Cult of the Factish Gods*. Durham: Duke University Press.

Leiviskä, A. (2015). 'The Relevance of Hans-Georg Gadamer's Concept of Tradition to the Philosophy of Education.' *Educational Theory* 65(5): 581–600.

Lévi-Strauss, C. (1962). *La pensée sauvage*. Paris: Plon.

Lewis, J. R. and O. Hammer, eds. (2007). *The Invention of Sacred Tradition*. Cambridge: Cambridge University Press.

Lima, V. da C. (2003 [1977]). *A família-de-santo nos candomblés jeje-nagôs da Bahia: um estudo de relações inter-grupais*. 2nd ed. Salvador: Corrupio.

Linnekin, J. (1992). 'On the Theory and Politics of Cultural Construction in the Pacific.' *Oceania* 62(4): 249–263.

Linnekin, J. and R. Handler. (1984). 'Tradition, Genuine or Spurious.' *The Journal of American Folklore* 97(385): 273–290.

Livingstone, E. A. (2013). 'Tradition.' In *The Concise Oxford Dictionary of the Christian Church*, 3rd ed. Oxford: Oxford University Press. [2015 online version]

Lochle, S. (2014). 'The Imposter as Trickster as Innovator: A Rereading of Carlos Castaneda's Don Juan-Cycle.' In *Fake Identity?: The Impostor*

Narrative in North American Culture, edited by C. Rosenthal and S. Schäfer, 81–96. Frankfurt: Campus Verlag.
Loyal, S., and B. Barnes. (2001). '"Agency" as a Red Herring in Social Theory.' *Philosophy of the Social Sciences* 31(4), 507–524.
Luhrmann, T. M. (1986). *Persuasions of the Witch's Craft: Ritual Magic in Contemporary England.* Cambridge, MA: Harvard University Press.
Luscombe, D. (2005). 'Dionysius Areopagita (Pseudo-).' In *Dictionary of Gnosis and Western Esotericism*, edited by W J. Hanegraaff, A Faivre, R. v. d. Broek and J.-P. Brach, 312–313. Leiden: Brill.
Machacek, D. and A. Fulco. (2005). 'Rights and Values in the American Constitutional Tradition.' In *Historicizing 'Tradition' in the Study of Religion*, edited by S. Engler and G. P. Grieve, 319–344. Berlin: De Gruyter.
MacIntyre, A. (2007 [1981]). *After Virtue: A Study in Moral Theory*, 3rd ed. Notre Dame: University of Notre Dame Press.
Magnoli, D. (2009). *Uma gota de sangue: história do pensamento racial.* São Paulo: Editora Contexto.
Mahmood, S. (2005). *Politics of Piety: The Islamic Revival and the Feminist Subject.* Princeton: Princeton University Press.
Malinowski, B. (1961 [1922]). *Argonauts of the Western Pacific.* New York: E. P. Dutton.
Mandair, A. (2009). *Religion and the Specter of the West: Sikhism, India, Postcoloniality, and the Politics of Translation.* New York: Columbia University Press.
Mani, L. (1998). *Contentious Traditions: The Debate on Sati in Colonial India.* Berkeley: University of California Press.
Mannheim, K. (1959). 'The Problem of Generations.' In *Essays on the Sociology of Knowledge*, translated by P. Kecskemeti and J. Floud, 276–322. London: Routledge.
Maples Jr., J. H. (2015). 'An Exclusivist View of History which Denies the Baptist Church Came Out of the Reformation: A Landmark Recital of Church History.' *Studia Historiae Ecclesiastica* 41(3): 131–146.
Maples Jr., J. H. (2018). *Forgotten but Not Gone: The Origin, Theology and Recurrent Impact of Landmarkism in the Southern Baptist Convention (1850-2012).* Eugene, OR: Wipf & Stock.
Marcel, J.-C. and L. Mucchielli. (2008). 'Maurice Halbwachs's Mémoire Collective.' In *Cultural Memory Studies: An International and Interdisciplinary Handbook*, edited by A. Erll and A . Nünning, 141–149. Berlin: de Gruyter.
Marriott, M. (1955). *Village India: Studies in the Little Community.* Chicago: University of Chicago Press.

Martín Alcoff, L. (2007). 'Mignolo's Epistemology of Coloniality.' *CR: The New Centennial Review* 7(3): 79–101.
Matory, J. L. (2001). 'The "Cult of Nations" and the Ritualization of Their Purity.' *South Atlantic Quarterly* 100(1): 171–214.
Matory, J. L. (2005). *Black Atlantic Religion: Tradition, Transnationalism, and Matriarchy in the Afro-Brazilian Candomblé*. Princeton: Princeton University Press.
Matthews, W. (2011). *World Religions*, 7th ed. Belmont, CA: Cengage Learning.
Mauss, M. (1931). 'La cohésion sociale dans les sociétés polysegmentaires.' *Bulletin de l'Institut français de sociologie*, 1: 4–68.
McArthur, Colin. (2003). *Whisky Galore! and the Maggie: A British Film Guide*. London: I. B. Taurus.
McCutcheon, R. T. (1997). *Manufacturing Religion: The Discourse of Sui Generis Religion and the Politics of Nostalgia*. Oxford: Oxford University Press.
McLennan, G. (2015). 'Is Secularism History?' *Thesis Eleven* 128(1), 126–140.
McNeil, K. (1996). "Aboriginal Governments and the Canadian Charter of Rights and Freedoms." *Osgoode Hall Law Journal* 43(1): 61–99.
Mead, G. H. (1938). *The Philosophy of the Act*. Chicago: University of Chicago Press.
Merlan, F. (2006). 'Beyond Tradition.' *The Asia Pacific Journal of Anthropology* 7(1): 85–104.
Mignolo, W. D (2012 [2000]). *Local Histories/Global Designs: Coloniality, Subaltern Knowledges, and Border Thinking*. Princeton: Princeton University Press.
Mignolo, W. D. and C. E. Walsh. (2018). *On Decoloniality: Concepts, Analytics, Praxis*. Durham: Duke University Press.
Minucius Felix. (160–250 CE?) *Octavius*, translated by A. Roberts and J. Donaldson. www.earlychristianwritings.com/text/octavius.html
Misztal, B. (2003). *Theories of Social Remembering*. Maidenhead: Open University Press.
Molloy, M. (2010). *Experiencing the World's Religions: Tradition, Challenge, and Change*, 5th ed. New York: McGraw Hill.
Morin, O. (2016 [2011]). *How Traditions Live and Die*. Oxford: Oxford University Press.
Morrill, S. (2005). 'Women and the Book of Mormon: The Creation and Negotiation of a Latter-Day Saint Tradition.' In *Historicizing 'Tradition' in the Study of Religion*, edited by S. Engler and G. P. Grieve, 127–143. Berlin: De Gruyter.
Morris, M. and N. Sakai. (2005). 'Modern.' In *New Keywords: A Revised Vocabulary of Culture and Society*, edited by T. Bennett, L. Grossberg and M. Morris, 219–24. Oxford: Blackwell.

Motta, R. (1996). 'A invenção da África: Roger Bastide, Edison Carneiro e os conceitos de memória coletiva e pureza nagô.' In *Sincretismo religioso: o ritual afro. Anais do IV congresso afro-brasileiro*, edited by T. Lima, 24–32. Recife: Fundação Joaquim Nabuco/Editora Massangana,.

Müller, F. M. (1873). *Introduction to the Science of Religion*. London: Longmans, Green & Co.

Naas, M. (2003). *Taking on the Tradition: Jacques Derrida and the Legacies of Deconstruction*. Stanford: Stanford University Press.

Nabokov, V. (2011[1962]). *Pale Fire*. New York: Knopf Doubleday.

Némedi, D. (1995). 'Collective Consciousness, Morphology, and Collective Representations: Durkheim's Sociology of Knowledge, 1894–1900.' *Sociological Perspectives* 38(1): 41–56.

Nongbri, B. (2013). *Before Religion: A History of a Modern Concept*. New Haven: Yale University Press.

Nora, P. (1989). 'Between Memory and History: Les Lieux de Mémoire.' *Representations* 26: 7–24.

Noyes, D. (2009). 'Tradition: Three Traditions.' *Journal of Folklore Research* 46(3): 233–268.

Nyíri, J. K. (1992). '"Tradition" and Related Terms: A Semantic Survey.' In *Tradition and Individuality: Essays*, 61–74. Dordrecht: Springer.

Oakeshott, M. (1962). *Rationalism in Politics and Other Essays*. New York: Basic Books.

Olick, J. K. (2008). 'From Collective Memory to the Sociology of Mnemonic Practices and Products.' In *Cultural Memory Studies: An International and Interdisciplinary Handbook*, edited by A. Erll and A. Nünning, 151–161. Berlin: Walter de Gruyter.

Olwig, K. F. (1993). 'Between Tradition and Modernity: National Development in the Caribbean.' *Social Analysis* 33, 89–104.

Otto, T. (2014). 'Transformations of Cultural Heritage in Melanesia: From Kastam to Kalsa.' *International Journal of Heritage Studies* 21(2): 117–132.

Parés, L. N. (2004). 'The "Nagôization" Process in Bahian Candomblé.' In *The Yoruba Diaspora in the Atlantic World*, edited by M. D. C. T. Falola, 185–208. Bloomington: Indiana University Press.

Parés, L. N. (2007). *A Formação do Candomblé: história e ritual da nação Jeje na Bahia*. 2 ed. Campinas: Editora Unicamp.

Parish, J. (2001). 'Black Market, Free Market: Anti-Witchcraft Shrines and Fetishes Among the Akan.' In *Magical Interpretations, Material Realities: Modernity, Witchcraft and the Occult in Postcolonial Africa*, edited by H. L. Moore and T. Sanders, 118–135. London: Routledge.

Parmentier, R. J. (1993). Review of P. Boyer *Tradition as Truth and Communication*. *American Ethnologist* 20(1): 191–192.

Partridge, C. ed. (2005). *Introduction to World Religions*. Minneapolis: Fortress Press.
Partridge, C. and R. Geaves. (2007). 'Antisemitism, Conspiracy Culture, Christianity, and Islam: The History and Contemporary Religious Significance of the *Protocols of the Learned Elders of Zion*.' In *The Invention of Sacred Tradition*, edited by J. R. Lewis & O. Hammer, 75–95. Cambridge: Cambridge University Press.
Pasi, M. (2005). 'Westcott, William Wynn.' In *Dictionary of Gnosis and Western Esotericism*, edited by W. J. Hanegraaff, A. Faivre, R. van den Broek and J.-P. Brach. Leiden: Brill, 1168–1170.
Pelli, M. (2010). *Haskalah and Beyond: The Reception of the Hebrew Enlightenment and the Emergence of Haskalah Judaism*. Lanham, MD: University Press of America.
Piercey, R. (2004). 'Ricoeur's Account of Tradition and the Gadamer-Habermas Debate.' *Human Studies* 27(3): 259–280.
Prandi, R. (2005). *Segredos guardados: orixás na alma brasileira*. São Paulo: Companhia das Letras.
Prandi, R., A. Vallado and A. R. de Souza. (2001). 'Candomblé de Caboclo em São Paulo.' In *Encantaria brasileira: o livro dos mestres, caboclos e encantados*, edited by R. Prandi, 120–145. Rio de Janeiro: Pallas.
Price, R. (1973). 'Introduction: Maroons and Their Communities.' *Maroon Societies: Rebel Slave Communities in the Americas*. New York: Anchor Books. E-book edition.
Quijano, A. (2000). 'Coloniality of Power, Eurocentrism, and Latin America.' *Nepantla: Views from the South* 1(3): 533–580.
Quinn, W. W. (1997). *The Only Tradition*. Albany: SUNY Press.
Quinn, W. W. (2005). 'Guénon, René Jean Marie Joseph.' In *Dictionary of Gnosis and Western Esotericism*, edited by W. J. Hanegraaff, A. Faivre, R. van den Broek and J.-P. Brach, 442–445. Leiden: Brill.
Radhakrishnan, R. (2000). 'Postmodernism and the Rest of the World.' In *The Pre-Occupation of Postcolonial Studies*, edited by F. Afzal-Khan and K. Seshadri-Crooks, 37–70. Durham: Duke University Press.
Radin, M. (1937). 'Tradition.' In *Encyclopedia of the Social Sciences*, edited by A. Johnson, 15: 61–67. New York: Macmillan.
Rahman, F. (1982). *Islam and Modernity: Transformation of an Intellectual Tradition*. Chicago: University of Chicago Press.
Rasmussen, T. (2005). 'Tradition.' In *The Oxford Encyclopedia of the Reformation*, edited by H. J. Hillebrand. Oxford: Oxford University Press. [on-line edition]
Redfield, R. (1956). *Peasant Society and Culture*. Chicago: University of Chicago Press.

Ricoeur, P. (1988 [1985]). *Time and Narrative*, vol. 3, translated by K. Blamey and D. Pellauer. Chicago: University of Chicago Press.
Ricoeur, P. (1995). 'Reflections on a New Ethos for Europe.' *Philosophy and Social Criticism* 21(5-6): 3-13.
Ricoeur, P. (2004 [2003]). *Memory, History, Forgetting*, translated by K. Blamey and D. Pellauer. Chicago: University of Chicago Press.
Robinson, I. (2005). 'Hasid and Maskil: The Hasidic Tales of an American Yiddish Journalist.' In *Historicizing 'Tradition' in the Study of Religion*, edited by S. Engler and G. P. Grieve, 283-296. Berlin: De Gruyter.
Rothstein, M. (2007). 'Scientology, Scripture, and Sacred Tradition.' In *The Invention of Sacred Tradition*, edited by J. R. Lewis and O. Hammer, 18-37. Cambridge: Cambridge University Press.
Roudomet, V. (2016). 'Theorizing Glocalization: Three Interpretations.' *European Journal of Social Theory* 19(3): 391-340.
Russell, N. (2006). 'Collective Memory before and after Halbwachs.' *The French Review* 79(4): 792-804.
Sahlins, M. (1993). 'Goodby to Tristes Tropes: Ethnography in the Context of Modern World History.' *The Journal of Modern History* 65(1): 1-25.
Said, E. W. (2003 [1978]). *Orientalism*. London: Penguin.
Sakai, N. (1997). *Translation and Subjectivity: On 'Japan' and Cultural Nationalism*. Minneapolis: University of Minnesota Press.
Sakai, N. (2022). *The End of Pax Americana: The Loss of Empire and Hikikomori Nationalism*. Durham: Duke University Press.
Santos, J. T. dos. (1995). *O dono da terra: o caboclo nos candomblés da Bahia*. Salvador: Editora Sarah Letras.
Sarot, M. (2001). 'Counterfactuals and the Invention of Tradition.' In *Religious Identity and the Invention of Tradition*, edited by J. W. van Henten and A. Houtepen, 21-40. Assen: Royal Van Gorcum.
Schaeffer, K. R. (2006). 'Ritual, Festival and Authority under the Fifth Dalai Lama.' In *Power, Politics, and the Reinvention of Tradition: Tibet in the Seventeenth and Eighteenth Centuries*, edited by B. J. Cuevas and K. R. Schaeffer, 187-202. Leiden: Brill.
Schönpflug, U., ed. (2009). *Cultural Transmission: Psychological, Developmental and Methodological Aspects*. Cambridge: Cambridge University Press.
Schudson, M. (1989). 'The Present in the Past Versus the Past in the Present.' *Communication* 11: 105-113.
Schwartz, B. (1982). 'The Social Context of Commemoration: A Study in Collective Memory.' *Social Forces* 61(2): 374-397.
Schwartz, T. (1993). 'Kastom, "Custom", and Culture: Conspicuous Culture and Culture-Constructs.' *Anthropological Forum* 6(40): 515-540.

Schwartz, B., Y. Zerubavel, B. M. Barnett, and G. Steiner. (1986). 'The Recovery of Masada: A Study in Collective Memory.' *The Sociological Quarterly* 27(2): 147–164.

Scott-Phillips, T. (2014). *Speaking Our Minds: Why Human Communication is Different, and How Language Evolved to Make It Special.* Basingstoke: Palgrave Macmillan.

Sedgwick, M. (2004). *Against the Modern World: Traditionalism and the Secret Intellectual History of the Twentieth Century.* Oxford: Oxford University Press.

Sedgwick, M. (2023). *Traditionalism: The Radical Project for Restoring Sacred Order.* Oxford: Oxford University Press.

Selka, S. (2007a). *Religion and the Politics of Ethnic Identity in Bahia, Brazil.* Gainesville: University Press of Florida.

Selka, S. (2007b). 'Mediated Authenticity: Tradition, Modernity, and Postmodernity in Brazilian Candomblé.' *Nova Religio: The Journal of Alternative and Emergent Religions* 11(1): 5–30.

Shanklin, E. (1981). 'Two Meanings and Uses of Tradition.' *Journal of Anthropological Research* 37(1): 71–89.

Shils, E. (1981). *Tradition.* Chicago: University of Chicago Press.

Silva, V. G. da. (1999). 'Reafricanização e sincretismo: interpretações acadêmicas e experiências religiosas.' In *Faces da tradição afro-brasileiro: religiosidade, sincretismo, anti-sincretismo, reafricanização, práticas terapêuticas, etnobotánica e comida,* edited by C. Caroso and J. Bacelar, 149–57. Rio de Janeiro/Salvador: Pallas/CNPq.

Silva, V. G. da. (2005). *Candomblé e Umbanda: caminhos da devoção brasileira.* São Paulo: Selo Negro.

Silva, V. G. da. and F. G. Brumana. (2016). 'Candomblé: Religion, World Vision and Experience.' In *Handbook of Contemporary Religions in Brazil,* edited by B. E. Schmidt and S. Engler, 170–185. Leiden: Brill.

Simpson, A. (2014). *Mohawk Interruptus: Political Life across the Borders of Settler States.* Durham: Duke University Press.

Singer, M. (1972). *When a Great Tradition Modernizes.* New York: Praeger.

Smith, C. and Vaidyanathan, B. (2010). 'Multiple Modernities and Religion.' In *The Oxford Handbook of Religious Diversity,* edited by C. Meister, 250–265. Oxford: Oxford University Press.

Smith, H. (1987). 'Is There a Perennial Philosophy.' *Journal of the American Academy of Religion* 55(3): 553–566.

Smith, H. (1989). 'Postmodernism's Impact on the Study of Religion.' *Journal of the American Academy of Religion* 58(4): 653–670.

Smith, H. (1992 [1976]). *Forgotten Truth: The Common Vision of the World's Religions.* New York: HarperCollins.

Smith, H. (1994). 'Bubble Blown and Lived in: A Theological Autobiography.' *Dialog: A Journal of Theology* 33(4): 274–279.
Smith, W. C. (1964). *The Meaning and End of Religion.* New York: Mentor Books.
Solomon, A. (2013). *Wonder of Wonders: A Cultural History of Fiddler on the Roof.* New York: Metropolitan Books. E-book edition.
Sontheimer, G.-D. and H. Kulke, eds. (1989). *Hinduism Reconsidered.* New Delhi: Manohar.
Sousa Júnior, V. C. de. (2005). *Nagô: a nação de ancestrais itinerantes.* Salvador: Editora FIB.
Sperber, D. (1996). *Explaining Culture: A Naturalistic Approach.* Oxford: Blackwell.
Spineto, N. (2001). 'Mircea Eliade and Traditionalism.' *Aries* 1(1), 62–87.
Spohn, W. (2006). 'Multiple, Entangled, Fragmented and Other Modernities: Reflections on Comparative Sociological Research on Europe, North and Latin America.' In *The Plurality of Modernity: Decentring Sociology*, edited by S. Costa, J. M. Domingues, W. Knöbl and J. Pereira da Silva, 11–22. Munich: Rainer Hampp Verlag.
Stausberg, M. (2007). 'A Name for All and No One: Zoroaster as a Figure of Authorization and a Screen of Ascription.' In *The Invention of Sacred Tradition*, edited by J. R. Lewis and O. Hammer, 177–198. Cambridge: Cambridge University Press.
Stausberg, M. and M. Q. Gardiner. (2016). 'Definition.' In *The Oxford Handbook of the Study of Religion*, edited by M. Stausberg and S. Engler, 9–32. Oxford: Oxford University Press.
Stewart, C. (2002). Review of M. Detienne, *The Masters of Truth in Archaic Greece. Anthropological Theory* 2(1): 116–117.
Stråth, B. (2013). 'Ideology and Conceptual History.' In *The Oxford Handbook of Political Ideologies*, edited by M. Freeden, L. T. Sargent and M. Stears, 3–19. Oxford: Oxford University Press.
Supreme Court of Canada. (2023). 'Summary 39856 Cindy Dickson v. Vuntut Gwitchin First Nation.' https://is.gd/g0GiS4 (accessed 3 August 2023).
Swiffen, A. (2019). 'Constitutional Reconciliation and the Canadian Charter of Rights and Freedoms.' *Review of Constitutional Studies/Revue d'études constitutionnelles* 24(1): 85–121.
Tall, E. K. (2012). *O papel do caboclo no Candomblé baiano,* In *Índios e caboclos: a história recontada,* edited by M. R. de Carvalho and A. M. Carvalho, 79–93. Salvador, BA: EDUFBA.
Tamanoi, M. (1998). *Under the Shadow of Nationalism: Politics and Poetics of Rural Japanese Women.* Honolulu: University of Hawaii Press.
Tanner, K. (2006). 'Tradition and Theological Judgment in Light of Postmodern Cultural Criticism.' In *Tradition and Tradition Theories: An International Discussion*, edited by T. Larbig and S. Wiedenhofer, 229–246. Berlin: Lit Verlag.

Tarde, G. (1903 [1890]). *The Laws of Imitation.* Translated by E. C. Parsons. New York: Henry Holt & Co.
Taves, A. (2011). 'Catholic Studies and Religious Studies: Reflections on the Concept of Tradition.' In *The Catholic Studies Reader*, edited by J. T. Fisher and M. M. McGuinness, 113–128, 404–406. New York: Fordham University Press.
Terpe, S. (2020). 'Working with Max Weber's "Spheres of Life": An Actor-centred Approach.' *Journal of Classical Sociology* 20(1): 22–42.
Therborn, G. (2003). 'Entangled Modernities.' *European Journal of Social Theory* 6(3): 293–305.
Thomas vs. Norris (1992), 2 C.N.L.R. 139 (B.C.S.C.) https://is.gd/27f1hJ (accessed 3 August 2023).
Thomas, N. (1992). 'The Inversion of Tradition.' *American Ethnologist* 19(2): 213–232.
Thomassen, E. (2007). '"Forgery" in the New Testament.' In *The Invention of Sacred Tradition*, edited by J. R. Lewis and O. Hammer, 141–57. Cambridge: Cambridge University Press.
Traphagan, J. W. and C. S. Thompson. (2006). 'The Practice of Tradition and Modernity in Contemporary Japan.' In *Wearing Cultural Styles in Japan: Concepts of Tradition and Modernity in Practice*, edited by C. S. Thompson and J. W. Traphagan, 2–24. Albany: SUNY Press.
Trevor-Roper, H. (2012 [1983]). 'The Invention of Tradition: The Highland Tradition of Scotland.' In *The Invention of Tradition*, edited by E. Hobsbawm and T. Ranger, 15–42. Cambridge: Cambridge University Press.
Tromboni, M. (2012). *A Jurema das ramas até o tronco: ensaio sobre algumas categorias de classificação religiosa.* In *Índios e caboclos: a história recontada*, edited by M. R. de Carvalho and A. M. Carvalho, 95–125. Salvador, BA: EDUFBA.
Truffaut, F. and H. G. Scott. (1985 [1983]). *Hitchcock.* New York and London: Touchstone.
Tull, J. E. (1975). 'The Landmark Movement: An Historical and Theological Appraisal.' *Baptist History and Heritage* 10(1): 3–18.
Turner, J. W. (1997). 'Continuity and Constraint: Reconstructing the Concept of Tradition from a Pacific Perspective.' *The Contemporary Pacific* 9(2): 345–381.
Turpel, M. E. (1993). 'The Charlottetown Discord and Aboriginal Peoples' Struggle for Fundamental Political Change.' In *The Charlottetown Accord, the Referendum, and the Future of Canada*, edited by K. McRoberts and P. J. Monahan, 117–151. Toronto: University of Toronto Press.
Twain, M. (2003 [1876]). *The Adventures of Tom Sawyer.* New York: Barnes and Noble. [epub edition]

Urban, H. B. (2001). 'Syndrome of the Secret: "Esocentrism" and the Work of Steven M. Wasserstrom.' *Journal of the American Academy of Religion* 69(2): 437–447.

van der Poel, F. (2013). *Dicionário da religiosidade popular: cultura e religião no Brasil*. Curitiba: Editora Nossa Cultura.

van der Port, M. (2005). 'Candomblé in Pink, Green and Black. Re-scripting the Afro-Brazilian Religious Heritage in the Public Sphere of Salvador, Bahia.' *Social Anthropology* 13(1): 3–26.

Van Gennep, A. (1975[1937]). 'Continuité et discontinuité du folklore.' In *Arnold van Gennep, textes inédits sur le folklore français contemporain*, edited by N. Belmont, 44–67. Paris: G.P. Maisonneuve et Larose.

van Henten, J. W. and A. Houtepen, eds. (2001). *Religious Identity and the Invention of Tradition*. Assen: Royal Van Gorcum.

Vansina, J. (1985). *Oral Tradition as History*. Madison: University of Wisconsin Press.

Verger, P. F. (1993). *Orixás: deuses Iorubás na África e no novo mundo*. São Paulo: Corrupio.

von Stuckrad, K. (2005). 'Whose Tradition? Conflicting Ideologies in Medieval and Early Modern Esotericism.' In *Historicizing 'Tradition' in the Study of Religion*, edited by S. Engler and G. P. Grieve, 211–227. Berlin: De Gruyter.

Vuntut Gwitchin First Nation. (2016). 'Vuntut Gwitchin Heritage Act.' https://is.gd/JWwqOE (accessed 3 August 2023).

Walker, S. S. (1990). 'Everyday and Esoteric Reality in the Afro-Brazilian Candomblé.' *History of Religions* 30(2): 103–128.

Wasserstrom, S. M. (1999). *Religion after Religion: Gershom Scholem, Mircea Eliade, and Henry Corbin at Eranos*. Princeton, NJ: Princeton University Press.

Waugh, E., G. Cardinal and N. Leclaire, eds. (1998). *Alberta Elders' Cree Dictionary*. Edmonton: University of Alberta Press.

Weber, M. (1978 [1922]). *Economy and Society: An Outline of Interpretive Sociology*. Berkeley: University of California Press.

Whitehouse, H. (1995). *Inside the Cult: Religious Innovation and Transmission in Papua New Guinea*. Oxford: Oxford University Press.

Whitehouse, H. (2000). *Arguments and Icons: Divergent Modes of Religiosity*. Oxford: Oxford University Press.

Whitehouse, H. (2004). *Modes of Religiosity: A Cognitive Theory of Religious Transmission*. Walnut Creek, CA: Altamira Press.

Whitehouse. H. (2006). 'Transmission.' In *Theorizing Rituals: Issues, Topics, Approaches, Concepts*, edited by J. Kreinath, J. Snoek and M. Stausberg, 657–670. Leiden: Brill.

Whitehouse, H. (2021). *The Ritual Animal: Imitation and Cohesion in the Evolution of Social Complexity*. Oxford: Oxford University Press.

Williams, R. (1983). *Keywords: A Vocabulary of Culture and Society*, rev. ed. New York: Oxford University Press.

Wilson, B. R. (1991). 'Secularization: Religion in the Modern World.' In *The Study of Religion: Traditional and New Religion*, edited by S. R. Sutherland and P. B. Clarke, 195–208. London: Routledge.

Wilson, D. (1970). *The Life and Times of Vuk Stefanović Karadžić, 1787–1864: Literacy, Literature, and National Independence in Serbia*. Oxford: Clarendon Press.

Winsor, M. P. (2003). 'Non-Essentialist Methods in Pre-Darwinian Taxonomy.' *Biology and Philosophy* 18(3): 387–400.

Wolfe, P. (1999). *Settler Colonialism and the Transformation of Anthropology: The Politics and Poetics of an Ethnographic Event*. London: Cassell.

Yates, F. A. (1964). *Giordano Bruno and the Hermetic Tradition*. London: Routledge and Kegan Paul.

Yerushalmi, Y. (1982). *Zakhor: Jewish History and Jewish Memory*. Seattle, WA: University of Washington Press.

Zambrano, E. (2001). 'Authority, Social Theories of.' In *International Encyclopedia of the Social and Behavioral Sciences*, edited by N. J. Smelser and P. B. Baltes, 978–982. Amsterdam: Science Direct.

Ziolkowski, M. (2013). *Soviet Heroic Poetry in Context: Folklore or Fakelore*. Newark: University of Delaware Press.

Index

How to use this index: This index can be used like any other: find key pages that address listed topics. But it is also designed to be a useful tool for a different task. Books in this series are each about one concept, so index entries tend to flag relations to that concept. This particular book is further designed to give not a cumulative argument but a series of snapshots of how 'tradition' intersects with other concepts. I prepared the index with this in mind. Beyond quick entries on people, religions, places etc., it tries to include all relevant pages (not a representative sample) for key concepts that intersect with 'tradition.' Reading through the book itself gives you something like a 2D picture of the discussion as it unfolds. You can use the index to build a more 3D model as you trace different cross-sections, using entries like 'agency/action,' 'authority,' 'modernity,' 'social boundaries/groups' etc.

Note: 'n' following a page number indicates a footnote.

agency/action 3, 6, 9, 11, 12, 21, 32, 36, 86, 91, 94–103, 105–108, 111, 115, 117–118, 126, 137, 143, 147–150, 154, 159
Africa 5, 72n, 73–74, 87–88, 112, 140
Afro-diasporic traditions 5, 72–76
Alfred, Taiaiake, 112, 113, 116
Althusser, Louis 104
American Academy of Religion 50–51
American constitutionalism 157
Arendt, Hannah, 78–79
art/artefacts 2, 21–22, 57, 83, 112, 126, 130, 135, 153, 157
Asad, Talal, 23, 25, 92, 107–108
Assmann, Aleida 126, 134–138, 153
Assmann, Jan 2, 126, 134–138, 153
Athanasius 39
Augustus 78, 158
authenticity 11, 22, 31–32, 35, 38, 49, 52–54, 57–58, 60–76, 79, 85, 108, 112–117, 119, 133, 156, 158

authority 3–8, 13, 18–20, 26, 31–33, 35–36, 42–46, 49, 52, 56, 57–76, 77–81, 86, 89, 98–102, 105, 114, 118, 133, 143n, 154–159
Ayoungman, Kent 11

Bastide, Roger 74
Bataille, Georges 102n
belief(s) 1–2, 4–6, 8–9, 13–14, 17, 20–26, 32–34, 35, 38–44, 48–49, 52, 58–61, 63, 70–71, 74, 75, 82, 85, 99, 100, 102, 108, 114, 124, 133, 140n, 155–160
Bernstein, Richard J. 138
Bible *see* scriptures
Blackfoot (*Niitsítapii*) 11–12
Blavatsky, Helena 28
Bloch, Maurice 98–99
Boer, Roland 25
Borella, Jean 56
Borges, Jorge Luis 64

Bourdieu, Pierre 96, 99n
Boyer, Pascal 86, 138–146, 148–149, 151, 153
Brazil 72–76
Brydon, Anne 141n
Buddhism 15–16, 19, 36, 65
bunka 12

caboclo spirits 74–76
Canada 114–115, 119–122
Candomblé 5, 72–76
canon(ization) 2, 6, 22, 66, 135–137, 153
Calvin, John 80
Carlyle, Thomas 64
Carneiro, Edison 74
Carrette, Jeremy 148n
Castaneda, Carlos 64–65
Celsus 46n
China 15–17
Christianity 13–15, 19, 45–47, 66, 72, 129–130
  Catholicism 39, 44, 72, 79–80
  Orthodoxy 39, 49
  Protestantism 41–42, 44, 78, 80, 81
  Revelation 46–47
  see also scriptures
Cicero 78
cognitive science 1, 127, 127n, 138–152, 158
colonialism/colonization 1, 4, 25, 59–60, 77, 82–85, 87–90, 91, 94, 100, 102–103, 108–122, 158
  see also postcolonial theory, decolonial theory, Indigeneity theory
continuity 2, 4, 6, 8, 12, 15, 22–23, 30–32, 36–39, 41, 49, 61–63, 66, 77–79, 86, 94, 109–111, 124, 132–133, 155–156, 159
Coomaraswamy, Ananda K. 55
Corbin, Henry 55
Coulthard, Glen 115–116
Cree 10–11
Cudworth, Ralph 47
cultural memory *see* memory

culture 1–2, 6–8, 10–12, 17–18, 26, 27–28, 29, 31, 37, 38, 41, 48, 59, 62–70, 78, 84, 88–89, 96, 102, 105–122, 125–127, 134–141, 144–148, 153, 154–157

Davidson, Donald 150–152
Davies, Philip 66
decolonial theory 4, 77, 102, 103–108
  see also colonialism/colonization, Indigeneity theory, postcolonial theory
definition/conceptual work (of tradition) 1, 5–6, 8–9, 10, 11, 20–34, 53, 62, 75, 86, 90, 95, 97, 102–103, 105, 107, 110–112, 114, 117, 122, 123–124, 130, 134, 137–139, 141, 142, 144–146, 146–147, 148, 153, 155–160
  as betrayal 13–15, 32, 97
  dynamic views 1–2, 4–5, 19, 26–27, 30–31, 36, 63, 82, 85, 87, 90, 95, 100–103, 109–122, 127–134, 137–138, 156
  levels of (zero-, first-, second-order) 20, 137
  and lineage 22, 26, 28, 33, 41, 47, 80
  relational view 27, 29–32, 71, 155
  as MacGuffin 21, 35
  as scripted 1, 30, 97–103, 117, 156
  as spectrum 15, 33, 39, 44, 57, 63, 66, 75–76, 85, 87, 92–93, 104, 143, 157
  as synonym for 'religion' 1–2, 14–17, 19, 20, 33, 86, 89, 94, 98, 105, 124, 154, 156, 159–160
  vagueness 10, 15–16, 19, 141, 154
  as verb 13, 96, 117
  see also tradition (minor topics)
Derrida, Jacques 104, 155, 159
descriptive/normative *see* normative/descriptive
Dorson, Richard M. 67, 69–70
Detienne, Marcel 142n
Droge, Arthur J. 45–46

188 • *Tradition*

Dugin, Alexander 55
Durkheim, Émile 86, 125–127, 131

Egypt 47, 54
Ehrenpreis, Mordechai 83
Eisenstadt, Shmuel N. 87, 92–93
elders 10–11, 22, 32, 119, 122
Eliade, Mircea 55
Enlightenment 78, 82–84, 131
  post- 3, 36
  counter- 89
esotericism 28, 37, 43, 45–56, 61, 72, 74, 80, 83
essentialism 26, 38, 54, 55, 63, 68, 75, 86, 97, 107–108, 116–117, 145–146, 156, 160
ethics *see* morality/ethics
Europe 6–7, 45, 52, 61, 69, 77–85, 87, 89, 90, 104, 107, 111–112, 118, 128
Evola, Julius 54–55

Fanon, Frantz 103–104, 106, 108
Ficino, Marsilio 47, 80
Fiddler on the Roof 6–7, 99
Fitzgerald, Timothy 19
folklore 8, 67–71, 135
  fakelore 67–70
Foucault, Michel 104
France 27, 68, 123–124, 125
Freemasonry 43, 54
Freud, Sigmund 50, 138

Gadamer, Hans-Georg 131–134, 152–153
Gardiner, Mark Q. 29–30, 41, 56, 145, 158
gender *see* women/gender
generations 2–3, 7, 13–14, 18, 20, 23, 37, 78, 88, 94, 95, 127, 134–136, 147–148, 157
Germany 14, 27, 43, 70
Giddens, Anthony 96
great-divide theories 82, 85–86, 89–90
Greece (ancient) 14, 39–40, 45, 142n
Griaule, Marcel 112

Grice, Paul 149–152
Grimm, Wilhelm and Jacob 68
Guénon, René 54–56
Gyatso, Sangyé 65

Habermas, Jürgen 132–133
habit(uation) 3, 6, 22, 30, 32, 82, 100–101, 103, 127, 132, 135, 154
Halbwachs, Maurice 110, 124, 125–131, 134, 150, 152–153, 158
Hammer, Olav 22, 58, 60–61
Handler, Richard 62–63
Hanegraaff, Wouter J. 45–46, 49
Hawaii 60
Hermes Trismegistus 47
Hermetic Order of the Golden Dawn 43
Hermetism 47, 49, 80
Herod the Great 128
Hervieu-Léger, Danièle 123–124
Hinduism 19, 24, 27, 54, 91–92, 105
history 2, 5–6, 9, 11, 22, 25, 31, 36, 38–40, 41–42, 45, 47–49, 51, 56, 59, 63, 66, 70, 72, 79, 82, 84, 86–87, 94, 116, 125, 126–127, 129, 131–135, 137, 155, 157–159
  and modernity 104, 106
  and pure tradition 8, 26, 28, 35–56, 106, 129, 157
  see also study of religion/s (historical-critical), great-divide theories
Hitchcock, Alfred 21, 35
Hobsbawm, Eric (and Terence Ranger) 59–60, 63, 91, 97, 129
Hofer, Tamás 58
humanities/human sciences 2, 6, 40, 47, 108, 145
Humphrey, Caroline (and James Laidlaw) 97–98
Huxley, Aldous 49–50
hybridity/syncretism 29, 72–76, 104, 108

Iamblichus 47
Ibn al-Hajj 59–60

ideology 2–6, 8–9, 16, 20, 22–34, 35, 40, 44, 50, 53, 57, 62–63, 67–71, 72–76, 77, 81–85, 89–92, 96, 100–117, 129–134, 137–138, 148n, 152, 155–159
India 56, 60, 91, 102, 105
Indigeneity theory 4, 77, 90, 102, 108–122
  see also colonialism/colonization, decolonial theory, postcolonial theory
Indigenous traditions 10–11, 69–70, 73, 74, 84, 102, 111–117, 119–122
innovation 3, 6, 11, 31, 46, 58–61, 65–66, 70, 79, 82, 87, 95–97, 99, 112, 117, 130–131, 133, 154, 156
insiders/outsiders 7n, 12, 20, 33, 35, 40, 44, 48, 51–53, 56, 60, 62, 66, 72, 76, 91, 96, 116, 158–159
invented traditions 1, 11, 22–23, 30–32, 43, 44, 57–76, 77–78, 89–91, 94–95, 97, 99, 103, 105–111, 116–117, 123, 128–130, 135, 137, 146–148, 152, 156–159
Islam 13–14, 19, 20, 27, 54, 55–56, 59–60, 92, 105
Israel 2, 128–129

Japan 11–12, 15
Josephson Storm, Jason Ānanda 29n
Josephus, Flavius 128
Judaism 2, 6–7, 13–15, 19, 47, 61, 66, 82–83, 87, 128–129

Kalevala 69–69
Karadžić, Vuk 68–69
kastam / kastom 109–111
Keesing, Roger M. (and Robert Tonkinson) 59n
Knox, Ronald 58
Korea 15

Lacan, Jacques 104
Landmarkism 41–42

language(s) 8, 9–14, 32, 51, 56, 67–69, 96, 131, 133, 142–143, 149–151, 156
law 14, 18, 59, 83, 86, 102, 109, 112–122
Lévi-Strauss, Claude 86
Lévy-Bruhl, Lucien 86
Lewis, James R. 60–61, 63
Linnekin, Jocelyn 62–63
Lönnrot, Elias 69–69
Lucia Day 58
Luhrmann, Tanya 140, 142
Luther, Martin 80

Machiavelli, Niccolò 78
MacIntyre, Alasdair 123
Macpherson, James 67–68
Mãe Aninha (Eugênia Ana dos Santos) 73–74
magic/witchcraft 43, 83, 88, 140, 142
Mahmood, Saba 105–106
Malinowski, Bronisław 58
Mannheim, Karl 135n
Mani, Lata 105
Maroon traditions 5
Marriott, McKim 91
Martin, Craig 25
Marx, Karl 86
Marxism 25, 50, 86, 104
Masada 128–129
Mathers, Samuel Liddell 43
McPhail, Angus 21
McCutcheon, Russell 19, 25
Mead, George Herbert 127n
memory 2–3, 4, 6, 22, 36, 39, 57, 124, 125–131, 134–138, 140–141, 150, 152–153
Mercredi, Ovide 119
Merton, Thomas 55
myth / metamyth 38–39, 50, 58, 64, 69–70, 74, 99, 104, 114, 137, 159
methodological solipsism 41
Minucius Felix 46
Mirandola, Giovanni Pico dela 47
modernity 2–6, 7, 12, 19, 27, 29–31, 36, 38, 45, 50–51, 54–55, 57–58,

60–62, 71, 78–93, 94–95, 100–109, 111–118, 122, 123–124, 132, 140, 154, 156–158
morality/ethics 1–2, 6, 7n, 8, 11–12, 22, 23–25, 27, 32, 54, 61–62, 75, 100–101, 103–104, 106, 108–109, 112–113, 116, 119, 123, 133, 150, 155–156
Morin, Olivier 1, 97, 146–152
Müller, Max 48, 51
mysticism 27, 49–50, 51, 68, 86, 130

Nabokov, Vladimir 64
Nasr, Seyyed Hossein 55
nationalism 17, 67–71, 73, 82, 84, 87, 105–106, 116, 119, 128–129, 135, 157
Needleman, Jacob 55
Neo-Platonism 47, 80
Nongbri, Brent 19
Nora, Pierre 57, 157–158
normative/descriptive 7, 16, 20, 23, 25, 27–28, 31–32, 75–76, 91, 103, 133
normative force of tradition 1–4, 7–8, 21, 23, 25, 29–32, 34–35, 58–59, 81, 116, 119, 133, 143, 154, 156

Oakeshott, Michael 3, 5
orientalism 27–28, 29, 31, 61, 91, 92, 102, 103, 112, 116
Origen 46n
origin(s) 4, 9, 30, 36–43, 45, 49, 52, 58, 63, 67–69, 94, 97–99, 118, 136, 154–155, 158–160
Ossian 67–68

Palestine 128–129
Papua New Guinea 109–110
perennialism 16, 28, 37, 40, 43, 45–56, 79–81
philosophia perennis / prisca theologia 45, 47, 49
Piercey, Robert 134
Plato 47

pluralism/multiculturalism/ 19, 22, 30–31, 38, 55, 75, 87–88, 104, 107, 113, 133
politics 3, 5–6, 8–9, 24–25, 30–31, 59–60, 69, 73–74, 78, 82–84, 89, 95, 102, 103, 107, 111–117, 122, 126, 134–135, 148, 155, 157
postcolonial theory 4, 77, 91, 102, 103–108
 see also colonialism/colonization, decolonial theory, Indigeneity theory
process (vs. content) 21–23, 25–27, 33, 37, 39, 44–45, 53, 62–63, 72, 91, 97, 106, 108–109, 113, 126, 128, 130–132, 134, 139, 141, 143, 149, 155, 157–159
pure vs. historical 4, 28, 35–45, 49, 51–56, 73, 75–76, 81, 85, 94–103, 106–110, 115–118, 122, 129–130, 152, 156–160
Pythagoras 47

race 69, 73, 104, 111–112, 114–115, 119
Ranger, Terence 59–60, 63, 91, 129
rationality / reason 2–3, 5, 6, 12, 25, 27, 30, 66, 77, 82–84, 86–87, 94–95, 100–103, 106–107, 109, 110, 117, 118, 123, 130–131, 149
reception 3–4, 13, 20, 22–23, 25, 28, 30–32, 35–37, 44, 69, 94–95, 98, 108, 113, 117, 124, 128–129, 133–138, 146–147, 155, 159
Redfield, Robert 91
reference/representation (semantic) 20, 25, 56, 59, 62–63, 97, 113, 124, 127, 129, 131, 133–134, 139–145, 148–152, 153, 159
religion
 and agency 9, 94, 159
 and belief 26, 38–40, 53
 and canonization 2, 134–138
 concept of 1n, 19, 23, 27, 45–56, 66, 92, 96, 102n, 117, 124, 130, 143, 158

death of 3
and ideology 5, 22, 25, 32, 35–36, 38–40, 44–46, 70, 75–76, 92, 105, 157
lived/popular 29, 68–69, 91–92
and memory 2–3, 129–130
and modernity 2, 5–6, 18, 19, 27, 33, 36, 44, 54–56, 77–93, 107, 123–124, 129, 154, 156
and pure tradition 29, 35–51, 72–76, 110, 117, 129–130, 152, 156–157
and social groups/boundaries 3, 5, 20, 27, 35–36, 38, 41–45, 52–53, 56, 61, 73–74, 92
and spirituality 32, 45, 53–54, 83, 85, 102, 112, 123–124
see also history, ritual(s), sacred/sacrality, secular(ization), study of religion/s, definition
religious studies *see* study of religion/s (SoR)
Renaissance 47, 49, 78–81
Ribeiro, René 74
Ricoeur, Paul 20n, 29, 33, 133–134, 137, 152–153
ritual(s) 1, 6, 9, 21, 22, 23, 32, 43, 44, 58–60, 65, 73, 75, 80, 83, 91–92, 97–101, 114, 117, 120, 124, 140–143, 145, 156, 159
Robbins, Jerome 7
Rocker, Joshua (Samuel) 87
Rome (ancient) 40, 45, 52, 77–78, 81, 128–129, 158
Rosicrucianism 28, 37, 43
Russia 6–7, 14

sacred/sacrality/divinity 1–2, 24, 29, 31–32, 39, 40, 45, 80, 100, 135
Sakai, Naoki 83–84, 88–89, 111
sati 105
Schuon, Frithjof 50, 55–56
science 27, 50, 56, 77, 81–83, 84, 106, 158
  see also social science(s), cognitive science

scientific revolution 78, 81
Scotland 67
Scott-Phillips, Thom 150
scriptures 2, 13–15, 25, 28, 36–37, 47, 60–61, 66–67, 79–80, 91, 126, 130, 135–136, 153
secular(ization) 3, 6, 40, 59, 80, 85, 87, 124, 157
Sedgwick, Mark 28, 47, 51, 53, 55
sex/sexuality 50, 115–116
  see also women/gender
Shils, Edward 36, 94
Sikhism 16, 18, 27
Singer, Milton 91
Smith, Huston 50–51, 55
Smith, Wilfred Cantwell 48, 51
social boundaries/groups 2–3, 5–6, 8, 12, 20, 24–25, 27, 31–34, 41–45, 52, 59, 62, 82, 85–89, 92–93, 95–96, 99, 104–106, 109, 110–122, 123–131, 134–138, 139, 147–153, 157–159
social roles 1–2, 22, 33, 38, 74, 101–102, 105–106, 141–142, 145, 148, 153
social science(s) 1, 6, 40, 47, 50, 62, 74, 108, 110, 127, 145
Sperber, Dan 148
Spiritualism 54
Stausberg, Michael 61, 145
Steuco, Agostino 47
study of religion/s (SoR) 1n, 2, 10, 14–20, 23, 33, 35, 38, 40, 43–56, 57, 90, 91, 95, 110, 156–160
  crypto-theological 47–48
  historical-critical 3, 19, 20, 25, 33, 35, 40, 44–45, 47–48, 50–56, 57, 137–138, 159–160
  perennialist 47–56
  religionist 47–56
  see also decolonial theory, Indigeneity theory, post-colonial theory
Sufism 54
syncretism *see* hybridity

Sweden 58
Szacki, Jerzy 25–26

Tarde, Gabriel 131
theology 27, 42, 45–48, 49, 52, 66
Theosophy 28, 49
Thomas, Nicholas 109
Thomassen, Einar 66
Tibet 28, 36–37, 65
time/temporality 2–6, 10–12, 14,
    19–22, 25–26, 30, 32–33, 36, 39,
    48, 51, 53, 57–67, 77–85, 88, 94,
    99, 109–114, 117, 122, 124–136,
    152, 155–159
Tönnies, Ferdinand 86
totalitarianism 84, 102
tradition (minor topics)
  death of 3
  in English 13–14
  great and little 91–93
  material basis of 2, 4, 85
  see also definition/conceptual work
Traditionalism (esoteric tradition)
    54–56
traditionality 20n, 21, 112, 113,
    133–134, 152

transmission 6, 8, 10, 14, 21–23, 25–26,
    33, 37–39, 41, 43–53, 58, 63,
    69, 96–97, 106, 131–133, 135,
    138–141, 143, 146–153, 154,
    158
Turner, James W. 62, 111
Twain, Mark 94

UK 43, 60, 67, 104
Umbanda 74
USA 69–70, 87, 128, 157

Valla, Lorenzo 79
Vansina, Jan 135n, 136
Vuntut Gwitchi 119–122

Warburg, Aby 126
Weber, Max 4, 27, 59, 82, 86, 100–102
Westcott, William Wynn 43
Whitehouse, Harvey 98, 140n
witchcraft *see* magic
women/gender 24, 104–106, 115, 116,
    118, 121–122

Zoroaster / Zoroastrianism 47, 61
Zwingli, Ulrich 80

www.ingramcontent.com/pod-product-compliance
Lightning Source LLC
Chambersburg PA
CBHW070547170426
43201CB00012B/1750